Victorian Fiction

Writers, Publishers, Readers

D1080880

Also by John Sutherland

Thackeray at Work
Victorian Novelists and Publishers
Fiction and the Fiction Industry
Bestsellers: Popular Fiction of the 1970s
Offensive Literature
The Longman Companion to Victorian Fiction
Mrs Humphry Ward
The Life of Walter Scott

Victorian Fiction
Writers, Publishers, Readers

John Sutherland

MACMILLAN

© John Sutherland 1995

First published 1995 by
MACMILLAN PRESS LTD
Houndmills, Basingstoke, Hampshire RG21 2XS
and London
Companies and representatives
throughout the world

ISBN 0–333–63286–9 hardcover
ISBN 0–333–64422–0 paperback

A catalogue record for this book is available
from the British Library.

10   9   8   7   6   5   4   3   2   1
04   03   02   01   00   99   98   97   96   95

Set in Computer Modern Roman at
the California Institute of Technology

Printed and bound in Great Britain by
Antony Rowe Ltd
Chippenham, Wiltshire

For my son
Jack Sutherland
with love and admiration

Contents

List of Plates

I am grateful to the Huntington Library for permission to reproduce the above illustrated covers. The illustrations in Chapter One ('Thackeray's Errors') are from the first editions of *Vanity Fair* (page 11) and *Pendennis* (pages 12, 13, 14, 15).

Preface and Acknowledgements

This book is devoted to the undogmatic belief that the more we know about the local conditions of Victorian Fiction, the better we shall understand it. Although undogmatic, the contention may seem somewhat cross-grained. The last thirty years have seen an explosion in techniques of explication of text—loosely subsumed under the term 'Theory'. There is no doubt that critics of literature—and the students they instruct—are infinitely more sophisticated than they used to be. But as a teacher in the two major English-speaking countries, I am consistently impressed with the fact that although students and colleagues read Victorian novels more intelligently than their predecessors, they often seem, in some ways, to *know* them less well.

My point may be put as a conundrum: if you had one trip on a time machine and—by some absurd whim—wanted to use it to find out more about Victorian fiction, would you go intrepidly forward (like Wells's traveller) to that far distant future point when the last PhD thesis is defended, the last MLA special panel sponsored, the last Dickens World conference at Santa Cruz held? Or would you go back to 1851?

I confess that I would put the machine in reverse. In the discussions that follow, I have attempted to recapture something of what these works of literature meant to their contemporaries—examining them for echoes of what, for want of a better word, might be called their 'Victorianness'. There is some investigation into the social, biographical, and historical context. But the circumstances that interest me most have to do with the composition, publication, distribution, and consumption of novels.

About half of the critical material in the following chapters is new, the other half draws (with some adaptation) on reprinted pieces. A section of chapter 1 appeared in *The Yearbook of English Studies*, 1971. Part of chapter 2 was published in the same journal, 1977. Another part of chapter 2 (relating to the manuscript of *The Woman in White* first came out in *Dickens Studies Annual*, 1991. The opening section of chapter 3 first appeared in *The Dickensian*, 1985. Chapter 4 was published first in *Dickens and other Victorians* (ed. Joanne Shattock), 1990. Chapter 5 was published in different form in *Biblioteck*, 1975. Chapter 6 first appeared in *Nineteenth-Century Fiction*, 1982, and chapter 8 in *Critical Quarterly*, 1988.

For readers who wish to refresh their memories, I have appended plot summaries of the less familiar novels substantially discussed in the text. Some of these synopses are adapted from my *Longman Companion to Victorian Fiction* (1988), and I am grateful to the publisher for permission to use them.

I have a number of debts: to the Huntington Library and its staff; to Mac Pigman, who helped me with the typesetting of this book, and to Guilland Sutherland, who helped with illustrations; to my former supervisor, K. J. Fielding, who was particularly helpful with chapter 3; to Alison Winter (who helped with the same chapter); to Rosemary Ashton, who helped with chapter 5; to N. John Hall, who helped with chapter 6; to Philip Horne, who helped with chapter 7; to Simon Eliot and Uzi Segal, who helped with chapter 8.

CHAPTER ONE

Thackeray's Errors

COUNTER-factuality in fiction can be illuminating. A striking example is found in the seventh chapter of Walter Scott's *The Antiquary*. Sir Arthur Wardour and his daughter Isabella have just left a dinner party at the house of Sir Arthur's fellow-antiquary Monkbarns. The two men have quarrelled (not for the first time) about their respective hobby-horses and Wardour has stormed off to walk back along the beach at sunset with his long-suffering daughter. They pass along the water line under a formidable (and unscalable) ridge of cliffs. It is July. The geographical setting is 'Fairport' (universally identified as Dundee)— 'a thriving seaport town on the north-eastern coast of Scotland'. What the elderly gentleman and his young companion do not realize as they make their way home is that the spring-tide will soon rush in and drown them for a certainty. Scott paints an ominous picture:

As Sir Arthur and Miss Wardour paced along, enjoying the pleasant footing afforded by the cool moist hard sand, Miss Wardour could not help observing that the last tide had risen considerably above the usual water-mark. Sir Arthur made the same observation, but without its occurring to either of them to be alarmed at the circumstance. The sun was now resting his huge disk upon the edge of the level ocean, and gilded the accumulation of towering clouds through which he had travelled the livelong day, and which now assembled on all sides, like misfortunes and disasters around a sinking empire and falling monarch. Still, however, his dying splendour gave a sombre magnificence to the massive congregation of vapours, forming out of their unsubstantial gloom the show of pyramids and towers, some touched with gold some with purple, some with a hue of deep and dark red. The distant sea, stretched beneath this varied and gorgeous canopy, lay almost portentously still, reflecting back the dazzling and level beams of the descending luminary, and the splendid colouring of the clouds amidst which he was setting. Nearer to the beach, the tide rippled onward in waves of sparkling silver, that imperceptibly, yet rapidly, gained upon the sand.[1]

As pedantic commentators have noted, the evening sun does not sink into the ocean on the east coast of Scotland. Scott, who had lived in and around Edinburgh all his life and had spent innumerable evenings on the Portobello and Musselburgh sands at his cavalry exercises, must have known this meteorological fact instinctively. Certainly it was pointed out to him after his novel was published. But he never changed the detail, even in his 1829, heavily-revised, 'Magnum' edition of *The Antiquary*.

Revision would not have been easy. Scott could not shift 'Fairport' to Scotland's west coast because a French invasion was to feature as the climax to the narrative, and the foe did not (historically) come from that quarter in 1794. And there was the Dundee connection. To have had the sun set behind the cliffs would have plunged the threatened walkers into murky twilight, and to have sacrificed a fine piece of luminous writing. Scott evidently decided to perpetuate the anomaly, claiming for himself the same freedom as the painter Claude in depicting imaginary landscapes of supernatural beauty. In the interests of a good scene, the planets themselves should change their course.

On other occasions Scott displayed what his biographer Herbert Grierson calls a 'noble contempt'[2] for literal or historical fact. *Kenilworth*, for instance, is shot through with what any schoolboy will detect as 'errors'. There is wild anachronism in the walk-on parts given Edmund Spenser and the 'player' Shakespeare in the narrative. Scott specifically identifies the date of the action as July 1575, when, in recorded historical fact, the great pageant which gives the novel its name took place at Kenilworth Castle. At that date, William Shakespeare was an eleven-year-old grammar school boy and the poetry (including snatches from one of his last plays, *The Tempest*) which is so popular with Elizabeth and her Court in the novel was decades in the future and long after the Virgin Queen's death. Nor had Spenser begun to write serious verse in 1575. Ralegh is congratulated on his daring in Ireland, five years before he went there. And Fuller's story about the cloak hurled down into the mud is almost certainly apocryphal (although Scott's novel was to make it a folkloric 'fact'). Amy Robsart died in 1560, fifteen years before the action of the novel in which she is the main character. None of this is attributable to historical ignorance on Scott's part. He was formidably knowledgeable about his country's past. These anachronisms were simply licences which he believed were available to the historical romancer wanting to devise an 'Elizabethan' amalgam.

Counter-factuality works rather differently with the following scene from Douglas Adams's *So Long, and Thanks for all the Fish* (1984), the fourth part of a trilogy [*sic*], dealing with Arthur Dent's aimless bouncing about the Milky Way. In quest of 'God's final message to his creation', Arthur and his girl-friend Fenchurch drop off for a brief tourist break in contemporary Los Angeles. They hire a car and cruise the freeways and boulevards:

Late in the evening they drove through Hollywood hills along Mulholland Drive and stopped to look out first over the dazzling sea of floating light that is Los Angeles, and later stopped to look across the dazzling sea of floating light that is the San Fernando Valley. They agreed that the sense of dazzle stopped immediately at the back of their eyes and didn't touch any other part of them and came away strangely unsatisfied by the spectacle. As dramatic seas of life went, it was fine, but light is meant to illuminate something, and having driven through what this particularly dramatic sea of light was illuminating they didn't think that much of it.

They slept late and restlessly and awoke at lunchtime when it was stupidly hot.

They drove out along the freeway to Santa Monica for their first look at the Pacific Ocean . . . Their mood gradually lifted as they walked along the beach in Malibu and watched all the millionaires in their chic shanty huts carefully keeping an eye on each other to check out how rich they were each getting.

Their mood lifted further as the sun began to move down the western half of the sky, and by the time they were back in their rattling car and driving towards a sunset that no one of any sensibility would dream of building a city like Los Angeles in front of, they were suddenly feeling astonishingly and irrationally happy and didn't even mind that the terrible old car radio would only play two stations, and those simultaneously. They were both playing good rock and roll.

The problem here is that if, starting from Malibu, you drive as Arthur and Fenchurch evidently do down the Pacific Coast Highway to Santa Monica then along the 10 Freeway to downtown Los Angeles, the sun is directly behind you, sinking magnificently into the Pacific Ocean (on 300 days a year). In other words, as Dent and Fenchurch are placed, if you drive 'towards' the sunset it will make better sense to rent a submarine. Since the 'Hitch-hiker' series is a whimsical exercise in science fiction one might hypothesize that Adams's characters have found themselves in an 'alternative universe', in which the motions of the planets are reversed (as time's arrow is supposed to be reversed at the other end of black holes). But the error seems more in line with Arthur Dent's endearing provincialism (whose emblem is his clapped-out Ford Prefect). He is like the package tourist who puts his holiday snaps the wrong way round in the projector and doesn't notice.

More than with other Victorian novelists there are anomalies and counter-factualities to be found in the fiction of Thackeray. They relate to what is a central issue in discussion of his craftmanship, namely how conscientious or careful was he in devising his fiction? It was something that worried his contemporaries. Even in the generosity of an obituary tribute, Dickens could not restrain himself from the complaint that he thought Thackeray 'too much feigned a want of earnestness, and that he made a pretence of undervaluing his art, which was not good for the art that he held in trust'.[3] In one of the most influential recent studies of Thackeray at work Peter Shillingsburg starts, as other critics have started, from Anthony Trollope's forthright denunciation, published in 1879, sixteen years after Thackeray's death. Trollope ('the lesser Thackeray') knew the other novelist personally, and had worked side by side with him on the *Cornhill Magazine* in the early 1860s. He was not impressed with everything that he had observed. Trollope indicted Thackeray as 'unsteadfast, idle, changeable of purpose . . . no man ever failed more generally than he to put his best foot foremost'.[4] Trollope laid the blame squarely on 'that propensity to wandering which came to Thackeray because of his idleness'. It led to what he called 'pervasive touches of vagueness'.

Shillingsburg dismisses Trollope's description as 'misleading, if not an outright falsehood'[5] (an allegation, incidentally, that only a very brave man would have made to Trollope's face). Together with other scholars—notably Edgar Harden who has studied Thackeray's literary manuscripts and Nicholas Pickwoad who has investigated the novelist's artwork—Shillingsburg has convincingly argued that Thackeray *did* revise his work, *did* plan ahead, *did* carefully correct his proofs, *did* give a great deal of thought to the composition and placement of his illustrations. The fruits of this scholarship are embodied in the new authorized edition of the novelist's works, and the extensive apparatus accompanying the texts.[6]

Nonetheless, some of the force of Trollope's accusation lingers. Although, as Shillingsburg demonstrates, Thackeray made (or sanctioned) some 280 alterations to the text of *Vanity Fair* after it was first published, the novelist left at least one massive blemish. In chapter 59 (in the 17th monthly number) Jos Sedley and Major Dobbin have returned to England after ten years' absence in India. In Brompton old Mr Sedley eagerly awaits the arrival of his son (on whom he is now financially dependent) and Amelia (with a more covert eagerness) awaits her faithful Dobbin. But Jos ('Waterloo Sedley' as the vain old buck is now called) chooses to linger three days at the Southampton tailors' shops and in the dining rooms of the inns along the road to London. Thackeray evidently misplaced by a couple of pages the 'slip' containing the proofs of two paragraphs of this section of the narrative.[7] As a result of this misplacing, Jos is described making his belated arrival at his father's house then—some pages later— is described delaying making the journey. He thus arrives at his destination before leaving his starting place, something as counter-factual as having the sun travel from west to east across the heavens.

Accidents happened in the press of month-on-month serialization. (Thackeray amusingly confesses to any number of them in a late 'Roundabout Paper', and craves the indulgent reader's pardon.) But what is interesting is that Thackeray evidently had pointed out to him the Southampton/London error shortly after the number was published. He wrote to his mother at this period: 'One or 2 people have found out how careless the last no of V.F. is, but the cue is to admire it and consider the author a prodigy. O you donkies!'[8]

Why, one may wonder, would a writer go to the trouble of making hundreds of corrections to the text of *Vanity Fair* (some of which required altering stereotype plates—a very laborious business) and not put straight a mistake of the kind that mars chapter 59? The blemish survives in every edition in the author's lifetime, and for the vast majority thereafter. It puts his apologists in an awkward position. Either they have to interpret Thackeray's remark to his mother as not necessarily meaning that he picked up the mistake—in which case he is that much less careful a corrector of his own narrative. Or, horrible thought, he knew and didn't give a damn. And what weight should one give to the contempt with which Thackeray evidently regards those 'donkies' who presume to 'admire' his work? The admiring Shillingsburg sidesteps the question with evident unease:

Of course, as [several scholars] have already pointed out, there are many errors and infelicities left in *Vanity Fair*, and it would be a mistake, in ignorance of the remaining lapses, to argue that Thackeray was flawless, meticulous, or dedicated to ferreting out every inappropriate word. But these changes [i.e. the 284 textual alterations] suggest Thackeray was fully cognizant of the tools of his trade and concerned over the minute details of this mammoth work.[9]

I used to believe that Thackeray's carelessness was indivisible from his opportunistic and improvisatorial method of composition. It was a tax paid for his 'touches of genius'. I have, however, revised that opinion. It now seems clear from the work of his recent editors that Thackeray was a scrupulous (if oddly fitful and sometimes inscrutable) critic and corrector of his own work on the sentence-to-sentence stylistic level. He did not like infelicities that offended his editorial eye and ear and would go to some pains to eradicate them. At other points it seems to me that Thackeray had a psychological need, connected with his *mauvaise honte* about being a writer of fiction, that drove him to leave unmended pot-holes in his work. It was his way of squaring accounts with the 'donkies' who made up his loyal readership. They are what the editor of the great 1908 'Oxford' edition of Thackeray's works, George Saintsbury, called his 'sign manual'. But, these apart, one can on other occasions detect a structural, sustained, and subtle play with anachronism and narrative anomaly which places Thackeray among the most experimentally advanced writers of fiction of his generation. It is this last which is, I think, the most challenging feature of his art for the modern reader.

Take, as an example, the handling of historical time in *Pendennis*. This was Thackeray's second major novel and, even by Victorian standards, immensely long (twenty-four 32-page monthly numbers, as opposed to the twenty that made up *Vanity Fair*). It took some twenty-six months in the publishing (November 1848–December 1850), interrupted as it was by the novelist's life-threatening illness which incapacitated him between September 1849 and January 1850. *Pendennis* is also long in the tracts of time its narrative covers. The central story extends over some forty years as the hero, Arthur Pendennis ('Pen') grows from boyhood to mature manhood. In passing, Pen's story offers a panorama of the changing Regency, Georgian, Williamite, and Victorian ages.

Pendennis is one of the first and greatest mid-Victorian *Bildungsromanen*. The central character, as Thackeray candidly admitted, is based closely on himself. As part of this identification, Thackeray gave Arthur Pendennis the same birthdate as himself—1811. This is indicated by a number of unequivocal historical markers early in the text. Pen is sixteen just before the Duke of York dies in 1827. We are told that Pen (still sixteen) and his mother recite to each other from Keble's *The Living Year* (1827), 'a book which appeared about that time'.[10] Pen's early years at Grey Friars school and his parents' Devonshire house, Fairoaks, fit exactly with Thackeray's sojourns at Charterhouse school and his parents' Devonshire house, Larkbeare. Both young men go up to university ('Oxbridge', Cambridge) in 1829. Both retire from the university, in rusticated disgrace, in 1830. Thackeray clinches this historical setting by any number of references to fashions, slang, and student mores of the late 1820s and 1830s, as well as by a string of allusions to the imminent and historically over-arching Reform Bill.

With the arrival of the aristocratic Claverings and their hangers-on in the seventh number, the chronological track bifurcates. It is, of course, 1830 by Pen's clock. But the raffish Chevalier Ned Strong (the baronet's aide-de-camp) recounts a chronologically irreconcilable military career with a curl of his moustache and a reckless laugh (he is talking to a thoroughly overawed Captain Glanders):

'I began, sir, as cadet of Hungarian Uhlans, and when the war of Greek independence broke out, quitted that service in consequence of a quarrel with my governor, and was one of the seven who escaped from Missolonghi, and was blown up in one of Botzaris's fireships, at the age of seventeen. I'll show you my Cross of the Redeemer, if you'll come over to my lodgings and take a glass of grog with me, captain, this evening. I've a few of those baubles in my desk. I've the White Eagle of Poland; Skrzynecki gave it me' (he pronounced Skrzynecki's name with wonderful accuracy and gusto) 'upon the field of Ostrolenko. I was a lieutenant of the fourth regiment, sir, and we marched through Diebitsch's lines—bang thro' 'em into Prussia, sir, without firing a shot. Ah, captain, that was a mismanaged business. I received this wound by the side of the King before Oporto—where he would have pounded the stock-jobbing Pedroites, had Bourmont followed my advice; and I served in Spain with the King's troops, until the death of my dear friend Zumalacarreguy, when I saw the game was over, and hung up my toasting-iron, captain. Alava offered me a regiment; but I couldn't—damme, I couldn't—and now, sir, you know Ned Strong—the Chevalier Strong they call me abroad—as well as he knows himself.' (p. 266)

This is an entirely plausible record for a nineteenth-century soldier of fortune. Strong, we apprehend, learnt his trade as a Hungarian irregular cavalryman. He was at Missolonghi, the town in Greece besieged by the Turks, where Byron died in 1824. Bozzaris attempted unsuccessfully to lift the siege with fireships in 1822. Jan Skrzynecki was a Polish general who was defeated by the Russians in 1831

(Strong seems always to fight for lost causes). Diebitsch was the opposing Russian general. Strong then fought for Dom Miguel in 1832–3, in the unsuccessful siege of Dom Pedro's forces (the 'stock-jobbing Pedroites') at Oporto. Bourmont was the French general aiding Dom Miguel. Strong then drifted on to fight in the army of Zumalacarregui (1788–1835), the ruthless Spanish guerilla commander, in the chaotic conflict over the Spanish succession. But Zumalacarregui, we note, died in 1835. This must therefore be three or four years ago for Strong to have washed up as an old soldier at Clavering Park. We have to assume a date of 1839, almost a decade later than the time zone currently inhabited by the hero. And still to come (in chapter 28) is the ball which precedes the 1832 Reform Bill, and which Strong graces with his presence. Time's arrow is zig-zagging backwards and forwards through history.

There is another apparently carefully contrived anachronism in the reader's introduction to Blanche Amory (Lady Clavering's daughter by a previous marriage). This is the young woman who is to be the *femme fatale* in young Pen's career, the 'mermaid' whose singing will almost drive him onto the rocks. Blanche's preferred reading matter reveals a dangerous predilection for free-thinkers, French feminists, Republicans, and 'modern' fiction:

Missy [i.e. Blanche] had begun to gush at a very early age. Lamartine was her favourite bard from the period when she first could feel; and she had subsequently improved her mind by a sedulous study of novels of the great modern authors of the French language. There was not a romance of Balzac or George Sand which the indefatigable little creature had not devoured by the time she was sixteen: and, however little she sympathized with her relatives at home, she had friends, as she said, in the spirit-world, meaning the tender Indiana, the passionate and poetic Lelia, the amiable Trenmor, that high-souled convict, that angel of the galleys—the fiery Stenio—and the other numberless heroes of the French romances. She had been in love with Prince Rodolph and Prince Djalma while she was yet at school, and had settled the divorce question, and the rights of woman, with Indiana before she had left off pinafores. The impetuous little lady played at love with these imaginary worthies, as a little while before she had played at maternity with her doll. (pp. 283–4)

As with Strong, this is all highly plausible and is dense with authentic detail. Lamartine (1790–1869) was a respectable poet prescribed in Blanche's early youth, the taste for whom led to less respectable reading. Balzac (1799–1850)—a novelist who clearly influenced Thackeray—would have been well advanced with his 91-strong *Comèdie Humaine* (1827–47) at the supposed period of the Claverings' arrival at Clavering Park. George Sand (1804–76), the most influential figure in Blanche's literary firmament, wrote novels advocating the rights of woman and condemning the iniquities of bourgeois marriage (such as *Indiana*, 1831—which we are told Blanche read as a little girl). Lelia, Trenmor, Stenio, are characters in Sand's *Lelia* (1833). The princes Rodolph and Djalma figure in Eugène Sue's *Mystères de Paris* (1842–3) and *Le Juif errant* (1844–5).

The last of these literary allusions are, of course, wildly anachronistic if we measure the historical setting by Pen's college and subsequent career. Blanche is steeped in books which were not available, even in France, their country of origin, until 1845. Thackeray was not blundering here. He knew Sue's work well (a couple of years before writing *Pendennis* he had seriously contemplated translating *The Mysteries of Paris* to raise cash). Moreover, all his literate readers would have registered Sue as a notorious contemporary author. And if Blanche—now a young woman of the world—were entranced by Djalma 'while she was yet at school', we must assume a date for the narrative of 1849, or nearly two decades ahead of the sleepy 1830 in which Pen (soon to fall in love with Blanche) resides. One can surmise what is happening here. Thackeray conceived Blanche as a fast young woman of the late 1840s. At the same time, and in the same narrative frame, he conceived Pen as he remembered himself having been in his early twenties, in 1830–1, unworldly, countryfied, innocent.

In the last instalments of the novel, as we are specifically told on a number of occasions, Pen is 26. And there are numerous historical allusions fixing the front-of-stage date as the mid-to-late 1830s. For instance: (1) Pen's visit to Vauxhall in Number 15, where Simpson—who retired in the mid-1830s—still presides; (2) the rage for 'silver fork' novels, which Thackeray pointedly recalls as a foible of 'that time' (p. 525); (3) London excitement at the performance of Taglioni in *The Sylphide* in the early 1830s (p. 478); (4) the huge box-office success of Bulwer's play, *The Lady of Lyons*, in 1838.

Pendennis is given its essentially nostalgic feel by historical and cultural events dredged up from the past, between ten and twenty years before the period of writing. And yet, there are a perplexing string of references which locate the action in the late 1840s, indeed at the very moment Thackeray was writing. In the highpoint scene of Derby Day in Number 19 we glimpse among the crowd at the racecourse the Prime Minister, Lord John Russell, who took up office in 1846, and Richard Cobden MP. Cobden did not enter Parliament until 1847. And, by cross-reference to Richard Doyle's well-known Derby Day panorama in *Punch*, 26 May 1849 (a work which inspired Frith's famous *Derby Day* painting) we can see that Thackeray is clearly describing the Derby of the year in which he wrote, which actually took place a couple of months before the number was published.

Thackeray is insistent in this final phase of his narrative that Pen is just 26 years old (p. 797), which gives a historical setting of 1837. But, at the same time, Pen is given speeches like the following (one of his more provokingly 'cynical' effusions to his *alter ego*, Warrington), in Number 20:

'The truth, friend!' Arthur said imperturbably; 'where is the truth? Show it to me. That is the question between us. I see it on both sides. I see it in the Conservative side of the House, and amongst the Radicals, and even on the ministerial benches. I see it in this man who worships by Act of Parliament, and is rewarded with a silk apron and five thousand a year; in that man, who, driven fatally by the remorseless logic of his creed, gives up everything, friends, fame, dearest ties, closest vanities, the respect of an army of Churchmen, the recognized position of a leader, and passes over, truth-impelled, to the enemy, in whose ranks he is ready to serve henceforth as a nameless private soldier:—I see the truth in that man, as I do in his brother, whose logic drives him to quite a different conclusion and who, after having passed a life in vain endeavours to reconcile an irreconcilable book, flings it at last down in despair, and declares, with tearful eyes, and hands up to heaven, his revolt and recantation. If the truth is with all these, why should I take side with any one of them?' (p. 802)

No well-informed Victorian reading this could fail to pick up the topical references. In his remark on the 'ministerial benches' Pen alludes to the great Conservative U-turn over the Corn Laws in 1846. His subsequent references are transparently to the theologian John Henry Newman (1801–90) and his brother Francis William Newman (1805–97). John went over to the Catholic Church in 1845. As Gordon Ray records, Thackeray attended his course of lectures on Anglican difficulties at the Oratory, King William Street, in summer 1850 (this number of *Pendennis* was published in September).[11] Francis, Professor of Latin at University College London, 1846–69, published his reasons for being unable to accept traditional Christian arguments in the autobiographical *Phases of Faith* (1850). According to Ray, Thackeray was much moved by the book. Clearly Pen's comments to Warrington only make sense if we date them as being uttered in mid-1850, at the same period that this monthly number was being written. And we have to assume that Thackeray was making his hero the vehicle for what he (Thackeray) was thinking on the great current question of Papal Aggression.

These examples of chronological dualism in *Pendennis* are systematic features of the novel's highly artful structure. Thackeray has devised a technique that was to be later explored and codified into a modernist style by the Cubists. Not to be fanciful, the author of *Pendennis* anticipates Picasso's multi-perspectival effect whereby, for example, more than one plane of a woman's face could be combined in a single image. Pen and his mentor Warrington in the above scene are at the same time young men of the 1830s and bewhiskered, tobacco-reeking, 'muscular' hearties of the early 1850s, verging on middle age. They inhabit the present and the past simultaneously, offering two planes of their lives to the reader simultaneously. The moment at which Thackeray discovered this technique can be located precisely in the early pages of *Vanity Fair*. At the conclusion of chapter 6 of the first edition we find the following footnote:

It was the author's intention, faithful to history, to depict all the characters of this tale in their proper costumes, as they wore them at the commencement of the century. But when I remember the appearance of people in those days, and that an officer and lady were actually habited like this—

I have not the heart to disfigure my heroes and heroines by costumes so hideous; and have, on the contrary, engaged a model of rank dressed according to the present fashion.

What Thackeray is asserting here is that his characters, while inhabiting the Regency world of 1813, will also be contemporaries (that is, Victorians of 1847). They are to be seen in two dimensions.

One must distinguish this constructive play with anachronism from lapses which arise from carelessness on Thackeray's part. An example is the confusion that surrounds Laura Bell's age at central points of *Pendennis*'s narrative. On page 36 we are told that the little orphan 'would be eighteen when Pen was six-and-twenty', at which point Pen's mother fondly intends that they shall be married. In fact, Pen pops the question when he is 'three and twenty' (p. 346). Laura (who has already attracted the attention of the local parliamentary candidate, Pynsent, who is looking for a wife) has a fine *embonpoint*, as Thackeray's illustration of the proposal scene shows:

But, if we calculate, this full-grown and handsomely developed woman is just fifteen, and perhaps a month or so short of that age. It is unthinkable that Pynsent and Pendennis would compete to break the law in marrying a girl a year short of the age of consent (given the later onset of menstruation in early nineteenth-century middle-class girls Laura might not even have reached puberty). It would have been quite simple to rectify this by going back and changing the earlier age reference to 'she would be eighteen when Pen was three-and-twenty'. Thackeray made numerous and fine-detailed changes to *Pendennis*, but did not change this anomaly which remains a mote to trouble the mind's eye.

At every point in *Pendennis* the alert reader has to discriminate between constructive errors and errors which unsettle the fictional illusion. Take, for instance, the episode in chapter 55 in which Captain Costigan is seen, 'one brilliant September morning' reeling back through Covent Garden after a night's debauch, 'with a crowd of hooting blackguard boys at his heels':

The Captain won't go home till morning.

The Captain is observed by Sam Huxter who, after his night's revels, is refreshing himself at a coffee stall, shadowily visible in the background of the picture. (Also visible, at the top right, is 'MMUMS', short for HUMMUMS, or Turkish Baths. At this period, it still carried the traditional overtone of 'bagnio', or 'stew'—that is, brothel—and reminds us that Sam, a young swell, has not been spending the night listening to opera.) A good-hearted fellow, Sam follows the Captain, whom he knows distantly. Sure enough, the old man falls down and Sam (who is a medical student) rushes forward to give first aid:

What is noticeable here is that both characters have changed their wardrobe. The Captain is no longer wearing his opera cloak (appropriate for a brisk September morning) nor does he any longer have tails, but a cutaway coat. Sam has replaced the huge bow cravat he was earlier wearing with more modest neckwear. One can reconstruct how the discrepancy came about. The first illustration was on steel, and had to be sent away to the engravers very early—before the copy was written, one may assume. The second illustration is a woodcut, done some weeks later while he was writing the number but before Thackeray had seen proofs of his steel engraving. Details of dress slipped his mind in the interval.

This oversight should be distinguished from the anachronism in chapter 10, showing the young swell Foker in jaunty conversation with the oafish lieutenant, Sir Derby Oaks, Pen's rival for the hand of 'La Fotheringay'. Phallic rivalry is hinted by the angle of Sir Derby's 'weapon' and the superbly erect Trafalgar cannon behind him (the cannon Captain Costigan is leaning against in the preceding picture has a distinct touch of brewer's droop):

One notes in passing that Foker wears the loose, dark-hued frock coat and is smoking the cheroot appropriate to a young fashionable of the 1840s. But more significant is that Sir Derby is corsetted in an absurdly tight 'shell jacket'—an item of military clothing not worn by young officers in home postings in 1828 (when this scene is set). There was, however, a huge controversy about shell jackets in 1848–9, when the narrow tunics were reintroduced as compulsory wear by the War Office, intent on making their peace-time army look more warrior-like. *Punch* had many jokes and cartoons about 'stout warriors' popping out of their shell jackets at the same period that Thackeray was writing and publishing these chapters of *Pendennis*. This is an example of him transmitting on two chronological channels, reconstructing the past and making a sly allusion to the present.

II

CLOSE CRITICAL attention has focused on the 'errors' in Thackeray's third full-length novel, *The History of Henry Esmond*. The novel was widely (and often pedantically) annotated as a historical novel for school use. *Henry Esmond* is also the only long novel of Thackeray's to be narrated autobiographically. Although the hero-narrator casts his account as a third-person narrative he regularly lapses into 'I narration' at moments of excitement, or when his guard slips. These inconsistencies are clearly contrived by Thackeray. Taking this as their cue, critics have persuasively argued that *all* the irregularities and contradictions in Harry's account are the product of Thackeray's artfulness. Like the fossils that God put in the rocks to fool the evolutionists, they are evidence of a higher plan. Persuasive and learned articles have been written on this subject and there have been authoritative disquisitions on the masterly 'irony' of *Henry Esmond*'s errors.[12]

It is again necessary to distinguish between one kind of error and another. Not even super-ingenious Freudianism could justify such authorial parapraxes as when Henry Esmond is made to call Frank Castlewood 'Arthur' (Thackeray's mind had momentarily slipped back to *Pendennis*). Nor can sense be made of the following exchange between Harry and Beatrix. She twits him with the suggestion (prophetic enough) that he should marry 'their' mother, Rachel:

'Mamma would have been the wife for you, had you been a little older, though you look ten years older than she does—you do, you glum-faced, blue-bearded, little old man! You might have sat, like Darby and Joan, and flattered each other; and billed and cooed like a pair of old pigeons on a perch. I want my wings and to use them, sir.' And she spread out her beautiful arms, as if indeed she could fly off like the pretty 'Gawrie', whom the man in the story was enamoured of.

'And what will your Peter Wilkins say to your flight?' says Esmond, who never admired this fair creature more than when she rebelled and laughed at him. (p. 294)[13]

The Life and Adventures of Peter Wilkins (by Robert Paltock) was published in 1751, some forty years after the Queen Anne period in which this conversation takes place and—by the best reckoning one can make—well after Esmond's death. The only way this literary jest can be rationalized (and it would be a fantastic if attractive hypothesis) is to assume that it is an interposition by Esmond's busybody daughter and the novel's 'editor', Rachel Esmond Warrington, rewriting the scene in the 1770s and unwittingly revealing the extent of her interference. There are other passages in *Henry Esmond* where (as with the transposed paragraph blemish in *Vanity Fair*) Thackeray seems on the face of it deliberately to have left contradictions in the text, as a kind of challenge to those 'donkies', his readers. Take the following paragraph, dealing with the conspiracy to bring the Pretender back to the Castlewoods' London house incognito, so that he may be smuggled to Court for a reconciliation with the Queen—the plot which Esmond has devised to restore the Stuarts to the throne of England:

Esmond's man, honest John Lockwood, had served his master and the family all his life, and the Colonel [i.e. Esmond] knew that he could answer for John's fidelity as for his own. John returned with the horses from Rochester betimes the next morning, and the Colonel gave him to understand that on going to Kensington, where he was free of the servants' hall, and indeed courting Mrs Beatrix's maid, he was to ask no questions, and betray no surprise, but to vouch stoutly that the young gentleman he should see in a red coat there was my lord Viscount Castlewood, and that his attendant in grey was Monsieur Baptiste, the Frenchman. He was to tell his friends in the kitchen such stories as he remembered of my Lord Viscount's youth at Castlewood; what a wild boy he was; how he used to drill Jack and cane him, before ever he was a soldier; everything, in fine, he knew respecting my Lord Viscount's early days. Jack's ideas of painting had not been much cultivated during his residence in Flanders with his master; and before my young lord's return, he had been easily got to believe that the picture brought over from Paris, and now hanging in Lady Castlewood's drawing-room, was a perfect likeness of her son, the young lord. And the domestics having all seen the picture many times, and catching but a momentary imperfect glimpse of the two strangers on the night of their arrival, never had a reason to doubt the fidelity of the portrait; and next day, when they saw the original of the piece habited exactly as he was represented in the painting, with the same periwig, ribands, and uniform of the Guard, quite naturally addressed the gentleman as my Lord Castlewood, my Lady Viscountess's son. (pp. 416–7)

Now clearly Lockwood cannot both be a member of the conspiracy, as he is in the first half of the paragraph, and a dupe as he is in the second half of the paragraph. To ascribe this to knowing 'art' on Thackeray's part would suggest that he conceived his narrator to be in the terminal stages of Alzheimer's disease. In order to understand how this nonsense came about, one has to reconstruct Thackeray's design for climax to his action and (probable) running changes that he made to it during the course of writing.

As Thackeray originally devised it, Esmond's plot to restore the Stuarts was to have three main elements: (1) the Prince was to be smuggled out of France into England on the Viscount's (i.e. Frank Castlewood's) passports, disguised as a servant, M. Baptiste. This precaution was necessary lest he be recognized by some keen-eyed official at the port of departure or entry; (2) once safely landed in England, the plan was that 'M. Baptiste' should switch with the Viscount, the better to allow him to gain entrance to the Court, where he might have his fateful interview with Queen Anne. Clearly as a French servant his way would be barred. Inexplicably, this switch was to take place on the morning *after* the party arrived at the Castlewoods' London house, not in some lane on the outskirts of the city; (3) as preparation for the switch, a portrait of the Prince (by Rigaud) purporting to be one of the Viscount should be sent ahead. Since the Viscount had been resident in France for a number of years, and was generally unfamiliar to the servants of the household, this portrait would allay any suspicions they might have as to the identity of the strange, Gallicised, master of the house.

What I surmise to have happened is that Thackeray had an original longer version of this episode (possibly in note form) in which an unwitting Jack Lockwood was sent ahead by several months with the portrait, ignorant of the ruse. But when he came to write the episode, Thackeray drastically reduced the space given to the portrait trick. Lockwood was reinstalled as part of the Esmond-Castlewood entourage and necessarily in the know. Thackeray, in the confusion of writing, did not sort out contradictions between the longer and the shorter version—hence the two quite different John Lockwoods inhabiting the above passage.

III

IN THE LAST section of this chapter I want to look closely at the eleventh chapter of the first book of *Henry Esmond*. General discussions of the novel make frequent reference to this chapter. Many central lines of plot and theme unwind from it. Here we have the most impassioned of the outbursts against the miseries of ill-assorted marriage (whose emotional source Gordon Ray has traced).[14] For the first time, the secret of Esmond's legitimate birth is opened to the attentive reader. The Jacobite conspiracies which are to culminate in the romantic adventure of the third volume are prefigured, and the most interesting of the psychological subplots, that of the jealousy between Rachel and Beatrix and their rivalry for Harry, is begun. This chapter also shows at its highest tension the hero's peculiar Oedipal tension towards his 'beloved patron' who is also the despised 'dullard' and 'boor' married to Rachel. It is, in short, the start of the novel's action proper. And yet it is, carefully read, a stretch of narrative which hinges on perplexingly sustained chronological contradictions.

The chapter begins, 'At his third long vacation, Esmond came as usual to Castlewood' (p. 113), which takes up the last sentence of the previous chapter, ' . . . he went to spend the last vacation he should have at Castlewood before he took orders' (p. 113). Harry is welcomed home from Cambridge by Rachel and her children. The mother's greeting is so melancholy as to astonish him, although the daughter is gay enough: 'Miss Beatrix was grown so tall that Harry did not quite know whether he might kiss her or no; and she blushed and held back when he offered that salutation, though she took it, and even courted it, when they were alone' (p. 113). Frank, we are told, is 'shooting up to be like his gallant father in look' (p. 113). In their turn they admire Harry who now sports a moustache and is told by the children that he is not to be a page any more 'but a gentleman and kinsman' (p. 114). This is probably slightly proleptic; in their enthusiasm the young people are thinking ahead a few months to when Harry, newly graduated, will be ordained. They conduct him to his old chamber in which, it appears, Lady Castlewood has put roses with her own hand and lit a fire, although it is, of course, June. Harry is left with the children and, prattling on his knee, Beatrix, who suddenly seems to have lost a few of her years, tells him: 'I don't think papa is very fond of mamma.' This explains Rachel's surprising sadness and inspires Esmond's inner soliloquy on domestic misery which carries over three pages. It concludes: 'This couple was living apart then; the woman happy to be allowed to love and tend her children (who were never of her own goodwill away from her) and thankful to have saved such treasures as these out of the wreck in which the better part of her heart went down' (p. 118).

The next paragraph tells us that 'These young ones had no instructors save their mother, and Doctor Tusher' (p. 118). We already know this, the same information is given two pages earlier in the conversation with Beatrix. But it seems that Thackeray is doing everything twice round. Once more the first impression of the flirtatious Beatrix is given: 'She put on a new ribbon to welcome Harry Esmond, made eyes at him . . . not a little to the amusement of the young man' (p. 118). Again we go over the plight of the Castlewoods, but although the description of the unhappy *ménage* is repeated and the universal hardship of the wife's lot again bemoaned, the tone is now calmer, even philosophic: 'Alas, that youthful love and truth should end in bitterness and bankruptcy! To see a young couple loving each other is no wonder; but to see an old couple loving each other is the best sight of all' (p. 119). And Esmond's seems to have been a very long long-vacation indeed since, in illustration of the marital discord now obvious, we are shown the different parental reactions to Frank's pie-eating exploits on the 'day after New Year's Day' (p. 119). This section ends with a passage describing how Harry is initiated into the 'sad secret of his patron's household . . . compelled to understand and pity a grief which he stood quite powerless to relieve' (p. 120).

The narrative then takes an abrupt turn from the domestic to the historical and political: 'It hath been said my lord would never take the oath of allegiance, nor his seat as a peer of the kingdom of Ireland' (p. 120). In fact something quite different was said in chapter 7: 'My lord went to London every year for six weeks, and the family being too poor to appear at Court with any figure, he went alone' (p. 73). But Thackeray (or possibly a forgetful Esmond) is not careful about the consistency of such details, so now we have a completely rusticated Viscount. More relevantly there follows a little essay on the assassination plot of 1695, sanctioned by 'King' James in exile, and for complicity in which Sir John Fenwick lost his head. Captain James (the Duke of Berwick), it appears, visited Castlewood with the Jesuit conspirator, Father Holt, on his secret embassy to promote this. But when Fenwick was executed in 1697 (Thackeray seems to make it 1696) and William burned the list of conspirators which included Francis Castlewood, the Viscount swore never again to plot against 'that brave and merciful man' (p. 121). In an attempt to coerce him Holt returns during Harry's 'first vacation from college' (p. 121) and, we guess, blackmails the reluctant conspirator with the truth of Harry's birth. This produces symptoms of disquiet which Esmond perceives, but cannot interpret. It takes place in 1696 and we can date Harry's last vacation (that is, when the chapter began) as

1700 from such unequivocal historical datemarks as William's death and the War of Spanish Succession.

We now go further back to 1690 when, we discover, the hero saved baby Frank from burning alive in the hall fire. This rescue was 'one of the causes why my Lord Viscount had taken Esmond into his special favour' (p. 122). It is a fact 'that hath not before been mentioned' (p. 122) says Esmond, modestly. It is, none the less, rather odd to double-back ten years at this stage when Esmond's adult career has been embarked upon. But one narrative reason for it becomes immediately apparent; it is staged so that Thackeray can indirectly let the reader into Holt's secret. It is worth quoting here at a little more length since from this passage springs much subsequent confusion:

My lady seldom drank wine; but on certain days of the year, such as birthdays (poor Harry had never a one) and anniversaries, she took a little; and this day, the 29th December, was one. At the end, then, of this year, '96, it might have been a fortnight after Mr Holt's last visit, Lord Castlewood being still very gloomy in mind and sitting at table—my lady bidding a servant bring her a glass of wine, and looking at her husband with one of her sweet smiles, said—

'My lord, will you not fill a bumper, too, and let me call a toast?'

'What is it, Rachel?' says he, holding out his empty glass to be filled.

''Tis the 29th of December,' says my lady, with her fond look of gratitude: 'and my toast is "Harry—and God bless him, who saved my boy's life!" '

My lord looked at Harry hard, and drank the glass, but clapped it down on the table in a moment, and, with a sort of moan, rose up, and went out of the room. What was the matter? We all knew that some great grief was over him. (p. 123)

Quite clearly, from the month and year, this cannot refer to Harry's long vacation, although it may belong to his first Christmas break. Even so the dates do not quite fit, since if he is home for his third long vacation in 1700 he must have gone up in the Autumn of 1697. But this is without doubt the 'now' of chapter 11 as it finishes, despite the impossibility of synchronising 1696 with the opening. The continuation from the passage above clinches this:

Whether my lord's prudence had made him richer, or legacies had fallen to him, which enabled him to support a greater establishment than that frugal one which had been too much for his small means, Harry Esmond knew not; but the house of Castlewood was *now* on a scale much more costly than it had been during the first years of his lordship's coming to the title. (p. 123)

The chapter ends a page later (with no resetting in time) on the visit from Sark Castle which is the means of introducing the serpent Mohun into Castlewood.

So our chapter begins with a moustached Esmond coming back in the summer of his final year (1700) and ends with a beardless Harry, barely a freshman, home for his first Christmas vacation (1696). And if we are really careful calculators we know that Esmond cannot have gone to Cambridge until 1697. Nor is it an encapsulated flashback; the next chapter and succeeding action takes off from this last point of the Sark visit which seems to be consecutive with Holt's mysterious business. To complicate the problem beyond the capacity of even the closest readers the final paragraph of the next chapter, 12, declares: 'It happened, then, that Harry Esmond came home to Castlewood for his last vacation, with good hopes of a fellowship at his college, and a contented resolve to advance his fortune that way. 'Twas in the first year of the present century' (p. 134). This is purportedly after the Sark visit in which Castlewood encountered and became crazed with Mohun's company, which in turn followed Esmond's return for 'the last vacation he should have at Castlewood before he took orders' (p. 113)—nothing about a fellowship then, we expected him to take up the living which Tom Tusher eventually gets. We may base this sequence on the argument between Castlewood and his wife over their first impressions of Mohun at the beginning of chapter 12 from which Esmond 'might see how hopelessly separated they were; what a great gulf of difference and discord had run between them' (p. 127). This presumably bears out the new 'I don't think papa is fond of mamma discovery'. Unfortunately for the logic of this episode, in chapter 13 Thackeray tries to get Mohun into an earlier stage of the narrative by recalling a visit which he and Castlewood had paid Esmond at the university the previous spring. The novelist does not tie this chronological loop in with what has gone before, trusting perhaps to the general haze of the narrative to cover it up.

Pedantic reading can find other anomalies in this section of the book. Consider these two quotations from chapter 11:

Waking up from dreams, books, and visions of college honours in which, for two years, Harry Esmond had been immersed, he found himself, instantly on his return home, in the midst of this actual tragedy of life. (p. 116)

So, into the sad secret of his patron's household, Harry Esmond became initiated; he scarce knew how. It had passed under his eyes two years before, when he could not understand it; but reading, and thought, and experience of men, had oldened him. (p. 120)

The main implication of these statements is that it is not until his return from Cambridge in his third year that Esmond has realized the wreck of the Castlewoods' marriage and that this realization comes as shock. Hence he is 'startled' by Rachel's appearance: 'A something hinting at grief and secrets, and filling his mind with alarm undefinable, seemed to speak with that low thrilling voice of hers, and look out of those clear sad eyes' (p. 114). The grief is, we must assume, the result of her having fallen out of love with her husband. But can we accept that this has, until 1700 and his own majority, been a 'secret' kept from Esmond, passing under his eyes without his understanding it? On the Viscount's return to Castlewood after the smallpox epidemic in 1695 we are told that 'Esmond began to divine how unhappy his adored lady's life was, and that a secret care (for she never spoke of her anxieties) was weighing upon her' (p. 193). Then it was that he discovered about 'the person at Hexton' (p. 122), her husband's mistress, and then it was, presumably, that Esmond became initiated into 'the sad secret of his patron's household', and this well before going up to Cambridge. On the face of it, Thackeray seems to have made Esmond discover the sad secret on two occasions separated by five years and two chapters.

The most persistent confusion, however, concerns Holt's visit to Castlewood to blackmail the Viscount, and how long the latter was in possession of the knowledge that Harry's title had been usurped from him. This is important because it determines the degree of villainy we impute to Castlewood, a principal character. On his return from his short spell in prison in 1701, Esmond tells the old Dowager Countess that his 'dear patron knew not the truth until a few months before his death' (p. 185), itself a few months earlier. This is confirmed when some pages later Esmond, now an officer enrolled in the fight against the French, which makes it 1702, mentions 'my poor lord's hurried confession that he had been made acquainted with the real facts of the case only two years since' (p. 192). How then do we explain the Viscount's 'sort of groan' and his 'great grief' at the toasting of Harry on 29 December 'this year '96, it might have been a fortnight after Mr Holt's last visit' (p. 123)? To cap it all we are told, only two pages after the assertion that Castlewood knew nothing until 1700, that Holt did not return as promised to follow up his disillusionment of Harry's patron because ''Ere the twelve hours were over, Holt himself was a prisoner, implicated in Sir John Fenwick's conspiracy' (p. 194). This would make it 1697 by historical reckoning and 1696 by Thackeray's slightly anachronistic chronicling of the event. Most readers, I think, will see this as an important discrepancy. If the Viscount had the secret four years and lied even on his death-bed then he must be considered a blackguard. If he knew about Harry's birth for only a few months then we, like Esmond, may forgive him.

In a letter of 1889 to Trinity College Cambridge, to whom he donated the manuscript of *Henry Esmond*, Leslie Stephen writes: 'there was no previous copy. Thackeray wrote (or dictated) the manuscript as it stands without previously putting anything on paper, and it was sent in this form to the printers.'[15] This is not quite right. There was originally another chapter 11 which Thackeray dropped. There was also some discarded narrative stocked with vital information about his birth left over from Esmond's earlier history, the important elements of which Thackeray had not reworked into the final pruned draft. These two ingredients were thrown into the final draft of chapter 11.

Although about a third of *Henry Esmond* was dictated to amanuenses, chapter 11 is in Thackeray's two handwritings.[16] The opening section (from the first paragraph on page 113 to the fourteenth paragraph on page 118) is on yellowish paper in Thackeray's sloping hand. It ends on 'the wreck in which the better part of her heart went down'. The second section (page 118 paragraph 15 to page 120 paragraph 18), that is the repeated description of Harry's arrival and the less furious reflection on married unhappiness, is written in Thackeray's upright hand on white paper. The third section (page 120 paragraph 19 to page 123 paragraph 34) covering Holt's visits, Harry's birth, the rescue of little Frank, and the anniversary toast, is written in the sloping hand but on blue Reform Club paper. The last section (page 123 paragraph 35 to page 125 paragraph 37), the Sark Castle visits, is, like the first, written on yellowish paper in the sloping hand.

With this information one can work out what happened. Originally Thackeray wrote a chapter centred on Harry's visit to Castlewood in the Christmas of his second year at Cambridge. This was to have stood where the present chapter 11 is. We even have the opening of this omitted chapter in the manuscript, crossed out but still legible, at the head of the second section in upright hand (the reason for its being there will appear in a moment). It goes:

If young Henry Esmond had any ambition to make a figure at the University, his hopes were disappointed, for fate and circumstance very soon put an end to his career there. In the second year of his residence, he being then nearly twenty years of age (and indeed older in years of experience than most of his college companions) he came home gladly to pass the Christmas vacation at Castlewood, and to revisit his dear friends and patron. He had been away from home more than a year—Mistress Beatrix was growing up to be a tall and bright-eyed lass, and little Frank Esmond shooting up to be a graceful stripling.[17]

It then continues as we have it in the published text from 'These young ones had no instructors save their mother, and Doctor Tusher' (p. 118). But having written all, or most, of this chapter Thackeray must have decided he was spending too long on Esmond's prehistory so he scrubbed out as much of his Cambridge career as he could, giving only half of chapter 10 to a summary account of these three years. This enabled him to jump ahead to the last summer of his hero's adult life, and the beginnings of the sexual complications of his adulthood, the Mohun entanglement and the imminent war. But while writing this later chapter 11 (i.e. the first section, as I have called it above), he realized that there was useful material about the second-year Harry in the deleted chapter and that his later version was dominated by an emotional *cri de cœur* that did nothing for the action. He therefore cut off the head and tail of his old chapter and grafted it in (this is what I have called the second section; its 'head' is the passage quoted above). This section transplants well apart from such discrepancies as Frank's New Year pies and a general sense of *déjà-vu*. Thackeray must also have realized at this point that he was being dilatory about moving the plot along and that he had left out some essential data about Harry's origins. So he exhumed an even earlier fragment from the chapter 9 area (this I have called the third section) which concerned Harry's pre-Cambridge life. This we may assume from the abrupt steps four and ten years backward and a modification which Thackeray made, in manuscript, to the account of Holt's last, and for the Viscount fatal, visit. Originally this read: 'It was in these days that Holt payed that final visit to his lordship and this left my Lord Viscount very much disturbed in mind.' Somehow, in its new later context, this visit had to be integrated with Harry's university period. And there was the added difficulty that the Fenwick affair tied it down closely to 1696, which was too early. Thackeray gambled that the reader would not notice if he jumped a year, so he made this the *first* Christmas vacation instead of the year before going up, and revised the above thus:

> The last conference which Mr Holt had with his lordship took place when Harry was come home for his first vacation from college (Harry saw his old tutor but for a half-hour, and exchanged no private words with him), and their talk, whatever it might be, left my lord viscount very much disturbed in mind. (p. 121)

Apart from this interpolation in a different and presumably later ink, there is nothing else in the third section about Harry being an undergraduate, as indeed he could not have been in 1696. But since the rescue anniversary was in December, Thackeray could at least mitigate the anachronism by having Esmond back at the earliest possible occasion, his first vacation. As we can see from the crossed-out preface to the second section it was originally the intention to have Esmond away from Castlewood for 'more than a year', thus making his ignorance of the gradual estrangement of the Castlewoods more plausible. This, though psychologically sound, had to go in the general shuffling of dates.

At this point, with the end of the chapter in sight, Thackeray must have been aware that he had introduced three chronologically different Harries, adult, adolescent, and juvenile, without any logical transitions; that he was entangled with two periods (1696 and 1700) and even two seasons of the year, long vacation and Christmas vacation. He may have toyed with changing the anniversary from 29 December to 29 June—but then Frank could scarcely have fallen into the fire, it would have to be something like the fountain in the great court. Rather than tinker in this way Thackeray simply latched the Sark visit (the fourth section which evidently dates from the same period of composition as the first) on to what he had already written. And this, with the other abrupt connexions, puts a large part of the chapter out six months seasonally and four years historically. It also renders for ever mysterious the nature of Viscount Castlewood, the villain who keeps Harry out of his inheritance for four years or the unlucky man who discovers just before his death that he has enjoyed his title and his possessions under false pretences.

The fact that no readers (as far as I know) have ever complained about Thackeray's rather clumsy footwork in chapter 11 of *Henry Esmond* (any more than they complained about the misplaced paragraphs in *Vanity Fair*) tells us something about the kind of relaxed reading his fiction encourages. Like the mosquito, which anaesthetizes its victim before getting to work with its proboscis, Thackeray induces in his readers a kind of indifference to fine points of detail. One has to read the text very much against the grain to see the contradictions. There is also something emotionally true about the confusion of dates and years in Esmond's university narrative. Most graduates, in later life, find that their memories run together and that it is difficult to separate one year's experience from another in the mind. There is another intriguing psychological aspect to the drastic shortening of the account of Esmond's years at Cambridge. Thackeray had done exactly the same in the previous novel, where Pendennis's college career (which Thackeray clearly intended to be a longish interlude) was brutally shortened. One explanation is that Thackeray was still bruised by the uproar caused by his 'University Snobs' chapters in *The Snobs of England* (1847). But it is tempting to detect deeper motives. Thackeray's closest friend at Trinity had been William Brookfield, the man whose wife he was in love with while writing *Pendennis* and *Henry Esmond*. It may be that revisiting the scenes of his early friendship at college (and the shared debauchery, and his disgraceful failure to get a degree) was too much for him.

CHAPTER TWO

Writing The Woman in White

THE GENERALLY accepted historical starting point for sensational fiction is 1859 and the serial publication of Wilkie Collins's *The Woman in White* in *All the Year Round* (26 November 1859–25 August 1860). *The Woman in White* was received by its first readers as a distinctly novel kind of novel. Specifically it was the originality of device that excited Collins's contemporaries and kept readers like Thackeray—someone who yawned over most popular fiction—turning pages 'from morning till sunset'.[1] The same originality made other contemporaries—writers such as Mrs Braddon, Charles Reade, and possibly even Dickens—aspire to imitate Collins's new tricks.

All witnesses testify to the amazing impact of *The Woman in White*, its 'shock' effect, as a not entirely approving Mrs Oliphant called it.[2] The newness of *The Woman in White* inheres, I suggest, in two cardinal features. First the detective feats of the heroic trio against their criminal rivals; second, the high-impact narrative. Disdaining conventional chapter structure, *The Woman in White* unfolds as a series of testimonies, or evidence given by involved parties, none of whom has the traditional fictional prerogative of omniscience. Collins's narrative has a pseudo-documentary surface and real-time chronology which teasingly negate the work's inner identity as fiction. Victorian readers were not used to this trick and they liked it.

What follows is primarily concerned with Collins's narrative innovations, but I shall digress briefly on *The Woman in White* and the science of criminal detection in mid-Victorian England. The idea that crime constituted an intellectual problem to be 'solved' (as opposed to an offence to be punished) was not something that originated in the imagination of writers of fiction—although it was quickly and profitably exploited by them. To mobilize detective intelligence against criminal cunning was a main motive in the Police Act of 1856. The strictly forensic procedures of law were no longer felt to be sufficient for the uncovering of serious felony, any more than hue and cry or the assistance of bribed street informants were now sufficient to capture the cleverer class of thief. Significantly, the first *OED*-recorded use of the word 'detective', in its modern sense of ingenious policeman, dates from 1856.[3] Underlying the 1856 Police Bill was a profound scepticism that crime would invariably uncover itself, that it never paid and that murders would out, though all the world overwhelmed them to men's eyes. These proverbial truths—truths very dear to the traditional novel with its canons of poetic justice—no longer held. A child of the time, Fosco waxes eloquently on the subject at Blackwater Park. 'It is truly wonderful', the fat arch-criminal observes:

how easily Society can console itself for the worst of its short-comings with a little bit of claptrap. The machinery it has set up for the detection of crime is miserably ineffective [he is talking in 1850]—and yet only invent a moral epigram, saying that it works well, and you blind everybody to its blunders from that moment. Crimes cause their own detection, do they? And murder will out (another moral epigram), will it? Ask Coroners who sit at inquests in large towns if that is true . . . Ask secretaries of life-assurance companies. (p. 202)[4]

Fosco concludes: 'there are foolish criminals who are discovered, and wise criminals who escape. The hiding of a crime, or the detection of a crime what is it? *A trial of skill* between the police on one side, and the individual on the other' (p. 210–11, my italics). Criminals ('Wise-guys'), it was felt in the 1850s, were becoming cleverer—geniuses in some cases. In fiction this conviction founded a line of anti-heroes which begins with Fosco—who discourses with scientists on equal terms—and leads to that strange contradiction, the academically distinguished arch-criminal like 'Professor Moriarty', and 'Doctor Nikola'. Before 1850 the liaison between erudition and low crime would have seemed freakish.[5]

Two varieties of clever crime particularly obsessed mid-Victorians—secret poisoning and forgery. At their most skilful, these felonies involved long premeditation, duplicity, and superior intellect. They, and crimes like them, called for enhanced police skills in detection. Hence Scotland Yard and all it implies to the popular mind. The 1856 Police Act was, of course, only concerned to set up a corps of professional detectives—sworn officers of the law.[6] A year later in 1857 the Matrimonial Causes Act—Britain's new and relaxed divorce legislation—mobilized a whole new army of amateur and unofficial detectives; namely, the suspicious spouse and his or her agent. What the 1857 Act decreed was that divorce should be a legal option if adultery could be proved against the erring wife; and if adultery—

aggravated by such additional offences as incest, violence, outrageous cruelty, bigamy, desertion, or sodomy—could be proved against the erring husband.

Adultery is notoriously an offence which has many participants but very few eyewitnesses. It may be, as the Latin phrase has it, delightful, but it is rarely flagrant. Typically the adulterous act must be reconstructed from circumstantial evidence—such things as hotel registers, private letters, travel movements, suspicious absences. Typically adulterers go to great length and use enormous ingenuity to cover their tracks. One thinks, for instance, of the lengths Dickens went to in concealing his connection with Ellen Ternan and Wilkie Collins his cohabitation with Martha Rudd. A demonstration of adultery that will stand up in court often requires formidable detective resources. The first use of the term 'private detective' recorded in the *OED* relates to Samuel Bozzle in Trollope's *He Knew He Was Right* (1869). Bozzle is the agent employed by Louis Trevelyan to spy on his wife and discover her (non-existent) adulteries. The 1857 Act gave a huge boost to the detective profession, more particularly the private investigator or 'eye'. Philip Marlowe, Sam Spade, and Magnum PI may all find a main line of their ancestry in the Victorian keyhole peeper like Bozzle.

The 1857 Act ensured that the relationship of wife to husband was subtly altered. Prudent partners realized that in their own interest they should keep a file on their other halves. Spouses became spies. This suspiciousness is not, of course, flattering to the holy state of matrimony. Victorian wives—angels in the house—cut a particularly poor figure steaming open their husbands' letters or rifling pocket books. Wilkie Collins sanitizes his saintly Laura by having the resourceful Marian do the actual snooping; snooping that includes listening at keyholes, intercepting mail and—in one heroic act of domestic espionage—perching on a window during a rainstorm in order to eavesdrop on Percival, the errant husband. The novel persuades us that such low acts are necessary, if a Victorian wife is to protect her rights.

In one of its main aspects, then, *The Woman in White* can be read as a study in divorce, Victorian-style. And one of the many narrative problems facing Collins as he galloped through the serialization of the novel, improvising resourcefully as he went, was how decently to cast asunder man and wife, Laura and Percival Glyde, so that she may eventually be free to marry Walter Hartright. The novelist eventually solved his problem by full-blooded melodramatic device. Glyde is burned to death in a church—whose sacraments he has defiled—attempting to destroy evidence of his illegitimacy. (This, rather disappointingly, is the great 'secret' about which eager readers of the serial were casting bets among themselves.) Glyde's immolation is poetically just but unlikely. The more realistic outcome in 1860 would have been for Sir Percival's private detectives to discover Laura and Walter cohabiting in the East End of London. This would constitute *prima facie* proof of adultery in the hands of any competent counsel who would make hay of the defence that the couple were living together as brother and sister.[7] They might afterwards be free to marry but Mr and Mrs Hartright would be for ever outcasts from respectable society.

I have suggested that 1856 and 1857 are significant dates if we want to reconstruct the idea of *The Woman in White* as it formed in Wilkie Collins's mind in 1859. There is another significant date—1855. In this year the last of the so-called 'taxes on knowledge' (i.e. the newspaper stamp) was removed. The result was what histories of British journalism record as a 'stupendous' growth in popular 1*d.* newspapers, of which the best known and most enduring was the *Daily Telegraph*.[8] These cheaper prints contained many more crime stories than their 4*d.* and 5*d.* rivals like *The Times*. More to the point here, the 1*d.* press with its larger circulation and more competitive tone fostered what we now call investigative reporting. The investigative reporter has close affinity with the detective (whether private or in the force) and in the modern thriller the two types are interchangeable as heroes. The *Telegraph*'s most famous investigative reporter was George Augustus Sala—who had learned his craft on *Household Words*. Sala was an exact contemporary of Wilkie Collins, a comrade on the *Household Words* team, and like Collins he went on to become a pioneer sensation novelist (if a less successful one). Among everything else, *Household Words* can be seen as a nursery of investigative journalism and a cradle of sensation fiction—stories with the immediacy of the day's newspaper headlines.

I want now to turn to Collins's idiosyncratic or 'high impact' mode of narration in *The Woman in White*. Collins expounds his technique to the reader in the 'Preamble' to the novel, using Hartright's voice:

As the Judge might once have heard it, so the Reader shall hear it now. No circumstance of importance, from the beginning to the end of the disclosure, shall be related on hearsay evidence. When the writer of these introductory lines (Walter Hartright by name) happens to be more closely connected than others with the incidents to be recorded, he will describe them in his own person. When his experience fails, he will retire from the position of narrator, and his task will be continued, from the point at which he has left it off, by other persons who can speak to the circumstances under notice from their own knowledge, just as clearly and positively as he has spoken before them. Thus the story here presented will be told by more than one pen, as the story of an offence against the laws is told in Court by more than one witness—with the same object, in both cases, to present the truth always in its most direct and most intelligible aspect; and to trace the course of one complete series of events, by making the persons who have been most closely connected with them, at each successive stage, relate their own experience, word for word. (p. 1)

The novel is as good as Hartright's word. A succession of witnesses lines up to address the reader, from principals like Hartright, Marian, Fairlie, and Fosco, to friends of the principals like the lawyers Gilmore and Kyrle and even humble bystanders like Hester Pinhorn the illiterate chambermaid or the gullible Eliza Michelson, housekeeper (dismissed) of Blackwater Park. Each offers his or her piece of evidence to the great jigsaw puzzle.

Wilkie Collins complacently claimed in his 1860 preface to *The Woman in White* that his evidentiary technique was entirely original: 'an experiment is attempted in this novel which has not (so far as I know) been hitherto tried in fiction' (p. xxxv). This is an over-statement several commentators have contradicted or modified. What about *Wuthering Heights*, they ask; or the final sections of Hogg's *Confessions of a Justified Sinner* and Bulwer's *Eugene Aram*, where the narratives dissolve into facsimile documents and reportage? As a number of reviewers pointed out, the eighteenth-century epistolary novel anticipated main aspects of Collins's technique in *The Woman in White*. Henry James—who disliked the novel's 'ponderosity'— called it dismissively 'a kind of nineteenth-century version of Clarissa Harlowe'.[9]

There were also two more direct inspirations for *The Woman in White*'s method, one at least of which was cited in reviews at the time. In 1856 *Household Words* offered in its extra Christmas number a tale 'by several hands' (principally those of Dickens and Collins) called *The Wreck of the Golden Mary*. This tale took the form of linked testimonies to a disaster at sea, given in the form of 'The Captain's Account', 'The Mate's Account', 'The Old Sailor's Story', and so on. The other commented-on forerunner of *The Woman in White* was Dinah Mulock Craik's *A Life for a Life*. This narrative takes the form of two intertwining diaries whose entries cumulatively tell the story of a doomed love affair. Craik's novel came out in late July 1859, while Collins was at Broadstairs, racking his brains how to begin *The Woman in White*.

The unoriginality of *The Woman in White* was pointed out, more or less small-mindedly, by Collins's contemporaries in a spirit of nothing new under the sun. But arguably they all missed the point. What Collins primarily stresses in his opening remarks is the analogy of *The Woman in White*'s narrative to the processes of *law*, as it is ritually played out in the English criminal court. The novel's technique is forensic, not historical. We know that Collins is not always to be trusted when he talks about his working methods, his inspirations and the sources for his stories. But that the central plot of *The Woman in White* was substantially drawn from an actual law case and trial is established.[10] The conspiracy against the heiress Laura Glyde, her being drugged and incarcerated in a lunatic asylum, are known to be taken from Maurice Méjan's *Recueil des causes célèbres* and its account of the Madame de Douhault case, which occurred in the late eighteenth century.

Collins's copy of Méjan's *Recueil* was published in 1808. Kenneth Robinson tells us that the novelist picked it up from a Paris *bouquiniste* in March 1856 while visiting the French capital with Dickens.[11] If true, this date—1856—is very interesting. Interesting, that is, in the light of something else that Collins said about *The Woman in White*, late in life:

One day about 1856 he had found himself at a criminal trial in London. He was struck by the way each witness rose in turn to contribute a personal fragment to the chain of evidence. 'It came to me then . . . that a series of events in a novel would lend themselves well to an exposition like this . . . one could impart to the reader that acceptance, that sense of belief, which was produced here by the succession of testimonies . . . The more I thought of it, the more an effort of this kind struck me as bound to succeed. Consequently when the case was over I went home determined to make the effort.'[12]

Collins does not identify the 1856 trial that he attended. But it is not hard to work out what it must have been. The trial of William Palmer, the Rugeley poisoner, was not just the crime sensation of 1856 but of the whole decade. It was, as the *Annual Register* observed, discussed at every fireside in the land over the summer of 1856.[13] The Rugeley poisoning was England's mania that year. An Act of Parliament was passed so that a show trial could be mounted in London. Public interest was at fever pitch. There was a cut-throat competition for courtroom tickets. Accounts of the trial dominated the newspapers for the twelve days it ran in May 1856, and it inspired books, pictures, doggerel verse, and a huge amount of rumour, some of it crediting Palmer with the poisoning of scores of victims. The trial also inspired the still-current salutation between drinkers—'What's your poison?'

Dickens was obsessed with William Palmer over the summer of 1856 (a period in which he was at his most intimate with Collins) and wrote an essay on the poisoner's infuriatingly inscrutable demeanour for *Household Words* in June 1856. Why would not 'The Poisoner' *look* like the criminal he manifestly was? Palmer was 'the greatest villain that ever stood in the Old Bailey dock',[14] yet he had the gall to appear as respectable as the lawyers who questioned him. It was maddening. Collins too, we may assume, was as fascinated by the monster of Rugeley as his friend and editor.

The details of the Palmer case were indeed fascinating. But the main importance of it to *The Woman in White* was in the legal precedent which the trial set. It was, above all, a triumphant vindication of the power of circumstantial evidence in the hands of a skilful prosecution. There was absolutely no material evidence against William Palmer. He was tried for one murder only, although rumour credited him with many more. And his victim's corpse could be found to contain no lethal amount of poison whatsoever. The alleged motive for the murder was flimsy and to the thoughtful observer virtually non-existent. There was no witness to the alleged crime. Palmer—who showed no remorse or anxiety—steadfastly denied his guilt and went to the gallows protesting that he was in fact the murdered man. The case was won, as everyone conceded, by the skilful accumulation of circumstantial evidence alone, which was brilliantly expounded to the jury by one of the most powerful prosecuting teams ever gathered for a murder trial in the nineteenth century.

II

THE MAIN EVENTS in the Rugeley poisoning can be summarized from four sources: reports in *The Times*, the *Annual Register* for 1856, the *DNB* entry on William Palmer, and Robert Graves's 1957 book, *They hanged my saintly Billy*.[15] William Palmer was born in 1824 in Rugeley—a small town in Staffordshire. His background was comfortably moneyed. His father had been a timber merchant. His mother was left a young widow in William's early childhood and was estimated to be worth some £70,000. William inherited £7,000 of this fortune on coming to man's estate in 1846. His childhood was easy and as a boy he was 'spoiled' by his fond parent. On leaving Rugeley grammar school, William was apprenticed to an apothecary in Liverpool. There he misconducted himself with a local girl, embezzled his master's money, and was dismissed. He was subsequently apprenticed to a surgeon in the Rugeley area, and again disgraced himself. Eventually, Palmer qualified at St Bartholomew's Hospital, London. He was admitted a member of the Royal College of Surgeons in August 1846 and set up as a general practitioner in his home town later that year.

Palmer was by all accounts a skilled surgeon. But he took to the turf and wasted his fortune and all his professional prospects by gambling and setting up a stable for brood mares. By 1853 William Palmer had lost most of his business and was in desperate financial straits, borrowing money at 60 per cent interest to stave off bankruptcy. He had married in October 1847 and had a family. But, as was commented on later, four of his five children had died within a month of their birth. Palmer, as it was recalled, frequently complained of the expense of raising offspring (although he was happy enough to raise foals). It was also noted that Palmer's mother-in-law, a wealthy woman whom he was treating, died prematurely of what was loosely called apoplexy.

But 1854 Palmer was forging bill acceptances using his mother's signature. In the summer of that year he took out a large insurance on his wife's life with the Prince of Wales company. He paid only one premium of 700-odd pounds before she died in September 1854 of what was termed 'English cholera' on the death certificate. Her husband had been dosing her with his own medicinal compounds. William Palmer duly came into £13,000 insurance benefit with his wife's death. But his debts and compulsive gambling soon ate up this second fortune.

Later in that same eventful year, 1854, he again forged his mother's acceptance to a £2,000 bill. And—using his London moneylender as intermediary—he took out another life insurance policy on his brother Walter for £13,000 (an oddly recurrent figure in this story) with the same insurance company, who did not realize that the beneficiary was the William Palmer who had just cost them so dear. Neither, apparently, did the Prince of Wales company appreciate that Walter Palmer was a chronic alcoholic with advanced delirium tremens which he treated with the homely remedy of a quart of gin a day. A corn factor, Walter had also squandered his £7,000 patrimony, and was now bankrupt. William Palmer—although evidently acutely short of money—undertook to pay the £1,000 a year premium for his brother.

By August 1855, William Palmer's debts, in the form of forged bills falling due for repayment, were again threatening to overwhelm him. At this crisis Walter conveniently died of 'apoplexy' after taking some pills made up by his brother. The insurers were informed. But, when they understood who was the beneficiary, they consulted the redoubtable Inspector Charles Field (Dickens's Inspector Bucket in *Bleak House*) and refused to pay up, defying Palmer to take them to court—which he declined to do. By now William's affairs were entangled with those of John Parsons Cook, a 28-year-old Leicestershire man. Cook was something of a dandy and like Palmer had run through his fortune (of around £13,000) on the race track where, it was reported, 'he did not bear a high reputation'. He too owned horses and gambled unluckily. Cook had also been unlucky in love and contracted syphilis, now in an advanced condition. It seems that William Palmer was treating his young friend confidentially for his complaint. The two sporting men also had some complicated financial arrangements which were never unravelled, even at the subsequent trials.

Palmer's problems boiled over in the middle of November 1855. He now owed London money-lenders £12,500 and renewals were becoming very difficult. Forgery of his mother's name would no longer serve. He needed £400 in cash immediately for interest payments, and at some not too distant point the principal would have to be repaid. He had other calls on his purse. He had consoled himself since his wife's death with a local girl of the lower classes and had procured an abortion for her. She was now blackmailing him for £100, for the return of thirty-five 'lascivious letters' that she would otherwise show to her father. Palmer was utterly destitute and had no way of meeting any of these demands. He had even to borrow £25 from a Rugeley butcher in order to attend the Shrewsbury races on 13 November. At the races, however, fortune at last smiled on him. Cook's mare, Polestar, was suited by the heavy going and won the main handicap event. This meant winnings of £800 and the horse became a valuable property for the purposes of breeding.

Cook celebrated his success at the ominously named Raven Hotel in Shrewsbury. There he was taken suddenly and violently ill after drinking what he called some 'strange-tasting grog' prepared by Palmer. In great distress he was removed to the Talbot Arms Hotel in Rugeley where, after swallowing morphine pills and drinking some broth (both prepared for him by Palmer), he died of a series of horrifically violent tetanic spasms. This occurred on 20 November 1855, a week after the race meeting. Cook's winnings were not to be found in his belongings at the Talbot Arms. Palmer meanwhile was settling various long-standing local debts in cash.

There was a universal prejudice that William Palmer was a mass murderer. Cook's stepfather, a man called William Stevens, vowed to bring his boy's killer to justice. Inquests were made on the deaths of Cook, Annie Palmer (William's wife), and Walter Palmer. On the basis of post-mortem examination and other evidence, the coroner found in December 1855 that all three had been murdered by William Palmer. He was duly arrested and imprisoned, but the charges relating to his wife and brother were later dropped for insufficient evidence. More specifically, the exhumed corpses of the two dead Palmers revealed no trace of poison. (The examinations had not been easy for the pathologists; Walter Palmer's corpse exploded when his lead-lined coffin was opened.)

The scantiness of their evidence and the fact that two charges had melted away alarmed the authorities. The case that Palmer had murdered Cook, the last chance to convict him, was at best flimsy. Certainly it was flimsier in regard to motive than the other two victims. No one doubted that William Palmer was a murderer— possibly of as many as sixteen people. But it looked as if he might be too skilful a murderer for the English legal system. This could not be allowed. A decision was made in high places to nail Palmer; and if necessary to bend the law to do so. An act of Parliament was passed in April 1856 allowing the case to be tried outside the original area of jurisdiction (Leeds), in the Central Criminal Court, London, where state resources and public opinion could be more effectively mobilized against the accused. The case was scheduled for two weeks in May 1856. Lord Chief Justice Campbell presided. Other big guns were recruited for the prosecution team. The Attorney General, Alexander Cockburn—the most brilliant barrister in England—and Mr Edwin James made the case for the Crown. No expense was spared. The prosecutors had the assistance of the best expert witnesses in the land, including such authorities in their fields as Sir Benjamin Brodie, professor of chemistry at Oxford and one of the country's foremost scientists.

Nonetheless, for all its official backing, the prosecution had an uphill road. His family had decided to stand by Palmer, and his mother was wealthy enough to retain a very able lawyer, Mr Serjeant Shee. The main evidence against Palmer was that he was alleged to have bought several grains of strychnine on 19 November (two days before Cook's death) and to have persuaded the chemist's apprentice he bought it from not to enter the transaction in the poison book. Palmer did not deny the purchase. His explanation was that he intended to poison some stray dogs that were worrying his brood mares. But he disputed the date, claiming that he was in London on 19 November. There was a strong suspicion that the witness might have been bribed or coerced by Stevens.

There remained other intractable weaknesses in the prosecution case. Palmer was desperately short of money in November 1855. But Cook's £800 (or what was left of it) would not have gone far towards the £12,500 he owed. And by Cook's death he was liable to further debts, incurred by them jointly. Very simply, William Palmer did not stand to gain much by murdering his friend. The post-mortem (which Palmer attended) and the organs which were sent to Guy's hospital for analysis were of no help whatsoever to the prosecution. Tiny quantities of antimony were detected, but not enough to hurt a baby. No trace of strychnine was found. The prosecution's allegation— far-fetched enough—was that Palmer had administered antimony (in the form of tartar emetic) sufficient to weaken Cook at Shrewsbury, then delivered the *coup de grâce* with strychnine (disguised as morphia pills) at Rugeley, judging the dose so accurately that the poison was absorbed in the body during the death throes, leaving no residue whatsoever. Pharmacologically this was unconvincing.

Great harm was done to Palmer's defence by the evidence of two maids at the Talbot Arms Hotel. One of them, Elizabeth Mills, claimed to have tasted some broth which Palmer sent Cook, and then to have been taken violently ill. This was confirmed by another maid. But it was alleged by the defence, quite plausibly, that these two women had been bribed to give false evidence by Cook's vindictive stepfather, Stevens. If nothing else, it was extremely unlikely that Palmer would have tried to kill Cook two different ways—with poisoned pills and poisoned soup. Palmer had other strong points in his defence. Cook's death bore all the signs of epilepsy, or of tetanus, both which are known complications of the syphilis from which he was suffering. The medical evidence on this matter was persuasive.

On the evidence, Palmer should have been acquitted. But had he got off scot-free, English criminal justice would have been thoroughly humiliated. The prosecution, aided by the judge, ruthlessly biased the proceedings against any such outcome. Whenever the defence brought forward some evidence, favourable to their client, the prosecuting lawyers would throw their arms in the air, and go through a pantomime of disbelief. They kept the most helpful defence witnesses out of court by threatening to divulge in cross-examination damaging information which the police had dug up. All in all, the trial was, as Shee complained, 'an organized conspiracy to hang our client'. But what clinched the case against Palmer was a superb summing-up by the prosecuting counsel, Alexander Cockburn. Without notes he dazzled the jury with his inductions from the purely circumstantial evidence. After the guilty verdict was delivered by the jury, Palmer scrawled a note to his counsel; 'It was the riding that did it'. His racing slang meant that Cockburn's rhetorical and narrative skill—not the quality of his evidence—had won the event for the prosecution. Palmer was sentenced to hang at Stafford gaol. He did not confess his guilt, even in the death cell. He maintained to the end his sober demeanour and only complained that he could not get the racing news in prison. He went to the gallows with the enigmatic remark that Cook 'was never poisoned by strychnine' (by what, then?).

William Palmer had a manifestly unfair trial, but one can see why it was necessary. Everyone *knew* that he was a killer, and quite probably a mass murderer. For him to have escaped justice because he was cleverer than the forces of law would have been intolerable. By hook or by crook (crook as it turned out) Palmer had to swing. I have

suggested that this trial—with its display of prosecutorial brilliance—
was the one which Wilkie Collins credits with inspiring him to write
The Woman in White, and I want now to look at the novel and various
points of connection between it and the Rugeley murder(s). There is
no need to summarize here all of *The Woman in White* (something
that is not easily done)[16] but it will help to go over the details of the
novel's poison plot.

The complications of the plot unfold when the obnoxious Percival
Glyde holds Laura to the engagement arranged by her dead father.
Glyde's motives are purely mercenary. Laura has a fortune of £20,000
at her own disposition and £3,000 a year when her Uncle Fairlie dies—
a remote eventuality, as it happens. It is evidently Glyde's expectation
that he can soon coerce his enervated wife into signing over her fortune
to him. After a six-month honeymoon in Italy, the Glydes return to
Hampshire, in company with the Foscos. Improbably, Fosco also has
an interest in Laura's fortune. On Lady Glyde's death, Fosco's wife
(Laura's aunt) will inherit £10,000. On their return, Glyde and Fosco
are financially embarrassed, to the amount of thousands and hundreds
respectively. One assumes that while abroad they have been gambling
at the tables or the *bourse*. They try to bully Laura into signing,
unseen, a deed making over her fortune to her husband. Her resolve
stiffened by her loyal half-sister, Marian, Laura refuses—unless she
is shown what it is she is signing. Baffled, Fosco and Glyde resort to
money-lenders, which gives them three months' reprieve until the bills
fall due.

Glyde meanwhile tells Fosco about Anne Catherick, the mysterious
lunatic with the uncanny physical resemblance to Laura. The Italian
virtuoso of crime sees a scheme—but one which is extraordinarily
complicated. As has been established early in the narrative, Fosco
is a 'chemist' of genius. Anne, as he plans, will be substituted for
Laura and then subtly poisoned. Meanwhile, Laura will be packed off
to Anne's private lunatic asylum, where her protestations that she
is in fact Lady Glyde will be taken as the ravings of a madwoman.
(In passing, it may be noted that this unidentified asylum must be
one of the most inefficient institutions in the history of medicine.
Not only can inmates apparently walk out whenever the whim takes
them, but the staff will not observe the fact that one of their long-
stay patients has overnight been transformed from a near-illiterate
peasant to a highly-cultivated woman capable of playing the piano,

painting watercolours, and speaking French.) It is a bizarre plan. Why not just poison Laura? She is chronically delicate. When the hero Walter Hartright first encounters her, she is resting in her room with a sick headache; the marital embraces of Glyde have evidently exhausted her even further. She could die at any time, without raising any great suspicion. The not very convincing reason for the complex shuffling of victims and the murder of just one of them is that it will kill two birds with one stone. Anne (improbably enough) knows of Glyde's illegitimacy, and the knowledge will die with her. But if the keepers at the asylum will not believe Anne's protestations that she is Lady Glyde, why should they believe Anne's protestations that Sir Percival's parentage is not what he claims? The sensible course for any unscrupulous gang would be to poison Laura during one of her many indispositions and do away with Anne Catherick during one of her frequent unauthorized leaves of absence from the asylum.

Anyway, Fosco and Glyde go ahead with their cumbersome scheme. It involves hiring two henchwomen in Hampshire (Mrs Rubelle and Margaret Porcher) and any number of accessories before and after the fact in London. All these represent a huge risk of detection and/or blackmail later. Nor does Fosco seem inclined to minimize his risks, even when opportunities drop, heaven-sent, into his lap. Marian, for instance, falls ill after her drenching night outside the window. Her fever develops into typhus—a perfect cover under which Fosco might slip her out of the world with a little friendly strychnine. Instead of which, with incredible perversity, he saves her life by over-ruling the doltish quack who is treating her. Meanwhile, Laura is drugged (again, with Dawson in attendance, this would seem the perfect time to kill her and blame the typhus currently raging at Blackwater Park). There ensues some jiggery pokery with rooms. Laura is made to think that Marian has gone on ahead and is bundled up to London without any friend to protect her. In St John's Wood she is drugged again and secreted in the asylum. As it was planned, Anne would have been poisoned immediately after the switch. But she had a weak heart and unluckily dies before Laura arrives in the metropolis on 25 July. This, then, is the fiendishly cunning plot devised by Count Fosco, the Napoleon of crime. It is, to put it charitably, no masterpiece of felonious art, nor would it have been even if Anne Catherick had survived long enough to be poisoned. But such is the brio of Collins's narrative technique, with all its pseudo-legalism, that we don't notice;

or do not care to notice how half-cocked Fosco's machinations are. What we take away is a vague conviction of how fiendishly cunning these à la mode poisoners are.

My argument so far has depended on four theses:

1. That *The Woman in White* is peculiarly a product of the 1850s.
2. That *The Woman in White* is the formative text in the evolution of the sensation novel as a genre.
3. That a main element in *The Woman in White*'s sensationalism is its use of the courtroom or forensic narrative technique.
4. That Collins was influenced in the invention of this technique by the Rugeley poisoning sensation.

The fourth thesis is the weakest. It relies on Collins's recollection that an unnamed 1856 trial inspired *The Woman in White* and the fact that Palmer's trial was the *cause célèbre* of 1856 and that the Dickens circle generally was abnormally interested in the affair. But the Palmer link seems plausible, at least to me. Collins's interest in poisoning (something not found before *The Woman in White*) seems more than a coincidence. But even I would not maintain that *The Woman in White* is a close transcript or a *roman à clef* version of Palmer's story—as Bulwer-Lytton's *Lucretia*, for instance, transcribes Thomas Wainewright's 'arsenical' crimes, or the Merdle subplot of *Little Dorrit* transcribes the forger John Sadleir's crimes. *The Woman in White* is more in the nature of a meditation on the Palmer affair, and the issues it raised in the mind of the thoughtful observer of the 1850s. Principal among these issues is the status of circumstantial evidence. The Palmer case depended, above all, on being skilfully *narrated* by Cockburn, so as to gloss over the inadequacy of his material evidence. (This was the 'riding' to which Palmer paid tribute.) In marshalling his circumstantial evidence to best effect, the lawyer became a kind of novelist. So might Collins's novel become a kind of legal transcript.

III

TROLLOPE'S DEROGATORY comment about Wilkie Collins in his *Autobiography* is well known:

When I sit down to write a novel I do not at all know, and I do not very much care, how it is to end. Wilkie Collins seems so to construct his that he not only, before writing, plans everything on, down to the minutest detail, from the beginning to the end; but then plots it all back again, to see that there is no piece of necessary dove-tailing which does not dove-tail with absolute accuracy. The construction is most minute and most wonderful. But I can never lose the taste of the construction.[17]

Nowhere is the mechanical perfection of Wilkie Collins's plotting more evident than in the early sections of *The Woman in White*. Collins took immense pains with setting up this story—'the longest and most complicated I have ever tried yet'.[18] In the summer of 1859 he took a cottage at Broadstairs (an expense he could ill afford) and worked away during the sweltering summer months, devising a story of needle sharpness. Even so he could not entirely satisfy himself. After the early numbers were set up in proof for *All the Year Round* he broke them down and rewrote them so as to get an even sharper plot opening.

The reader with detective inclinations will find clues enough in the early sections to the farsightedness of Collins's writing. Pesca's political affiliation, which is the machinery used to engineer the climax, is parenthetically mentioned in the first number; no further reference is made to it until the thirty-eighth number. Similarly farsighted preparation is made for other important elements such as Countess Fosco's £10,000, her husband's strange aversion to Italy, and Anne Catherick's poor health. Arguably the early parts of the story are over-complex and baited. Dickens thought so and lodged an editorial complaint with Collins on 7 January 1860, after the seventh number had just come out:

I seem to have noticed, here and there, that the great pains you take express themselves a trifle too much, and you know that I always contest your disposition to give an audience credit for nothing, which necessarily involves the forcing of points upon their attention, and which I have always observed them to resent when they find it out—as they always will and do.[19]

Collins, to judge from the subsequent narrative, seems not to have taken too much notice of Dickens's instruction. But the wonder is that when he got into his stride he was actually able to maintain the cat's cradle intricacy of his plot. In what he called his 'weekly race' with *All the Year Round* he was, for most of the novel, no more than a week or so ahead of publication (i.e. a month before 'magazine day' in England, so as to get the American sheets off in time). This may be deduced from occasional comments in letters and from the speed with which he absorbed his own proof corrections into the subsequent narrative.[20] In manuscript Number 50 the maid appears as 'S̶u̶s̶a̶n̶ Fanny' and in Number 51 without any crossing out as 'Fanny'. This sequence of alterations could only occur if the novelist were one number ahead of himself. The dates of composition which Collins himself records on the manuscript (15 August 1859 to 26 July 1860) taken together with the dates of serial publication (26 November 1859 to 25 August 1860) suggest that after the first third of the novel Collins was obliged to work against the calendar and even the clock.

It must have been a gruelling year for the novelist. In his letters he reports himself 'horribly fagged' and '*slaving* to break the neck of the Woman in White'.[21] Under this pressure Collins was obliged to rely very heavily on the proof stage for any correction, adjustment, or afterthought improvement. In this respect *All the Year Round* was kinder to the novelist than the 32-page monthly number. He did not have to worry about accommodating 'over-matter'. In the periodical's double-columned format any reasonable over-run could be absorbed and there was never any mutilation of the manuscript copy Collins provided. But in other ways *All the Year Round* with its 'teaspoonful' instalments and its frequency of issue was the epitome of the furnace-like conditions in which the nineteenth-century serialists worked.

In these conditions a writer not entirely clear on where he was going might easily have found himself rushed into an inextricable muddle. To prevent this Collins seems to have relied very much on the blueprint which he laid down in his mind during the early planning stages of the novel at Broadstairs. The manuscript, in fact, is a marvel of spontaneity for a work of such narrative complication. Although there is much scoring out, almost all the improvements pertain to felicity of expression. What we find are mainly minor polishing changes which give a little more suspense, clarity of definition, or perfection of statement. Otherwise Collins seems to have written with the master plan firmly held, guiding him inexorably onwards through the narrative maze to the tremendous denouement.

On two occasions during the narrative progress, however, Collins was shaken out of his rhythm. One of these emergencies he turned to profit with a brilliant improvisation that enhances the story. The second resulted in what remains as the weakest link in the carefully interconnected plot. In what follows I shall examine these two emergencies and their consequences for the novel as a whole.

In the manuscript preface to *The Woman in White* Collins wrote:

The first chapters (forming the first week's part, and the opening of the second) were rewritten, after they had been set up in type . . . The whole of the rest of the MS was written for the press, once, and once only—exactly as it is here preserved. In all cases where there is any important difference between the printed copy and the original manuscript, the additions and alterations (Miss Halcombe's *Dream*, for example, among the number) were made on the spur of the moment, upon the proofs—which I have not preserved.

With reference to the example Collins gives we can elaborate on his account. The Numbers concerned are 46, 47, and 48 (although originally they were intended to be only 46 and 47). The stretch of narrative concerned is that which is told through Marian Halcombe's diary and records the opening exchanges in her epic duel with Fosco. Number 46 begins with the diary entry describing Marian's and Laura's evening walk to the boathouse at Blackwater Park. The newly-wed wife confesses the misery of her marriage, and her continuing guilty love for Walter Hartright (who has, of course, gone off on an expedition to Central America to forget *his* love for Laura). As the heroines walk back they hear themselves followed through the dark wood by what seems like a woman. They run in terror back to the safety of the house. In the drawing-room, Fosco makes some sinister small talk before the ladies retire and Marian, by cross-questioning the servants, ascertains that it was none of them who stalked her and Laura in the wood. Number 46, as published, finishes on this point.

The next day Marian receives (by messenger) an expected letter from Mr Kyrle, the solicitor, which confirms her suspicions of Sir Percival and the legal document which he wants Laura to sign. Marian arranges to meet the messenger in the grounds. Fosco, however, has followed her and escorts her back to the house where Sir Percival has just come back from some mysterious business. The nervous strain of the cat-and-mouse game begins to tell on Marian. She is exhausted and beginning to sicken. Although she does not yet know it the poisonous miasma of Blackwater lake has infected her with typhus. In this state she falls into a disturbed slumber. She dreams vividly of Walter Hartright in the American jungles. She is awoken from this vision by Laura who has discovered who it was that pursued them last night—'Anne Catherick!' Number 47, as published, finishes on this ejaculation.

The manuscript shows that 46 and 47 were originally meant to have been one Number. They are continuous in the manuscript and

48 is, in fact, renumbered by Collins 47/48. As it is they make two unusually short Numbers in the periodical. The invariable length of the preceding Numbers in *All the Year Round* is between 12 and 17 columns. Numbers 46 and 47 are eight-and-a-half and seven-and-a-quarter columns respectively, easily the briefest in the whole run of the novel.

The reasons for Collins having to bisect a single Number must be conjectured. It could not have been indisposition on his part since he had to perform heroically, and at very short notice, to carpenter each of the halves into a respectable whole for the journal. Writing the supplementary material must have been harder work than writing a complete new instalment. My guess is that Dickens wanted the extra space for a current affairs article and, uncharacteristically, took from his serial to do so. Normally, of course, the serial, always the lead item in *All the Year Round*, was sacrosanct.

For whatever reason, Collins at short notice had to improvise, and improvisation meant expansion to bring the numbers up to the minimum length tolerable. In Number 46 he added in proof the long conversation (in fact more of an inquisition) in which Fosco presses Marian as to where she and Laura have been. At the same time Collins took advantage of the by now hopelessly unjustified proofs to expand considerably Marian's enquiries of the servants whether it was any of them who had followed the ladies from the boathouse. Economically the novelist left the proofs of the first half of the Number intact, for which the printer was doubtless grateful.

In the same spirit of economy Collins did not tamper with the first half of Number 47. But the addition he made in the second half of that Number is more exciting and less in the nature of routine inflation than what we find in Number 46. In the manuscript Marian falls asleep and is woken soon after by Laura. In the revised, printed version there intervenes the following dream:

The quiet in the house, and the low murmuring hum of summer insects outside the open window, soothed me. My eyes closed of themselves; and I passed gradually into a strange condition, which was not waking—for I knew nothing of what was going on about me; and not sleeping—for I was conscious of my own repose. In this state, my fevered mind broke loose from me, while my weary body was at rest; and in a trance, or day-dream of my fancy—I know not what to call it—I saw Walter Hartright [in her vision she sees him escape death in the jungle from fever, from pigmies' arrows, and from shipwreck. It is, he tells her, all part of the 'Design' leading to

'the unknown Retribution and the inevitable End'] . . . I saw him for the last time. He was kneeling by a tomb of white marble; and the shadow of a veiled woman rose out of the grave beneath, and waited by his side. The unearthly quiet of his face changed to an unearthly sorrow. But the terrible certainty of his words remained the same. 'Darker and darker', he said; 'farther and farther yet. Death takes the good, the beautiful, and the young—and spares *me*. The Pestilence that wastes, the Arrow that strikes, the Sea that drowns, the Grave that closes over Love and Hope, are steps of my journey, and take me nearer and nearer to the End.'
My heart sank under a dread beyond words, under a grief beyond tears. The darkness closed round the pilgrim at the marble tomb; closed round the veiled woman from the grave; closed round the dreamer who looked on them. I saw and heard no more. (*All the Year Round*, 47, 479–80; 249–50)[22]

Judged by itself, this is a brilliant piece of coloratura writing. *The Woman in White* continually hovers on the brink of Gothic supernaturalism, and the visionary dream fits perfectly here. It is possible, too, that Collins was thinking of the memorable stanza which concludes Lyric 56 of Tennyson's *In Memoriam*:

> O life as futile, then, as frail!
> O for thy voice to soothe and bless!
> What hope of answer, or redress?
> Behind the veil, behind the veil.

It is certain, on the other hand, that in the last sentence of Marian's dream Collins was thinking ahead to the tremendous scene that finishes the second epoch (Number 56) where Walter, believing Laura dead and grieving over her tombstone, encounters a veiled woman:

. . . the veiled woman had possession of me, body and soul. She stopped on one side of the grave. We stood face to face, with the tombstone between us. She was close to the inscription on the side of the pedestal. Her gown touched the black letters.
The voice came nearer, and rose and rose more passionately still. 'Hide your face! don't look at her! Oh, for God's sake, spare him—.'
The woman lifted her veil.
'Sacred to the Memory of Laura, Lady Glyde—.'
Laura, Lady Glyde, was standing by the inscription and was looking at me over the grave. (*All the Year Round*, 56, 128–9; 377–8)

This dovetails beautifully with the previous dream, and with the first appearance of the woman in white all those months ago. At the same time it emphasizes the main theme of the novel; that in all the apparently impenetrable mystery there lies 'Design'. The increasingly evident purposes of Providence in this design are hinted at (but with no more than hints). The process of the novel is that of a gradual unveiling. This theme was, of course, introduced with Marian's improvised dream and the visionary Hartright's address to her:

I shall come back. The night when I met the lost Woman on the highway, was the night which set my life apart to be the instrument of a Design that is yet unseen. Here, lost in the wilderness, or there, welcomed back in the land of my birth, I am still walking on the dark road which leads me, and you, and the sister of your love and mine, to the unknown Retribution and the inevitable End. (*All the Year Round*, 47, 480; 248)

As well as the encounter over the gravestone Collins exploited the afterthought still further in the 'Brotherhood of the Veil' through which Hartright and Pesca bring about the downfall of Fosco. In the manuscript Collins went on to explain the significance of the society's name: 'the name signifying that, except by superior permission and for matters of life and death, the veil is never lifted between the members, and that they remain, from first to last, mysteries to one another.' (This would have come in *All the Year Round* 68, 416.) Collins may have thought that this was rubbing in the symbolism rather too hard so he cut out the above and renamed the secret society simply 'The Brotherhood'. Nonetheless, the image of the mysterious woman unveiling remains the most powerful and explicatory which we can find in the novel.

IV

COLLINS'S HANDLING of this emergency may be scored a brilliant success. He showed himself quite capable of masterly improvisation in spite of his notorious propensity for carefully laid and worked-out plots. Few novelists on *All the Year Round* can have corrected their proofs so effectively. In the second emergency, however, Collins does not come out quite so well. We can catch him in what seems almost a fumble and there remains as evidence of it in the printed text of the novel an incongruity which may well worry more pedantic readers. With other novelists, this incongruity might not matter so much; but with Collins, as Trollope noted, we are encouraged to be small minded about such things: 'the author seems always to be warning me to remember that something happened at exactly half-past two o'clock on Tuesday morning; or that a woman disappeared from the road just fifteen yards beyond the fourth milestone.'[23]

In the largest sense the second emergency concerns the machinery by which Fosco is defeated. Fosco and Glyde, it will be remembered, intend to murder Anne Catherick (should she not oblige them by dying), pass off her corpse as Lady Glyde's, and return Lady Glyde to the asylum as Anne Catherick. It is a complicated and somewhat unlikely scheme and it is made more complex for the villains because Anne, who has a weak heart, dies before Laura can be spirited away from Blackwater Park to London. This creates a dangerous flaw in their plan since if the departure from the country by Laura can be shown to post-date the death certificate then, demonstrably, it would be impossible for her to be Anne Catherick with delusions that she is somebody else.

The possibility of denouement via this chronological discrepancy is raised on a number of occasions in the last third of the novel. Collins evidently intended the reader to be aware of this weak spot; disproof of the villains' machinations by comparison of dates is, we are made to expect, the climax towards which the action is moving. To condition the reader on this point, apparently, Collins added in proof two hundred words of dialogue between Marian and Walter in which he firmly states his resolve to uncover evidence of the inconsistent dates: 'We must persist, to the last, in hunting down the date of Laura's journey. The one weak point in the conspiracy, and probably the one chance of proving that she is a living woman, centre in the discovery of that date' (*All the Year Round*, 59, 197).

Why, one may wonder, did Collins raise the reader's expectation in this way? For in the event the discrepancy of dates turns out to be a gigantic red herring. Hartright can prove nothing on this score despite all his frantic endeavours and the denouement is worked out quite otherwise. Hartright goes to Fosco's hideout and blackmails him with the threat of exposure to the Brotherhood. Thus threatened, the Napoleon of crime makes a signed confession. As part of this confession he gives the name of the cabby who delivered Lady Glyde to London, and the letter from Glyde which proves the impossibility of her having been in town on the day she 'died'. But it is merely confirmatory evidence and strikes the reader as something of an anticlimax after all the pointers we have had.

The more one thinks about this business the stranger it appears.

Why all this build-up for what turns out, finally, to be a very minor piece of plot machinery? Has Collins deliberately misled the reader into thinking that the end will be brought about by Hartright's turning up the missing evidence? To understand how this puzzle came about it is necessary to reconstruct a crucial segment of the narrative, the account of Mrs Michelson in Number 56. It will be helpful, once more, to synopsize the narrative in close detail.

Mrs Michelson, housekeeper and clergyman's widow, is a gullible but incorruptibly honest witness to what took place during her time of service at Blackwater Park. Unfortunately, however, her account suffers from imperfect observation and bias. To our superior knowledge the main events at this period of the narrative are the Count's duping Anne Catherick and the loyal servant Mrs Clements while Marian is disabled with typhus. Fosco has insulted and driven away the local physician Dawson, the servants have been all dismissed, and a mystified Mrs Michelson has been sent on a wild-goose chase to Torquay. Blackwater is thus left in sole possession of the villainous trio and their hench-woman, Mrs Rubelle. They use their freedom to secrete Marian in a disused part of the house, under the superintendence of Mrs Rubelle. When Laura recovers from her nervous collapse she and the now-returned Mrs Michelson are told that Marian has recovered and is now staying with Fosco in St John's Wood, London. Laura is persuaded by this lie to follow her friend there. What has happened, of course, is that Fosco has Anne Catherick in London and intends to switch her with Laura.

This is where the crux occurs. 'Towards five o'clock on the . . . same day' (*All the Year Round*, 55, 102) of Laura's departure, Mrs Michelson discovers that Marian Halcombe has not, after all, left Blackwater but is still convalescent there. Indignant beyond words at the deception played upon her she gives notice and then:

I stole back, leaving the sick lady still peacefully asleep, to fetch writing materials from the inhabited part of the house. Returning with them to the bedside immediately I there wrote three notes. One was to Mr Dawson, begging him to resume his attendance, and telling him that the next day Blackwater Park would have nobody in it but Miss Halcombe and myself. The other two were duplicates addressed to Lady Glyde. In each I told her Ladyship very briefly, what had happened; taking care to preface the statement in consideration for her frail state of health, by mentioning that I was then writing by Miss Halcombe's bed, and that I saw her before me, comfortably asleep. I directed one of these notes to the care of Frederick

Fairlie, Esquire, and the other to the care of Mrs Vesey, whose address I had particularly noticed, when I put Lady Glyde's letter into the post. Being ignorant of Count Fosco's address, it was impossible for me to send a third note to his care. I did all I could—it is some comfort to me, now, to know in my own heart and conscience that I did all I could.

I gave the letters, with instructions, to the gardener—a steady man, on whom I could rely. He brought me back word that he had posted the two notes to Lady Glyde in going through the village, and that he had driven round to Mr Dawson's residence.

This was how the passage was put down in the manuscript. But Collins altered it in proof, so that it appears very differently in the printed version that we have:

I stole back, leaving the sick lady still peacefully asleep, to give the gardener instructions about bringing the doctor. I begged the man, after he had taken Mrs Rubelle to the station, to drive round by Mr Dawson's, and leave a message, in my name, asking him to call and see me. I knew he would come on my account, and I knew he would remain when he found Count Fosco had left the house.

In due course of time, the gardener returned, and said that he had driven round by Mr Dawson's residence, after leaving Mrs Rubelle at the station. The doctor sent me word that he was poorly in health himself, but that he would call, if possible, the next morning. (*All the Year Round*, 56, 123; 363)

Mrs Michelson, at the end of her account, apologizes for 'my own inability to remember the precise day on which Lady Glyde left Blackwater Park for London. I am told that it is of the last importance to ascertain the exact date of that lamentable journey; and I have anxiously taxed my memory to recall it . . . We all know the difficulty, after a lapse of time, of fixing precisely on a past date, unless it has been previously written down' (p. 124; 366). As an added misfortune, it emerges that Mr Dawson has 'forgotten' the date on which the gardener came to him with Mrs Michelson's message.

It is not hard to see that Collins was in something of a tangle here. It seems he originally intended the denouement to be sprung by these three posted letters which Mrs Michelson sent off. The date would be 'written down' there in her own hand on the 'same day' that Lady Laura left for London. In 1850 letters would also have on the envelope two postmarks, one marking the office and day of despatch, the other the office and day of delivery. These would clinch matters. Evidence would have been lodged with Fairlie, Mrs Vesey, and Dawson, two at least of whom were absolutely reliable.

The disadvantage of this scheme seems to have struck Collins almost immediately. It was too efficient. He had still over a third of his novel to spin out. These letters would not permit the kind of postponement and winding up of suspense he required. It would all be too open and shut. Therefore the possibility of proof or disproof was removed with Mrs Michelson's three letters. Unfortunately, however, this did not clear things up very tidily. It is clear that Collins had set up the foregoing narrative for this kind of denouement by means of the anachronism of Anne's death and Laura's arrival in London. Its possibility could not be erased altogether from the narrative. Moreover the amended version of the plot which tries to leave Mrs Michelson's memory of the day plausibly uncertain has some gaping holes in it. Take, for instance, the Torquay visit; there must surely have been some corroborating evidence from the hotel keepers she spoke to there, or ticket collectors, or railway porters, any of whom could easily have helped ascertain when she came back to Blackwater. And her return could be quite easily correlated with Laura's departure.

This embarrassing likelihood occurred to Collins. Consequently he removed from the printed text the following sentence which we find, uncrossed-out, in the manuscript: '[Marian] was in a deep sleep at the time, when naturally or artificially produced she could not say. *Reckoning by her own calculation of days and nights, her removal must have been accomplished on the first evening after I had been sent out of the way to Torquay.* In my absence . . . ' (p. 123; 365). It was just this kind of reckoning that Collins had to discourage in the reader. Obscurity and vagueness must shroud the episode to protect its superficial credibility. In the short term the measure worked, but at the cost of a very weak link which was very evident in the three-volume issue of the novel (where the reader could more easily refer back to earlier narrative). Reviewing the third edition of *The Woman in White* in *The Times*, 30 October 1860, E. S. Dallas made an objection about the impossibility of the novel's time scheme (reckoning from Marian's diary, Laura must have gone up to London a fortnight later than the narrative asserts her to have done) and went on to point to the no less glaring improbability of the general ignorance of Laura's day of departure and, in particular, Mrs Michelson's convenient amnesia:

The date might be very easily recovered if the author chose—but he doesn't choose, and he insists, against all probabilities, upon everybody forgetting it. The person who would be most likely to remember it is the housekeeper at Blackwater Park, who pretends to some education, who is the widow of a clergyman, and who writes a pretty long narrative, in which she contrives to remember with wonderful accuracy a great number of minute facts in the precise order of their occurrence. On the day in question her mistress leaves Blackwater Park, she herself resigns her position as housekeeper, and during the day several remarkable incidents occur, the whole being wound up by the master of the house leaving it in a fury at night. The lady who has such a wonderful memory for everything else cannot remember this day of days, what day of the month, or what day of the week it was.

As we have seen, Collins's first instinct was to leave the date recoverable through Mrs Michelson's letters. Had he kept to his original idea he might have satisfied Dallas, but at the cost of a novel whose end could not be sufficiently postponed for the necessary suspense to gather.

What the time error and Mrs Michelson's improbable vagueness reveal is something of the crisis conditions in which Collins composed the last third of his serial. Its unexpected popularity brought an embarrassingly alert public attention to the weekly development of the plot and a much-voiced scepticism that Collins would ever be able to pull everything together. The American correspondent of the *Publishers' Circular*, 1 June 1860, reported:

I see that Mr Wilkie Collins's *The Woman in White* is announced for completion in book form. Will it then really be completed? People here, who have read it in *Harper's Weekly*, have been so excited by it, and so anxious to find out the denouement of the plot, that they have begun to doubt if there can ever be a conclusion to it.

Meanwhile in June and July Collins was complaining of pressure from *All the Year Round*: 'I am *slaving* to break the neck of the Woman in White—and get done in five numbers more' he wrote in June and on 5 July: 'I am *obliged* to end the story in August to avoid running into a new volume [of *All the Year Round*] and with the prospect of *one* double number at least to write.'[24]

If this were not enough, the novelist was further harassed by the need to get a complete manuscript to the publisher Sampson Low for the three-decker version to be issued, as it normally would be, three weeks before the serial came to an end in the journal. There was obviously some problem with this. The work had been advertised in the *Publishers' Circular* of 2 April 1860 to be 'complete in July'. It was announced as 'immediate' throughout July by Sampson Low. In the event it appeared in volume form around 15 August, only a week or so before the serial came to its conclusion in *All the Year Round.*

It was under these circumstances that the novelist was forced into the impossibilities and improbabilities which Dallas notes. The wonder is less that we can find them, if we look hard enough, than that they do not protrude to ruin the novel utterly. Even Dallas, after pointing to the chronological error which rendered 'the last volume a mockery, a delusion, and a snare' was generous enough to acknowledge the novel's power to triumph over its own flaws:

What must that novel be that can survive such a blunder? Remember that it is not now published for the first time. It was read from week to week by eager thousands in the pages of *All the Year Round.* In those pages a blunder which renders the whole of the last volume, the climax of the tale, nugatory, escaped the practised eye of Mr Dickens and his coadjutors, who were blinded, as well they might be, by the strong assertions and earnest style of the narrator. A plot that is worked out of impossibilities, like that of robbing the almanack of a fortnight, may be treated as a jest; but we vote three cheers for the author who is able to practise such a jest with impunity.

CHAPTER THREE

Dickens, Reade, Hard Cash *and Maniac Wives*

THE CLOSING years of the 1850s and the beginning of the 1860s saw an explosive growth in magazines largely devoted to the serialization of fiction. The best-selling of these was Dickens's *All the Year Round* which he erected on the remains of *Household Words* after his break with Bradbury and Evans, in 1858–9. From the first Dickens's independent journal was supremely successful. 'Our success here,' wrote W. H. Wills, *All the Year Round*'s assistant editor, 'has exceeded the most sanguine expectations. One hundred & twenty thousand of No 1 have already been sold and we are settling down to a steady current sale of one hundred thousand'.[1] Dickens's rivals might occasionally attain these figures as a sales peak but none could boast it as a steady current circulation.

Finding a regular supply of fiction to keep 100,000 discriminating purchasers happy was not always easy. Not every author could adapt to the 'tea-spoonfull'[2] measurements and the 'weekly race' of the paper's instalments. (Charles Lever's *A Day's Ride* was a notable failure, and forced Dickens to adapt his novel in progress, *Great Expectations*, for the paper.) And even if he secured the right kind of man for the journal, the editor could not rest content. *All the Year Round* used up novelists at prodigious speed. Twenty thousand words a month, a three-decker in just over half a year was a faster rate of production than many could trust themselves to keep up to. Dickens, moreover, was in the market with other periodicals, all looking for the same kind of talent. Although he outsold them, his main competitors, *Once a Week*, the *Cornhill Magazine*, and *Macmillan's Magazine*, had the advantage of him in that they could offer more attractive—or at least more convenient—remunerations. Since these rivals were all affiliates of large houses they could make a bid for serialization and subsequent volume publication combined. Dickens whose proud claim it was that there was 'no publisher whatever associated with *All the Year Round*'[3] was somewhat embarrassed when it came to making the four-figure offers required to get the best writers. In 1861 he lost his star serialist to George Smith (proprietor of *Cornhill*) who—with the coffers of Smith, Elder & Co. to draw on—could offer an unprecedented £5,000 for a serial and volume deal (*Armadale*, as it was to be).

In his search for contributors Dickens had Charles Reade frequently in mind. In September 1860 he wrote an elaborately courteous letter of invitation to the other novelist:

My dear Sir,—I address you without apology in the spirit of the Art we both profess, and for which you have done so much.

May I ask you if it would suit your convenience and inclination, to write a serial story for *All the Year Round*, reserving the free copyright in a collected form for yourself? It would give me the highest gratification to grace these pages with your name, and to have you for a fellow-labourer.

I do not doubt that all terms and conditions could be easily arranged between you and me . . . [4]

Reade, however, was not immediately available. He was struggling to deliver the oversized *The Cloister and the Hearth* (for Bradbury and Evans and *Once a Week*) and had a priority agreement with his American publishers which obstructed him from contracting a new novel with Dickens.

All the Year Round went on with Dickens's *Great Expectations*, Lytton's *A Strange Story* and Collins's *No Name*. Reade, however, was not forgotten. Yet in the end it was he who made an overture to Dickens in January 1862. Would *All the Year Round*, he asked, like to bid for a serial? Wills communicated the enquiry to Dickens who was in Plymouth and the editor replied:

[Reade] seems to me, to be the best man to be got for our purpose. But I think his terms will be rather higher than yours. Seeing that we shall not be paying Wilkie's salary [Collins had just retired as a staff member on the magazine] then, I think you might at once (if you saw it to be necessary) go up to five and twenty pounds a week. But he *may not* be used to such receipts as I suppose. I would decidedly pursue the idea, with the intention of getting him, as the best man to be got. No doubt he would be glad to work with me. I believe he has a respect for me.[5]

But Reade, however much he might 'respect' Dickens, was thinking in much more materialistic terms:

I think they *must* have me for *All the Year Round*, for Dickens is working on a shilling serial and Collins going to 'Cornhill.' So I shall stand firm about the American sheets [i.e. the American rights], and, please God, shall publish the new story *hot* [i.e. *pari passu* with publication].[6]

Reade's terms, as put to Wills, were reasonable; he would accept the £25 a week. But he would want as much length as his previous massive novel, *The Cloister and the Hearth*. Apart from anything else this would mean a fee of close on £1,000. Dickens wrote a hurried note to Wills: 'Reade, good. I would give him what he asks, holding him to a certain space within which the story shall be comprised.'[7] But Reade was not to be 'held' in this way. Finally a compromise was arrived at and Wills wrote to Reade from the journal's office on 22 January:

Dear Reade,

It would be a great pleasure to us to close with your proposal without another word; but, large as our sale is, our arrangements past present and to come really will not justify the outlay of £925 on your story—which would be the cost of 185 pages at £5 per page.

Will you kindly consider *this* proposition?—Eight hundred pounds (£800) for a story to occupy not less than 160 of *All the Year Round*. Any greater quantity of matter that you might find indispensable to your art, still to be included in that payment.[8]

Despite some last minute counterbids by George Smith of *Cornhill*, Dickens secured his man. The contract was signed on 31 January 1862.

Dickens had some warrant for feeling pleased with the way things had turned out with Reade—he had snaffled a leading novelist from under the noses of his rivals. His troubles were, however, far from finished with the signing of the contract. The stipulation as to delivery of copy was straightforward and not all that stringent for an experienced serialist like Reade. The first portion of the new story was to be with Wills 'on or before the first day of October next' and:

It is intended that the publication of such story . . . shall be commenced in the month of December next (or so soon thereafter as the principal story which may then be in course of publication in the said periodical in weekly parts shall have been finished).[9]

Yet, as we know, *Hard Cash* did not appear in the journal until 28 March 1863. What went wrong? Although the period is particularly bleak as regards extant correspondence we can reconstruct the erratic course of *Hard Cash*'s production from circumstantial evidence. Originally, as Reade put it, he was to have written *hot*—that is with a minimum of delay between composition and publication. At the end of May 1862 he went down to Oxford (where he had a fellowship) to start work on the novel. In his manuscript he suggests the start of writing as having been in June. Ocular evidence suggests that he

wrote rapidly, not to say furiously, from the first penstroke on. But
his stamina does not seem to have been up to the strain of launching
the novel by Autumn. On 3 September we find him writing to the
American, Mrs J. T. Fields:

Your welcome letter of July 4th. found me here trying to qualify myself by
hard reading to write a story of the day. I don't know whether you remember
a dome shaped building called the Radcliffe Library. This building has lately
been made a reading room for students, in connexion with the Bodleian; and
unlike all other public libraries in this country it is well lighted & kept open
till ten at night. This affords me facilities I cannot meet with in London.
Unfortunately a set off has come in the shape of Gout or something very
like it, which impairs my powers, so behold me in anxiety and despondency
about my forthcoming production.[10]

Nonetheless, while cricket was still being played at Oxford he had
three numbers of *Hard Cash* written. Presumably, therefore, Wills
got his copy by November. But the manuscript is, as Reade himself
observes in his preface to it, 'disgracefully disordered'. Though there
might be mass enough to satisfy the publishers it was hardly in any
shape for the printer. It is not until beginning of the thirteenth number
that Reade seems to have arrived at some sense of the proportions of
his novel and at this point he jots down alongside his manuscript
narrative: 'I propose to treat each Number as a distinct work. This
will get rid of all difficulties as to paging.' Thereafter something like
order begins to appear in the pagination and division of the story.

  Confronted by this tangle it seems that Dickens suggested that
Reade might like to take a few extra weeks over his novel's opening,
so as to get it into acceptable shape. Reade replied on 18 November,
rather guardedly:

I have six numbers finished: five of which are copied for Press. A delay of
six weeks, though not necessary, might be advantageous to the work; and
I should say 'Yes' at once if I [had] not some misgiving about Harper [the
American publisher to whom Reade had sold rights in the form of early
proof sheets]. He agreed with me for sheets under an impression that I was
to follow Collins in A.Y.R.[11]

Harper seems in the event to have given no difficulty. But not having
a story to carry on with when Collins's *No Name* finished would
precipitate a real emergency for *All the Year Round.* It was very short
notice—almost a matter of days since as Wills pointed out 'to reap
the American advantage you must be a month beforehand with the

proofs'. Dickens and Wills had no time to await Reade's agreement to the six weeks' delay. Luckily they had another iron in the fire. Mrs Gaskell had submitted a manuscript story at about the time when arrangements were being finally settled with Reade. Dickens had liked it and Wills had written to her to say so adding:

But . . . as we have a serial story now in progress, and have even engaged for its successor, it is at present impossible for us to propose any exact time for the appearance here of your story. This is not of importance to you perhaps: but it is right to mention that we shall be obliged to hold it back for a good and suitable opportunity.[12]

Mrs Gaskell would appear to have been one of those invaluable authors who did not mind going to the end of an indefinitely long queue. With Reade's writing difficulties the 'good and suitable opportunity' had arisen. On 6 December there was inserted in *All the Year Round* a notice that when Collins's *No Name* finished it would be followed by Mrs Gaskell's *A Dark Night's Work* and that in turn by 'a new serial work' by Charles Reade the following March (1863).

Even now, Dickens's editorial problems with *Hard Cash* were not over. In fact the worst was still to come. That climactic part of the story which has the hero incarcerated in a lunatic asylum by his villainous father shocked, alarmed, and eventually turned away readers. Dickens had evidently bought a pig in a poke. When he ordered his novel from Reade he did not clearly know, and did not specify, what it should be about. Reade chose to make it a one-man-crusade of near hysterical passion against the abuses of private lunatic asylums. Little wonder that *All the Year Round*'s family readership was turned off. It is still repulsive to read such descriptions as that in Number 32 of the forcible 'tanking' of patients after which the hellish keeperesses 'make them drink the foul water for meals'. 'The dark places of the land', Reade wrote, anticipating Conrad, 'are full of horrible cruelty.' Many readers, it appeared, preferred not to know about such places and were disinclined to pay 2*d.* a week to have them brought into their homes.

To lose readers was bad enough but in addition Reade, now writing *hot* indeed, was showing dangerous signs of having the bit between his teeth. In the advertisement for the novel Wills had declared that *Hard Cash* would finish in about eight months. On the other hand the contract allowed Reade to produce 'any greater quantity of matter that you might find indispensable to your art'. Should he want to,

Reade could go on for ever. The prospect gave Dickens and Wills concern:

Wills called [wrote Reade in August] and reassured me with 'Hard Cash'. They would not care if it ran fifty numbers; but they want to end their tenth volume with the conclusion either of 'Hard Cash' or its successor. Peevish nonsense! The story has done them no good, in fact they print 3,000 copies less than at the outset.[13]

Reade was a notoriously prickly man and Dickens seems to have withheld from any personal contact with him. There is no evidence that, as with works by Lever, Lytton, or Collins for *All the Year Round*, he involved himself in the composition of his contributor's novel. He seems also to have moderated any expression of his editorial anxiety, restricting himself to an indirect 'hint' in September that Reade would 'find leisure for a little dash for the Christmas number' and congratulating him on *Hard Cash*'s 'admirable art [and] surprising grace and vigour'.[14]

Dickens's diplomatic nudges seem to have had some success. Reade drew his narrative to an end in a frantic gallop of events. The hero escapes the asylum, gains a first at Oxford, gravels his opponents in court, and wins his true love all within five weekly numbers. Altogether the serial lasted 40 weeks and took some 275 pages of *All the Year Round*. This meant that Wills and Dickens had 115 pages for nothing, a gift whose generosity they may have wished curtailed. The serial in fact span out until 26 December.

There had been urgent pressure on Dickens to interfere with *Hard Cash*—more particularly to curtail the severity of Reade's attack on the medical profession. Dickens chose to answer in the edition of *All the Year Round* containing the novel's last number. On 23 November he wrote to Wills, insisting that Reade should not be privy to what he was doing:

I wish the enclosed note to [be] printed, *in rather larger type* than usual, and across the page or after the end of Very Hard Cash. Without consulting Reade about it. I should like him to know it is going in, and therefore will you have it appended to the proof of the end of his book when it is sent to him for Revise:—printed, I mean, upon the slip. The case as to Conolly and Sutherland is a very serious and painful one indeed. It would be exceedingly strong if I knew neither of them; but knowing both of them it becomes perfectly shocking.[15]

The declaration appeared, capitalized, in the 26 December issue of *All the Year Round*:

THE STATEMENTS AND OPINIONS OF THIS JOURNAL,
GENERALLY, ARE OF COURSE, TO BE RECEIVED AS
THE STATEMENTS AND OPINIONS OF ITS CONDUC-
TOR. BUT THIS IS NOT SO, IN THE CASE OF A WORK
OF FICTION FIRST PUBLISHED IN THESE PAGES AS
A SERIAL STORY, WITH THE NAME OF AN EMINENT
WRITER ATTACHED TO IT. WHEN ONE OF MY LITER-
ARY BROTHERS UNDERTAKES SUCH A TASK, I HOLD
THAT HE EXECUTES IT ON HIS OWN LITERARY RE-
SPONSIBILITY, AND FOR THE SUSTAINMENT OF HIS
OWN REPUTATION; AND I DO NOT CONSIDER MYSELF
AT LIBERTY TO EXERCISE THAT CONTROL OVER HIS
TEXT WHICH I CLAIM AS TO OTHER CONTRIBUTIONS.

II

THE PUBLICATION of *Hard Cash* constitutes an illuminating episode in
its own right, showing as it does the delicately poised balance of forces
between author, editor, publisher, and reading public. But Dickens's
enigmatic comment to Wills about the 'shocking' references in Reade's
novel to 'Conolly and Sutherland' and his embarrassment at 'knowing
both of them' uncovers an argument seething beneath the surface
of fiction of the mid-Victorian period, an argument which is framed
within the larger social context of sane men and women (particularly
spouses) being incarcerated in lunatic asylums by vindictive relatives.
It was, in the late 1850s and 1860s, an explosive issue. Tracking this
argument as it surfaces in a string of major novels, climaxing in *Hard
Cash*, usefully illustrates the codes by which Victorian novels talked
to each other on such awkward matters.

It is necessary to start three decades earlier with Edward Bulwer's
bestseller, *Pelham* (1828). The aristocratic author had married Rosina
Doyle Wheeler in August 1827 after a stormy courtship and in the
face of implacable disapproval on the part of Edward's mother.[16] In
the most drastic of parental rebukes she cut her disobedient son off
without a penny. This it was that induced the dandiacal young man
(who saw himself as the destined inheritor of Byron's mantle) to the
manufacture of fashionable novels—not, in the 1820s, an occupation
for gentlemen.

Pelham is constructed as a mystery. The secret which the hero eventually discovers to have blighted the life of his friend Reginald Glanville is that Gertrude, the woman Reginald once loved, was seduced by the villain Tyrrell. Tiring of her, Tyrrell has consigned his prostituted victim to the horrors of a private madhouse. Glanville finds Gertrude on the brink of death in a locked cell. The keeper, 'with a sort of smirk', informs him that 'her madness is of a very singular description . . . sometimes she is conscious of the past, sometimes utterly oblivious of everything; for days she is perfectly silent . . . though, at times, she raves so violently, that—that—*but I never use force where it can be helped.*'[17] The unfortunate woman is rescued but dies soon after. Glanville, in revenge, murders Tyrrell. (Ironically, in view of events thirty years later, Rosina claimed to have given her husband the idea for *Pelham*'s plot.)

Pelham, as marketed by the 'Prince of Puffers', Henry Colburn, a publisher notorious for his unscrupulous advertising, went on to become one of the biggest and most enduring bestsellers of the nineteenth century and promoted Lytton into the class of £1,000-a-work novelists. Meanwhile the marriage failed spectacularly. On a trip to Italy in 1834 (on which Edward was allegedly accompanied by his mistress) relations between the couple broke down beyond repair.[18] There were by now two children—a daughter Emily born in 1828 and the son and heir, Robert, born in 1830. A legal separation was enacted in April 1836. Two years later Rosina's children were removed from her care on the grounds of her neglect and indifference to them. This charge was almost certainly untrue. But Edward wanted custody of his son who would be eventual heir to the Lyttons' Knebworth estate. Rosina had a strong moral case but the law—as another famously abused wife, Caroline Norton complained—was firmly biased towards the father on custody issues. In the same year, 1836, Lytton became a baronet, a title of which he was inordinately proud.

In the rage of losing her children Rosina wrote a furious *roman à clef* against her husband—*Cheveley, or the Man of Honour* (1839) publicising to the world his brutalities, his meanness (he kept her on a meagre allowance of £400), and his gross adulteries. Over the subsequent years she did everything she could to embarrass him. She bombarded the press with 'revelations' of his infamy and confected innumerable lawsuits. She wrote as many as twenty letters a day to his clubs, with obscenities scrawled on the envelopes. Lytton bore her persecutions as best he could, taking consolation in his mistresses, the brilliant success of his novels, and his promising political career.[19]

In the years immediately after the separation Rosina had her champions in the press, notably the Irish editor of *Fraser's Magazine*, William Maginn, and his young protégé, W. M. Thackeray. Ostensibly the *Fraser's* campaign against Lytton was political. The magazine was rabidly Tory; he was (at this period) a Reform Liberal with 'Radical' sympathies. The Fraserians, particularly Thackeray, habitually descended to gross personality in their attacks on the 'Knebworth Apollo' and made frequent sly reference to his marital problems. Lytton was tormented and at one particularly distressed juncture contemplated calling Maginn out to a duel. After his connection with *Fraser's* ceased, Thackeray continued to lampoon Lytton until well into the 1840s. Indirectly he continued to strike at the other writer with his protracted satire on 'baronets'—a rank which is, in Thackeray's fiction, invariably associated with moral depravity (see, for example Sir Pitt Crawley in *Vanity Fair* and Sir Francis Clavering in *Pendennis*).

As it turned out, Lytton's tormentor was to have a no less unhappy married career. Thackeray had married Isabella Shawe, in the face of the disapproval of her family, in August 1836. Like Rosina, Isabella was Irish. But she notably lacked the other woman's independence of spirit and as a girl had been dominated by her widowed mother. She was only 18 at the time of her marriage to Thackeray, who was seven years older and infinitely more experienced in the ways of the world. The young couple were very hard up in the early years of the marriage. Thackeray had run through his inherited fortune gambling and in injudicious business speculation. He was obliged to support his family by his precarious earnings from his pen. The family grew quickly. As Thackeray had confided to his best friend, William Brookfield, a main motive in marrying had been to provide for himself a morally acceptable outlet for his powerful sexual appetites (appetites which had already led to his contracting venereal disease).[20] There was a first daughter, Anne, born in June 1837, less than a year after marriage. Another daughter, Jane, followed in July 1838. The subsequent months were difficult and the little girl died in March 1839. A third daughter, Harriet, was born in May 1840.

In the weeks following her last daughter's birth Isabella began to show ominous signs of 'langour and depression'. In a letter of

August 1840 she informed her mother-in-law that 'my head flies
away with me as if it were a balloon'.[21] The standard remedy—
'change of air'—was tried. But Thackeray's money problems were
acute, nor was there any sign that he would ever be anything more
than an impecunious penny-a-liner. He could not provide domestic
comforts or prolonged convalescence. Under pressure he may have
said unkind things. He is on record as expressing regrets that he had
ever married.[22] Although all his recorded references to Isabella herself
are tender he was unremittingly savage on the subject of her mother,
to whom she had been very close as a girl. Mothers-in-law were to
be the blackest of beasts in Thackeray's fiction. He represented them
with satirical ferocity in fiction throughout his life (see, for example,
the unspeakable Mrs Major Gam in *Dennis Haggarty's Wife*, the 'Old
Campaigner' in *The Newcomes*, Mrs Baynes in *Philip*).

Isabella was, by all accounts, a timid young woman—evidently
somewhat apprehensive of her husband's exuberant personality, genius, and sexual passions. She was torn between the two most powerful
personalities in her little world. The crisis in her condition occurred
in September 1840 on a trip to Ireland (where the Shawes lived). The
Thackerays were to visit her family while William prepared a travel
book on the country (*The Irish Sketch Book*, as it was to be). Letters
written just before departure record that Thackeray felt he was being
driven 'mad' by Isabella's 'lowness' of spirits and that he intended
to deposit her with her mother 'while she is unwell'.[23] It could easily
have been felt that she was being abandoned, returned as damaged
goods. The crossing to Ireland turned out a nightmare. One day out of
port, on the pretext of visiting the water closet, Isabella threw herself
out of a porthole. She was twenty minutes in the sea before being
found by the circling vessel 'floating on her back, paddling with her
hands'. The next night she made further unspecified attempts at self
destruction. She had left England 'melancholy' and landed in Ireland
'quite demented'.[24]

It is hard not to see some symbolism in the occasion and place
Isabella Thackeray chose for self destruction—the watery gulf between
her mother's and her husband's homes. She is on record as having
expressed feelings of unworthiness and the conviction that she was
'never fit to be a wife'. But after the crisis of the crossing Isabella
made no more attempts at suicide. It was her last futile assertion of
her right to decide her own destiny.

In Ireland Thackeray was abused by his mother-in-law for making her daughter undertake a trip while in a precarious state of postnatal depression. Mrs Shawe flatly accused him of ill-treatment and of having brought the young woman to this extremity by cruelty.[25] The principal symptoms, as far as one can make out, were confusion and autistic withdrawal. In January 1841 Thackeray confided the woes of his marriage to his friend Edward FitzGerald, with a novelist's acuteness of observation:

At first she was violent, then she was indifferent, now she is melancholy and silent and we are glad of it. She bemoans her condition and that is a great step to cure. She knows everybody and recollects things but in a stunned confused sort of way. She kissed me at first very warmly and with tears in her eyes, then she went away from me, as if she felt she was unworthy of having such a God of a husband.[26]

That 'and we are glad of it' was ominous.

In the early months recovery was hoped for. Thackeray had knowledgeable friends foremost among whom was Bryan Waller Procter (1787–1874). Procter was a poet, attorney, and—most importantly at this point—a Commissioner in Lunacy. It was a lucrative position, worth between £1,500 and £2,000 a year, involving the monitoring of the provision of treatment for the insane. Procter evidently carried out his duties conscientiously. He gave informed advice to his friend. But treatment was an expensive and protracted business. The period of Isabella's breakdown coincided with the most straitened years of Thackeray's career. He was in perpetual financial hardship. At some sacrifice he placed Isabella at Esquirol's Maison de Santé, at Ivry, but was alarmed by glimpses of 'wild fierce women rambling about in the garden'.[27]

There was, Thackeray told Mrs Procter, 'nothing the matter with her except perfect indifference, silence and sluggishness. She cares for nothing.'[28] Most distressing was her unmotherly indifference towards her children. Thackeray—evidently still advised by Procter—tried other treatments which represented the latest thinking in 1840s psychiatry. They included a month's vigorous hydropathy in Germany (a very modish therapy, currently being taken by two notable melancholics of the period, Lytton and Alfred Tennyson). There was a disastrous interlude in 1841 when Thackeray attempted to keep Isabella at home as a semi-invalid with her children around her. Then she was placed with another French psychotherapist, Dr Puzin, at Chaillot. Here she remained until 1845. The Thackeray children meanwhile were looked after mainly by his mother, currently living in Paris. Procter showed Thackeray his 'favourite' London asylum, but the husband was 'appalled'.

Finally Thackeray made the momentous decision to remove Isabella from his life. It warrants the briefest of epitaphs in Gordon Ray's authorized biography: 'Isabella's behaviour had become so erratic, indeed, that Thackeray was forced to abandon his fond scheme of entirely reuniting his family. He brought her to England in October 1845, where she was henceforth looked after by Mrs Bakewell, "an excellent worthy woman" at Camberwell.'[29] Mrs Bakewell's charge was a modest £2 a week. Even by mid-Victorian standards this was a less than munificent sum and one assumes that the care Isabella received was basic. Secrecy from the world's eyes seems to have been at least partly a motive in the choice of keeper. Thackeray lived in Kensington and (unfashionable) Camberwell was well to the south, across the river and at this period virtually in the country. Procter probably arranged the business of the medical certificates which would have been required for long-term confinement.

It was a rational decision and quickly justified itself in career terms. Thackeray was liberated to go on and write his first major hits: *The Snobs of England* (1846-7) and *Vanity Fair* (1847-8). At £104 a year, Isabella was—with Thackeray's authorial success—a negligible expense. Nonetheless he complained about Mrs Bakewell's bills, noting tartly that Isabella's mother never offered to help with them.[30] It was less meanness than the underlying conviction that the Shawes were to blame, genetically or by their mode of upbringing, for Isabella's calamities.

In the early days of Isabella's confinement at Camberwell Thackeray made visits—sometimes unobserved by her. She evidently enjoyed occasional lucid spells, but committed unspecified 'nasty pranks' in 1846 which were possibly sexual in nature. After a couple of years she was no longer visited by her husband or children. In 1848 Thackeray noted that 'she cares nothing for us now'. If they cared for her it was a perfunctory and remote emotion. Thackeray's daughters were brought up with an idealized picture of their absent mother who was, during the whole of their girlhood, never more than five miles away. After 1845 Isabella has only a few passing mentions in Ray's biography. She lived with the Bakewells until 1893.

Thackeray was not cruel and in the early years of marriage was ostentatiously fond of his 'little woman'. But in erasing her from his and their daughters' lives he lessened the chance of her recovery to zero. Comfortable confinement was all that Isabella could hereafter expect from her husband. There was no further treatment, no attempt to keep her in touch with the children to whom she had given birth. She had become a non-person. At the *Punch* table (whose conversations were faithfully recorded by Henry Silver) Thackeray freely talked about the venereal infection which he had contracted as a young man and which had damaged his urethra; he talked about his homosexual experiences at Charterhouse school; he talked bawdy. But he never mentioned his wife.

Thackeray's treatment of his wife—more particularly his decision to erase her from public existence—was complicated in an unexpected way by *Jane Eyre* (1847). In that novel the governess heroine discovers—in the very church where she is to be married—that her prospective husband has a mad wife living whom he has kept in an upstairs room, under the superintendence of a housekeeper. They return from the interrupted ceremony and Jane sees for the first time the bloated, half-caste monster whose nocturnal pyromaniac mischief has nearly destroyed her. Brontë, who fervently admired *Vanity Fair*, dedicated the second edition of *Jane Eyre* to Thackeray in 1848. Her novel was, of course, put out under a pseudonym ('Currer Bell') but was universally apprehended to have been written by a woman not unlike Jane Eyre.

Brontë's gothic bigamy plot sparked wild rumours that swept round London like wildfire. They fed on earlier gossip about Thackeray's mad wife and (for those close to him) other gossip that he had had sexual adventures with his children's governesses (he and his mother had some unpleasant words on the subject and his vexation spilled over into the spiteful depiction of Helen Pendennis in the later numbers of his novel in progress). A sexually opportunistic governess, Becky Sharp, is the main character in *Vanity Fair*. A sexually victimized governess is the main character in *Jane Eyre*. In the *Quarterly Review* for December 1848, the reviewer Elizabeth Rigby (writing anonymously) put into print the scurrilous *canard* that the pseudonymous 'Currer Bell' had once herself been a governess in Thackeray's household. He could not marry her, of course, because of the mad Mrs Thackeray (to whom Rigby distantly alluded). *Jane*

Eyre was written in revenge by a discarded lover. A 'surreptitious family' was invented to embellish the rumour of sinister goings-on in Kensington.[31]

Bertha Mason's incarceration was certainly not based on Isabella Thackeray's. At Haworth Charlotte Brontë can have known nothing of Thackeray's domestic arrangements. But the author of *Jane Eyre* was not ignorant of what it was to have deranged relatives in the house: her eccentric father, Patrick, and her alcoholic, opium-addicted brother, Branwell, might well, in less loyal families, have found themselves institutionalized. *Jane Eyre* also reveals that Miss Brontë had developed some strong opinions about the proper treatment of the insane—more particularly she had views on the current fad for 'non-restraint'. In describing to Jane his decision to keep Bertha at home, Rochester—rather surprisingly—reveals himself to be a strong proponent of the non-restraint doctrine. He reveals that he has recruited Mrs Poole and her son from 'Grimsby Retreat' where both worked and where he occupied a senior position as a keeper. The term 'retreat' indicates that Rochester adheres to the system successfully pioneered by the Quakers at their famous York Retreat (headed by Henry Tuke) in the late eighteenth century. This non-coercive, highly-civilized treatment (centred on 'moral therapy') of the mentally ill was Dr John Conolly's principal inspiration for his own, widely publicized, reforms at Hanwell asylum (in Middlesex) in 1840. Hanwell had popularized his doctrine of non-restraint in his 1847 book, *The Construction and Government of Lunatic Hospitals for the Insane*. It is clear that in her attic Bertha is held in a minimum security environment, except when she is, as Mrs Poole puts it, 'rageous'.

The disastrous consequences of Rochester's misguided enlightenment on the question of restraint are shown in the string of fires that Bertha starts. The first of them almost kills Rochester, the second blinds and maims him. It is less Mrs Poole's love of the bottle than Rochester's faith in non-restraint that costs him his eyes. Jane (and, we apprehend, Charlotte Brontë) firmly believed in the panoply of straitjackets, locked cells, and manacles. Given the fact that the Brontë sisters had to manhandle Branwell in the extremes of delirium tremens (in which he nearly burned himself and his family to death) and a pistol-packing father, Charlotte's uncompromising and reactionary views are wholly understandable.

III

BY 1850 LYTTON had put his life back together very satisfactorily. He was now a successful novelist, the laureate of domestic bliss in such novels as *The Caxtons, a Family Picture* (1849). His own family picture remained, however, less than blissful. He had abandoned his daughter Emily to die of typhoid in a London lodging house. After her lonely and wretched death, the body was taken back to the magnificent family home at Knebworth and it was given out to the world that she had expired there, at her father's side. It is the most despicable of Lytton's actions (unless one credits Rosina's allegation that in 1855 he hired an assassin to poison her). Rosina was not even informed her child was dying and was anyway denied access even in such extremities (on the grounds that she was a negligent parent). She furiously publicized the facts of Edward's parental neglect and his lies.

As always, Lytton rose above his wife's 'calumnies', drawing on the immense advantage of fortune, title, and his powerful friends (notably John Delane, editor of *The Times*). He had inherited a huge fortune (and another 'Lytton' to his string of names) when his mother died in 1844. His political ambitions were growing. He became Lord Rector of Glasgow University in 1853. In the same year he received £20,000 from Routledge for the reprint rights to his novels. It was the largest single deal in British literary history. He had returned to Parliament (now as a mature Whig) in 1852. His second career in the House was crowned with prompt success when he was made Colonial Secretary in Lord Derby's ministry. He was a cabinet minister as a relatively young man and could look forward to the very highest position in his party (like Disraeli, another fashionable novelist).

Rosina, now in her fifties, was more bitter than ever. Unlike her husband she had never committed adultery (his agents were always vigilantly spying on her, hoping to discover grounds for divorce). Her novels—not very wonderful but certainly readable library fare— were boycotted by respectable publishers, who feared her husband and his friends in high places. She was socially ostracized and kept on a pittance of a pension, as she saw it. The £400-a-year which Edward allowed her was little more than the fortune she had brought to the marriage and which had—by the law of the land—become her husband's property. She was convinced that the newspaper silence about her grievances was engineered by her malignant husband in collaboration with what she termed 'the Dickens press gang'.

Dickens and Lytton were, by the 1850s, intimates. Dickens named one of his luckless sons Edward Bulwer Lytton Dickens in 1852. The two men had collaborated to set up the Guild of Literature and Art early in the decade. What they had in mind was a colony of cottages on Lytton's Knebworth estate. It would be an 'asylum' for destitute writers and painters. The Guild was designed as a rival to the Royal Literary Fund which did its good work with grants, handouts, and doles. As with his reform institution for fallen women, Urania Cottage (which he set up with the heiress Miss Burdett Coutts in 1847), Dickens believed firmly at this stage of his life in the totalitarian institutions which took benign charge of all aspects of an inmate's life, in the interest of benevolently reconstructing that life to greater social utility.

In 1851 Lytton wrote a fund-raising comedy for the Guild of Literature and Art, with the title (provocative enough to Rosina) of *Not so Bad as we Seem*. Dickens put on amateur productions of the piece, together with a distinguished amateur company which included two versatile men of letters who coincidentally were experts in madness—John Forster (secretary to the Lunacy Commission) and Robert Bell (co-proprietor of a private lunatic asylum at Chiswick). The cast which Dickens assembled for this and other fund-raising performances also included Wilkie Collins (who was to become Dickens's favourite protégé) and a young professional actress, Ellen Ternan, later to become Dickens's mistress.

Coming as it did after the death of her daughter, the 'charitable' performances of *Not so Bad as we Seem* drove Rosina frantic. When she learned that the play was to be put on at the Duke of Devonshire's house in June 1851, she showered the noble patron with letters abusive of her husband ('Sir Liar'), the 'arch-humbug' Dickens, and the 'Guilt' (i.e. the· Guild) generally. She threatened to irrupt into the first night dressed as an orange girl, like Nell Gwynn. She drew up spoof programmes, and wrote a burlesque. In an extremity of nervousness, Dickens consulted his Scotland Yard friend, Inspector Field (Bucket of *Bleak House*) and posted detectives at the doors to apprehend Lady Lytton, should she make good her threats.[32] Wisely, perhaps, Rosina kept away, although Dickens remained apprehensive of some act of 'desperation' from her for some months afterwards. In reaction to her husband's new-found enthusiasm for charitable causes she published a pamphlet in 1857 entitled 'Lady Bulwer Lytton's Appeal to the Justice and Charity of the English Public'. It cost her a lot of money and did not, as she fondly expected, win her justice from the public or charity from Knebworth.

In June 1858, exasperated to the point of distraction, Rosina went down by train to Hertford where her husband was putting himself forward for renomination to the town's voters. Such occasions (twenty years before the secret ballot) were traditionally rowdy. But few election meetings were as dramatic as that which now took place in the High Street at Hertford. Rosina's own account of the occasion is almost certainly melodramatically exaggerated, but nonetheless conveys her luckless husband's consternation and her implacable spite against him. Having arrived at the hustings, as she recalled:

I touched with my large green fan the arm of the first man near me [and] said in a loud clear voice, 'My good people, make way for your member's wife, and let me pass, for I have something to say to him,' whereupon the mob began to cheer and cry, 'Make way for Lady Lytton, that we will, God bless her, poor lady.' And instantly a clear passage was made for me to the very scaffolding of the hustings. 'Thank you, friends,' said I. And then steadily fixing my eyes on the cold, pale, fiendish, lack-lustre eyes of the electioneering baronet, I said, 'Sir Edward Earle Bulwer Lytton, after turning me and my children out of our house to run an unexampled career of vice, you have spent years in promulgating every lie of me, and hunting me through the world with every species of outrage . . . etc. . . . . etc.'[33]

According to Rosina, her astounded husband's jaw fell, 'like that of a man suddenly struck with paralysis, and he made a rush from the hustings.' The mob began to cheer 'and vociferate, "Ah! he's guilty, he's guilty, he dare not face her. Three cheers for her ladyship".' *The Times* (which was controlled by friends of Lytton's) did not report anything other than Lytton's successful address to his constituents.

Lytton did not delay long in taking his revenge. On her return to London, on 22 June, Rosina was abducted by hired strongmen in the streets (with the brutal instruction that she 'behave like a lady'—a line echoed in the parallel scene in the 1993 film of Michael Hastings's play, *Tom and Viv*). Without any chance to alert her friends she was bundled away to a private lunatic asylum, Wyke House, in Brentford. The establishment was run by Robert Gardiner Hill, an early and prominent advocate of the non-restraint system. It was chosen carefully and evidently on the best medical advice. Rosina was convinced that behind the scheme was 'that vile old Doctor Conolly [who] would sell his own mother for money'.[34] Other accounts claim that six doctors were called on to certify her as mad, with the legally requisite personal examination. It is all very muddy but the facts of the physical abduction, as reported by the *Daily Telegraph*, writing on 21 July 1858, seem clear enough:

Upon whose authority was Lady Lytton captured and sent to Brentford? Not originally, as has been stated, upon that of Dr Conolly. The certificates were signed by a Mr Hale Thompson, once known at Westminster Hospital, and by a Mr Rose, an apothecary of Farringdon Street, whose medical reputation seems to have travelled providentially from east of Temple-Bar [i.e. the slums of London] to an official residence in Downing Street [Lytton's office]. The sanction of these 'eminent' gentlemen enabled the policemen and nurse to place Lady Lytton by force in a carriage, but through a humane afterthought Dr Conolly was ultimately called in and dispatched to the residence of Mr Robert Gardiner Hill at Brentford. There he certified that Lady Lytton was a demented patient.

According to Rosina, writing to Charles Reade in 1864, Lytton paid Hill £800. He probably paid Conolly as much (his price for such services, as was to emerge a few months later, was not cheap). Rosina was probably correct in suspecting Conolly's hand behind the plot. Another likely adviser was John Forster ('One of Sir Liar's tools', as Rosina called him), as was Lytton's and Dickens's lawyer friend William Ballantine, and, probably, the omnipresent literary man Procter, a close friend of both Dickens and Forster. Forster, as has been said, had been Secretary to the Lunacy Commission since 1855 and was well placed to advise on legal technicalities. In preparation for the abduction Dickens and Lytton evidently intervened with friends on the papers (notably *The Times* and *Punch*) to suppress all reference to Lady Lytton. *Punch*'s not mentioning the outrage (at a period when their treatment of Disraeli verged on Jew-baiting) is particularly striking. Bradbury and Evans, the magazine's proprietors, were, of course, also Dickens's publishers. *The Times*, under the editorial supervision of Lytton's friend Delane, confined itself to the tersest of official comments although it carried in the summer of 1858 a number of items relating to the Colonial Secretary's political activities.

In preparation for the abduction, the ground was laid with a whispering campaign. As Rosina later recorded: 'Sir [Edward] was giving out all over London, *via* a Mr Robert Bell, one of the Dickens literary clique, that I was *quite mad*.'[35] She was convinced 'that brute

Dickens' was a co-conspirator. On his part, Robert Bell (1800–67) was well qualified to spread malicious rumours of this kind. He was a middle-ranking *littérateur*, clubman (the Garrick and the Reform), and a friend of both Dickens and (more closely) Thackeray. He dined with everyone. He was intimate with Thackeray at the period when he was working out what to do with Isabella, and an amateur actor in Dickens's troupe in early 1851, when Rosina was threatening her Nell Gwynn stunt.[36] More importantly, for Lytton's immediate purposes in June 1858, Bell had strong connections with the lunatic business. From 1844 to 1850 he was the licensed owner of the Manor House private asylum at Chiswick. (In 1850 it passed into the ownership of a member of Bell's family, Thomas Harrington Tuke, who was also a son-in-law of John Conolly's.) It was through Bell, probably, that Dickens was introduced to Conolly and his family. The subsequent social connection seems to have been principally conducted through the grown-up daughters of the men.[37]

The abduction and incarceration of Rosina, although it could be suppressed in the columns of the nation's newspaper of record, provoked a huge outcry from people in Taunton, among whom the lady had lived for some time with the public reputation of a perfectly sane citizen. Committees were formed and indignant petitions drawn up. Political opponents to Lytton were mobilized. The *Telegraph* took up her case (possibly with the motive of embarrassing the Derby administration). At Hill's Wyke House asylum, Rosina was duly visited by commissioners. They included, as she reported, Procter. Conolly (who had earlier certified her as 'demented') was in attendance. Rosina found Procter to be sympathetic and 'gentlemanly'. Conolly she cordially loathed. These gentlemen now drew up new certificates, testifying that she was sane. On 17 July, having spent three-and-a-half weeks in custody as a madwoman, she was released. Rosina was now allowed to travel on the Continent in the company of her son, Robert. A notice to this effect was placed in *The Times*. It was accompanied by a letter from Conolly asserting that, despite his earlier 'decided opinion' that Lady Lytton was mad when committed earlier in the summer, he was now quite happy to see her released 'in the society of her son and her female friend'.

What had Lytton intended? To lock up his wife permanently and erase her as Thackeray had erased Isabella? This was what Rosina believed. She maintained that she had only been preserved from a lifetime's incarceration by the heroic efforts of her friends and Lytton's enemies. But for them she would have ended up like the man in the iron mask. In fact, Lytton probably did not intend to bury his wife for ever in a lunatic asylum. She was not so easily subdued. On advice, he had chosen one of the best-conducted institutions in the land and one which was accessible to investigators (he could very easily have secreted her somewhere off the beaten track in Yorkshire). What Lytton presumably intended was to frighten her, by showing her the instruments, as the Inquisition had done with Joan of Arc. Rosina could work out clearly enough what had happened to wives like Mrs Thackeray and could foresee what would happen to her if she again tried an escapade like that at Hertford on 9 June 1858. The imprisonment seems to have been designed as a demonstration to persuade her to control herself in future and allow her husband to get on with his career. There was a carrot. If Lady Lytton behaved herself she would have her allowance raised to £500 and she might have access to her son. Ideally, she should stay outside the country. Lytton achieved his end. Rosina never again publicly humiliated her husband.

IV

IT IS NECESSARY at this point to outline in more detail the character of John Conolly (1794–1866), one of the most ambiguous figures in nineteenth-century medicine. Originally from an obscure, impoverished, but genteel background, Conolly had drifted into medicine, qualifying at Edinburgh in 1821. During an early residence in France he had been impressed with the country's mental health reforms and as a medical student he displayed a prophetic interest in melancholy. On leaving Edinburgh he failed as a general practitioner. He was, throughout life, improvident and restless. He was not particularly gifted intellectually nor was he a particularly able physician. But he had a winning manner ('oily' as Rosina called it) and he invariably impressed people with his benevolence. In the late 1820s he took up a position at the new University of London medical school. And it was at this point in his career that Conolly published what was to be his most influential work, *An Inquiry Concerning the Indications of Insanity* (1830). In it he advocated radical reform of the policy of restraint of lunatics, drawing on the pioneer work of the Quaker retreats

and of Pinel in France. Conolly argued against asylums generally as
non-therapeutic, and more likely to produce madness than cure it.
Although it was later to be taken very seriously, Conolly's *Inquiry* fell
flat at the time. There were squabbles with the university authorities
about stipends and Conolly resigned in 1832, having held his academic
post only four years.

There followed nine debt-filled years.[38] Finally in 1839 Conolly
was appointed Resident Physician (effectively governor) at Hanwell
Lunatic Asylum. It was a large institution, with 800 beds, serving
greater London. With maximum publicity Conolly put into action a
policy of drastic reform. He abolished the panoply of strait-jackets,
manacles, and whips by which the inmates had traditionally been
regulated. He converted Hanwell from a madhouse—a prison for the
insane—to a a 'lunatic asylum', a refuge for the unfortunate. Conolly
was taken up by *The Times* and became, as Elaine Showalter puts
it, 'a symbol of the aspirations of the age'.[39] Although he was only
in charge of the asylum for just over four years, Conolly put the
humane treatment of lunatics on the social agenda for the well-
meaning British middle class. The reforms at Hanwell made him a
great national hero, overshadowing the more solid achievements of
non-restraint predecessors like the Tukes, Pinel, and Robert Gardiner
Hill, a contemporary who lacked Conolly's brilliant public relations
skills.

As his fame grew so Conolly enlarged his definition of what it
was to be mad. He was in the forefront of the popularization of
'moral insanity', a theory formulated by James Cowles Prichard in
the mid-1830s. The exoneration of madness as a dangerous condition
received something of a check with the McNaghten case in 1843, when
a murderer (intending to assassinate the Prime Minister and killing
his secretary instead) was spared the gallows on grounds of mental
incompetence. The subsequent 'McNaghten Rules' were devised to
limit moral insanity as an extenuating circumstance. Nonetheless,
throughout the 1840s, Conolly was extending his definition of what it
was to be mad. By 1850 he was prepared to certify as qualifications
for incarceration in the asylum an extraordinary range of behaviours:
'excessive eccentricity', 'utter disregard of cleanliness and decency',
'perversions of the moral feelings and passions', a disposition 'to give
away sums of money which the subject cannot afford to lose', indeed
all cases where the person's 'being at large is inconsistent with the

comfort of society and their own welfare'. Conolly had a particular
bee in his bonnet about the madness of Hamlet, on which he was
to publish a monograph in 1863. He was, in the eyes of some of
his colleagues, at risk of becoming himself a monomaniac on the
subject of mania. Once an opponent of all asylums, he now apparently
yearned to put a majority of the English population into a non-
restraint institution with himself as benevolent governor. Conolly's
more conservative colleagues were alarmed by his 'eagerness to consign
the morally perverse and socially inadequate to the asylum'.[40] Apart
from other objections it was a very useful weapon in the hands of
vindictive spouses.

In the 1850s Conolly became a close acquaintance of Dickens. They
frequently met socially and Dickens refers glowingly to Conolly's
reforms at Hanwell as early as 1852 in *Household Words*. The character
of Mr Dick in *David Copperfield* and Betsey Trotwood's care for him
is a florid tribute to Conolly's non-restraint system. Dick is presented
as a charming and utterly harmless lunatic rendered into a desirable
household pet by his keeper's kindness. Miss Trotwood has earlier
rescued Mr Dick from a private asylum, where he was consigned by
heartless relatives, and whose horrors are hinted at. She treats him
as a guest, allows him the freedom of the house, gives him money to
jingle in his pocket, and asks his advice on household problems. He
gives Delphic and occasionally shrewd answers. Symbolic of Mr Dick's
freedom is his kite flying, a therapy which allows him to control his
delusions by loosing them into the air. He is himself as free as air,
inhabiting a utopia of Conollyan non-restraint. There is no suggestion
that Mr Dick can ever be cured. The last picture we have of him is of
a happy old lunatic, still flying his kite, and writing the interminable
testimonial that is forever invaded by King Charles's head. Only a
sadist would put Mr Dick in a straitjacket or lock him up.

In May 1857 at a dinner for the Royal Hospital for Incurables,
Dickens proposed to the company the health of Dr Conolly. To
resounding cheers he went on to describe him as 'a distinguished
gentleman who was not more remarkable for his talent than he was
for possessing the kindest and tenderest heart'.[41] This was the public
image of Conolly in the 1850s—the Cheeryble of the lunatic asylum.
Dickens enhanced his friend's public image by publishing a eulogistic
article (by Morley) in *Household Words* (28 November 1857), 'Things
within Dr Conolly's Remembrance'. Morley painted the doctor in

glowing colours as the pioneer of the civilized treatment of lunatics not just in England, but in Europe. In fact, for all the tributes and honours showered on him, Conolly's circumstances were becoming increasingly difficult. He had only been in charge of Hanwell from 1839 to 1843. He remained there tenuously as a visiting physician until 1852, when all connection ceased. Why he was dismissed or resigned is unknown (perhaps it had something to do with the McNaghten backlash). As at the University of London he showed himself chronically unable to hold down a salaried permanent position. To support himself in the mid-1850s Conolly went into business as a freelance 'alienist', taking any kind of consultancy work. He was short of money and getting on in years. His children were a source of never-ending expense and anxiety.

By the end of the 1850s, Conolly had descended to the condition of a psychiatric harlot, exploiting his reputation for whatever money it would bring. He, who had excoriated private asylums in 1830, turned his own house into a private asylum for nerve-wracked women. He was now a 'trader in lunacy'. He had a commercial interest in other private asylums—institutions which he now justified as necessary for the middle classes who could not face the stigma of 'pauper asylums', like the county institution at Hanwell. In contravention of the Madhouse Act of 1828, which prohibited a link between certification and profit, Conolly referred patients to asylums owned by friends and by his son-in-law, Thomas Harrington Tuke (Robert Bell's relative).

It is clear that Conolly was one of Lytton's main henchmen in his 1858 difficulties and that (for a price) he lent the necessary medical cover to an act of flagrant assault, kidnap, coercion and blackmail. He certified Rosina was demented when the certificate was needed to seize her on the London streets. Three weeks later, he blandly certified that she was quite sane, when that declaration was required. Her mental condition had not changed (if anything it was more deranged after three weeks' of Mr Hill's unwanted attention). What had changed was Lord Lytton's wishes in the matter. His remittances determined whatever opinion Conolly put his name to. Rosina was probably right to think that John Conolly would have sold his mother for money.

V

CONOLLY WAS ALMOST certainly advising and serving Dickens in the same capacity as Lytton at exactly the same period. Over the months June–August 1858 the Dickens marriage was falling apart. The causes for the breakdown are complex and have been the subject of much speculation, most recently in Claire Tomalin's *The Invisible Woman* (1989, a biography of Ellen Ternan) and Peter Ackroyd's 1989 biography of Dickens. Much remains obscure. What is certain is that in 1858 Dickens, aged 46, had fallen out of love with his 43-year-old wife and had fallen in love with a 19-year-old actress, Ellen Ternan. Dickens was dependent in this crisis on a number of confidential advisers, notably Forster. But Conolly's hand seems clearly visible in one of the most enigmatic pieces of documentation from this vexed period, the so-called 'Violated Letter'. Ostensibly a private communication for the benefit of his manager, Arthur Smith, Dickens evidently intended that it should be made public—if circumstances required. Apparently he wanted it be available as evidence if things ever came to court. (The letter was 'violated' when it came into the hands of the *New York Herald-Tribune*, who published it without permission.)

The Violated Letter is dated 25 May 1858—a period when separation between the Dickenses was inevitable. There are, however, a number of features in the Violated Letter which have always perplexed Dickensians. Dickens, for instance, asserts that during the course of their marriage Mrs Dickens has always been indifferent to her children. He specifically attributes this to 'the peculiarity of her character', with the implication that she is emotionally defective. The day-to-day care of the children had fallen, Dickens claims, to his long-suffering sister-in-law, Georgina Hogarth—a woman with whom it was popularly supposed in London at the time he was enjoying intercourse. (Since brother and sister-in-law were within the degrees of incest, the slander was all the more infuriating.) Dickens goes on:

For some years past Mrs Dickens has been in the habit of representing to me that it would be better for her to go away and live apart, that her always increasing estrangement made [worse] *a mental disorder under which she sometimes labors*—more, that she felt herself unfit for the life she had to lead as my wife, and that she would be better far away.[42]

Forster, he continues, has advised a separation.

The above descriptions of Catherine Dickens have baffled the novelist's biographers. There is no evidence that Mrs Dickens was ever anything but a loving mother. According to some accounts she seems to have been if anything over-solicitous of her children's welfare. As Michael Slater puts it: 'A great mass of evidence could be heaped up showing that Catherine was a loving mother (she evidently liked children generally as she gave many children's parties even after her separation from Dickens) and that she was loved by her children . . . but it is hardly necessary.'[43] Nor is there any evidence, beyond Dickens's allegation in this letter and some communications with his patron Miss Burdett Coutts at the same period, that Catherine Dickens before, during, or after the separation 'laboured under a mental disorder'.[44] She seems to have been remarkably sane.

Biographers have assumed that Dickens's perceptions were temporarily warped by the emotional turmoil of the separation and by the 'disgusting and horrible' allegations that he was having a sexual relationship with his sister-in-law Georgina Hogarth (allegations which he believed to emanate from his hated mother-in-law, Mrs Hogarth).[45] Dickens was seeing what he wanted to see. What is likely is that the Violated Letter of 25 May was directly provoked by a previous letter of 20 May from Catherine to Mark Lemon, who was acting as her intermediary. The letter has not survived but, as Michael Slater surmises, it may well have hinted at a divorce action. This would have been feasible in terms of the 1857 Act which permitted a woman to sue for divorce on grounds of adultery where cruelty, perversion, or incest was involved. The contents of the letter were apparently communicated to Forster, who evidently passed them on to an appalled Dickens.

On her part, it is not hard to reconstruct what must have gone through Catherine Dickens's mind on discovering the contents of the Violated Letter. To be accused of motherly indifference to children and 'mental disorder' with Dr John Conolly and John Forster (now a Commissioner in Lunacy) hovering in the background was highly ominous. It is significant that Catherine would not accept Forster as an intermediary, insisting instead on Lemon (the homespun editor of *Punch*). Forster, she may have thought, knew far too much about locking up women with 'mental disorders'. For a physician like Conolly, Mrs Dickens's alleged 'langour' and her excitability about her husband's infidelity with a younger woman would have been quite sufficient for a certificate of 'moral insanity' to be drawn up. He did it for Lord Lytton, would he not do the same for his friend Mr Dickens? And if she escaped the dreadful fate of Isabella Thackeray at the very least Catherine might, like Rosina Bulwer in 1836, be forcibly separated from the children whom she was alleged not to care for.

It is extremely unlikely that Dickens intended to incarcerate Catherine. It is equally unlikely that he wanted to alienate her permanently from her children. What he may have intended was, like Lytton at the same period, to 'show her the instruments'. Give her and her mother a terrifying glimpse, that is, of what he *might* do, if she were to bring Ellen Ternan's name into play, or not join with him in putting down the outrageous allegations of incest with Georgina. It is the kind of 'take no prisoners' warfare aggrieved partners still resort to in divorce actions (nowadays with trumped-up accusations of 'sexual abuse' of the children).

Within a few days, in early June, Catherine agreed to the terms of the separation. She was bought off and put into obscure retirement. She was given an annual allowance of £600 (originally the offer was '£400 and a brougham'). In the same month, Rosina—after infinite haggling—got an improved pension from Lytton of £500. These sums were considerably more than the £104 a year it cost Thackeray to keep Isabella. And, as Michael Slater points out, the £600 allowed Catherine was 'generous' by the standards of middle-class income at the period. But Dickens and Lytton were earning, from writing alone, over £10,000 a year in the late 1850s. Thackeray was in the £5,000 class. Between them the three dismissed wives had borne their husbands some fifteen children and seen them through their most trying authorial years. None had committed adultery (that we, or their husbands apparently, knew of). A modern divorce lawyer would not have been fobbed of with a few hundreds.

By the end of 1858 the three leading novelists of the age, Thackeray, Dickens, and Lytton (authors of such celebrations of domesticity as *Our Mutual Friend*, *The Newcomes*, and *My Novel*) all had put their wives away. There was an overlapping network of aides knowledgeable in madness involved behind the scenes: Procter, Conolly, Bell, Forster. The private lunatic asylum was an actual (or in Dickens's case an obliquely threatened) weapon in all three husbands' establishing their social and authorial freedom from vexatious spouses and their in-laws. Each achieved his independence at very affordable cost. Each made other amatory arrangements. Thackeray fell in love and conducted a long (and probably unconsummated) affair with his best friend's wife; Lytton took a string of mistresses; Dickens set up house with an actress many years his junior.

VI

IN THE CROWDED SUMMER of 1858 things began to go badly wrong for John Conolly. Ten months earlier, in November 1857, Lawrence Ruck, a Welshman possessed of property worth £1,500 a year, had been committed to a lunatic asylum by his wife. The circumstances of Ruck's committal were highly irregular. A 'surgeon' (unqualified in psychiatric medicine) saw him separately. Ruck was subsequently visited by Conolly. On the strength of their joint opinions, Ruck was seized and put in a private lunatic asylum, Moorcroft House, owned by a Dr Stillwell. By the terms of the 1828 Act, the physicians should properly have examined their patient together and have drawn up a formal report. Certified insane, Ruck was held in Moorcroft House, under protest, until 24 August 1858, when a jury—to whom he gave an eminently lucid account of himself—found him of sound mind. It came out at the trial that Ruck was 'intemperate' and had been suffering an attack of delirium tremens at the time of his commital. It also emerged that there had been marital difficulties between him and Mrs Ruck, provoked by his 'Mormonite' promiscuousness. In short, he was a drunk and she, angry at his philandering, had him locked away and took his money.

It was humiliating enough for Conolly to have his professional judgement publicly overturned. But worse was to come. In June 1859, Ruck brought a civil action against Stillwell and Conolly for false imprisonment. Some extraordinary facts emerged during the case (in which Conolly prudently did not testify, although his reputation was thoroughly blackened). It emerged that Conolly was receiving £800 a year from Stillwell, representing 15 per cent of the fees for every patient he referred to the asylum. It further emerged that he was paid for consultations at Moorcroft—that he had received hundreds of pounds for 'treating' Ruck when, it was demonstrated, he had never seen the man. Ruck, of course, was paying for this non-treatment, via Mrs Ruck, who now had command of his fortune. This exchange of financial favours was grossly unprofessional, and flatly against the law. Conolly was fined £500 damages and roundly censured. He was not, however, struck off the list, nor were further proceedings brought against him, presumably because of his eminence, his earlier services to medicine, and his advanced age.

The Lytton and Ruck scandals were accompanied by other highly publicized instances of spousal misuse of the Lunacy Act. Considerable publicity was given to the case of Mary Jane Turner. A Yorkshire woman of means, Mrs Turner had been put away by her husband. Her plight was exacerbated by the gross sexual misconduct of her keeper (who was paid three guineas a week—rather more than the going-rate it was revealed in court). *The Times* covered the case in great detail in July 1858. On the Continent, commentators saw this spate of vindictive spousal incarceration as evidence of a peculiarly Anglo-Saxon style of divorce. As Rosemary Ashton notes: 'Julius Rodenberg, a bourgeois exile who wrote hack-journalism in German newspapers, described in his collection of "scenes of everyday life", *Alltagsleben in London. Ein Skizzenbuch* (1860), how the papers were full of accounts of English men and women declaring their spouses insane in an attempt to shake off the loathed partner.'[46] There is a symptomatic indication of the fear this epidemic of punitive incarceration induced in susceptible wives recorded in Thomas Carlyle's *Reminiscences.* His wife, Jane, had fallen and injured herself, and during her protracted convalescence, in November 1863, she was further afflicted with what the doctors termed 'disease of the nerves'. As Carlyle recalls:

A hideous pain, of which she used to say that 'common honest pain, were it cutting off one's flesh or sawing of one's bones would be a luxury in comparison,' seemed to have begirdled her, at all moments and on every side. Her intellect was clear as starlight, and continued so; the clearest intellect among us all; but she dreaded that this too must give way. 'Dear,' said she to me, on two occasions with such a look and tone as I shall never forget, 'promise me that *you will never put me into a madhouse,* however this go. Do you promise me now?' I solemnly did. 'Not if I do quite lose my wits?' 'Never, my darling; oh, compose thy poor terrified heart!'[47]

It may have been harder for Jane to compose her heart with the examples of Lady Lytton and Mrs Thackeray in her mind.

There is strong evidence that Dickens became disenchanted with both Lytton and Conolly after the scandals of 1858 and the parliamentary select committee of investigation which they inspired. (The committee's report led to legal reforms in the treatment of the insane in 1862.)[48] In particular Conolly's hypocrisy and unprofessional conduct must have revolted Dickens, when he was belatedly made aware of it. But, bound as he was to both men by links of friendship and confidential assistance, he could not break directly. Nonetheless in *Great Expectations* (1860), there is a clear indication that Dickens had revised his earlier views about non-restraint of the criminally insane. Miss Havisham is no Mr Dick—harmlessly free as the birds in the air. Like the pyromaniac Bertha Mason, in her uncontrolled violence, Miss Havisham arsonizes her house, and destroys herself. Pip is haunted by the image of the madwoman 'running at me, shrieking, with a whirl of fire blazing all about her, and soaring at least as many feet above her head as she was high.' Better, the reader might think, that the poor woman had been confined and manacled than that she should do such harm to herself and others.

There are other clues to Dickens's sense of dissociation from his former allies. In his new magazine, *All the Year Round, The Woman in White* was the first great hit in late 1859. Collins's narrative has as its mainspring a plot in which a wicked baronet (the rank is stressed) imprisons a woman—his sane wife, no less—in a private London lunatic asylum. Collins was a journalist and was up with all the London gossip. He was closely associated with G. A. Sala, another Dickens protégé, and now a principal journalist on the *Daily Telegraph*, the main London newspaper to take Rosina's side in summer 1858. It is inconceivable that Collins did not know what he was doing in devising the plot of *The Woman in White*. It is equally inconceivable that Dickens—who was Wilkie's confidant and who read the proofs as they were returned—did not tacitly approve. Where he disapproved, as with Charles Lever's unfortunate serial *A Day's Ride*, Dickens was not slow to use his editorial prerogative to intervene. He gave his imprimatur to the first numbers of *The Woman in White*, which were delivered well ahead of publication.

Dickens used the diplomatic power of his position with consummate skill. Of course, it was implied, he could not interfere with the creative work of a brilliant 'fellow labourer' like Collins. At the same time he put into print (and paid handsomely for) a novel which blackguarded baronets who locked up their wives for nefarious purposes in lunatic asylums and who plotted to poison them (as Rosina alleged Lytton had plotted to poison her). Rosina could not have done better herself, and she wrote to Collins congratulating him on his percipient depiction of villainous wife-murdering baronets. At the end of *The Woman in White*'s run, Dickens wrote a magisterial letter of commendation to his protégé on the skill of his narrative technique. He studiously avoided any reference to the contents of the plot.[49]

At the same time, Dickens made flattering overtures to Lytton, inviting him to contribute a serial to *All the Year Round*, thus forestalling any suggestion that he was at all antagonistic to his former colleague and fellow thespian. So too with *Hard Cash*. Dickens must have known that since 1859 Reade had been gathering material with which to attack the private lunatic asylum racket, and had been active in court cases on behalf of victims of false imprisonment. Collins, who was close to Reade, would surely also have informed him that the novelist had a particular vendetta against Dickens's former friend and counsellor, John Conolly.

In the event *Hard Cash* devolved in its later numbers into a massive *ad hominem* attack. Reade's depiction of Conolly—particularly as regards the facts of the Ruck case—was plainly libellous; or would have been had Conolly not been too frightened to go into court and expose himself to cross-examination (Reade, incidentally, had been trained as a barrister). The direct assault on Conolly begins in chapter 31 of *Hard Cash*, when the hero is visited in his private apartment by a Dr Wycherley, 'a gentleman he scarcely knew by name'. With an air of 'benevolent superiority' Dr Wycherley asks a few aimless questions as to Alfred Hardie's general health. Alfred wearies of the impertinent interrogation and turns him out of the room. Wycherley is followed by a seedy apothecary, who asks a series of similarly irrelevant questions. Alfred vexed out of all patience turns Mr Speers out of the room with even more violence. What he does not realize is that he has been examined prior to certification (the irregularities in this procedure exactly match those of the unfortunate Mr Ruck in November 1857). Wycherley, it emerges, is in the pay of Alfred's incredibly villainous father.

Alfred is lured to an asylum and imprisoned. In the hero's subsequent encounters with Wycherley, Reade depicts Conolly with photographic closeness. He is 'the very soul of humanity. Here are no tortures, no handcuffs, nor leg-locks, no brutality', he informs Alfred. All the 'benevolent' Wycherley does is incarcerate sane men and women for money. Reade even guys Conolly's *idée fixe* about Hamlet (Alfred has to agree the Prince is mad before he can be considered for release). Finally, Wycherley is called to account in court. Counsel drags 'out of him that he received 15 per cent from the asylum keepers for every patient he wrote insane; and that he had an income of eight hundred pounds a year from that source alone.'

Although posterity has been harsh to Reade, seeing his satire in *Hard Cash* as excessive, he was clearly justified in his assault on Conolly. The doctor, whatever his great works in the early 1840s, had sold himself to some very sordid causes in the following decade. He had completely backtracked on his earlier position on the undesirability of private asylums—and was himself now the proprietor of such an institution. Worse, he was a huckster feeding other dubious institutions, prostituting his medical qualifications for the purpose. Reade believed, with some justice, that the whole non-restraint policy was a sham. There remained, he believed, hideous violence at places like Hanwell to which the authorities turned a blind eye. As an eccentric and sexual fetishist Reade must have realized that—by Conolly's elastic criteria—he too could easily be incarcerated.

In his preface to the book version of *Hard Cash*, Reade asked for further cases of wrongful imprisonment in lunatic asylums to be sent to him. The request elicited a massive 'letter' from Rosina Lytton which could not—while Lytton, 'that brute Dickens' (as she called him), and Conolly lived—be published for libel reasons. It was privately printed as a book called *Blighted Life* in 1880 by Edward Keneally after all the principals in the episode had gone to their reward. Keneally was a disciple of William Maginn who had led the *Fraser's* campaign against Bulwer, fifty years before.

During the course of the publication of *Hard Cash*, Dickens was approached by Conolly's son-in-law, Thomas Harrington Tuke, asking that Reade be controlled. Dickens was awkwardly placed. He had been friendly with Conolly, who probably was of great assistance to him (as he had been to Lytton) in the summer of marital discord in 1858. His daughters were, apparently, still friendly with Conolly's family. He replied to Tuke on 15 November 1863 (as *Hard Cash* was reaching its offensive climax): 'I cannot imagine that Mr Reade had the least knowledge of what you tell me concerning Dr Conolly . . . Reade is enormously mistaken and damages a good cause. But I cannot believe that he would wilfully be personal and cruel.'[50] This was disingenuous. It was abundantly clear that Reade intended to be as cruel as he could be, as Dickens of all people must have realized. Conolly evidently feared that *Hard Cash* would provoke more civil suits against him. He himself could not take legal action against Reade without adding to the disastrously bad publicity his malpractice had already accumulated. Dickens could, of course, have intervened with

Reade had he so wished. But he did not so wish—at least not on behalf of John Conolly, as he now regarded him in 1863. The most he would do, and it was in fact less than nothing, was to insert his equivocal capitalized statement at the end of the serial's run.

CHAPTER FOUR

Dickens's Serializing Imitators

THE SUBJECT OF THIS CHAPTER is serialization; that is, the division of narrative into separately issued instalments, usually for commercial convenience but occasionally for art. Specifically the subject is that mode of serialization pioneered by Dickens in April 1836 with his first novel, and which he was still triumphantly practising in September 1870, the month of his death. A majority (nine) of his novels came out this way. The features of Dickensian serialization can be given Bitzer-style as: 'The new novel in twenty monthly, self-contained, illustrated parts, each 32 pages long, selling at one shilling, wrapped in a uniformly illustrated paper cover and accompanied by an advertiser.'

Extended discussions of Dickens invariably become meditations on his uniqueness. Although the main interest here concerns imitators and imitations the conclusion I shall arrive at is the usual one: that Dickens was the great inimitable. The novel in monthly parts proved a bow of Ulysses which apparently only one man could consistently draw and fire on target. Dickens himself called it 'a very unusual form'[1] and for most writers that is what it remained. Only three major Victorian novelists used Dickensian serialization for the bulk of their novels: Dickens (obviously), Thackeray and Lever. And of the three, Thackeray and Lever ultimately gave it up as unworkable. The yellow cover and the pink finally gave way to the all-conquering duck-egg green. In sum, the number of Victorian novels brought out in monthly numbers is tiny. Over the period 1837–70 an estimated 8–9,000 works of fiction were produced in England. At the beginning of this period (its boom time) there were at maximum some 15 part-issued shilling serials a year. The number settled down by the 1840s to around five. By the end of the 1860s, it had dwindled to one or two. And by September 1870, there was only one.

Why, for everyone but Dickens, the novel in shilling monthly numbers should have proved so intractable is a fascinating question. Another question which suggests itself is why, against the tide of publishing progress, Dickens remained so happily wedded to the novel in numbers for 35 years (about ten years longer than he was happily married to his wife, Catherine).

The straight answer, of course, is that Dickens could make the novel in numbers pay handsomely, as others evidently couldn't. But the fact is that Dickens could have made any form of publication pay. If he had inscribed his novels on marble tablets, Victorians would have fought each other to buy. More than any other novelist Dickens had a choice. This was a privilege of his pre-eminence. And for 35 years, his choice was curiously repetitive and apparently unimaginative. No other first-rank novelist of the mid-nineteenth century was as faithful to one mode of publication as Dickens. Where they weren't forced into change or new fashion, they sought it; often as middle-aged people do, to escape their own sense of impending superannuation. Why didn't Dickens? Why was a man otherwise so restless in literary and personal matters so automatic in his publishing practice? I'll leave these prefatory questions hanging. The central part of this discussion will be a survey of the rise and fall of the novel in monthly numbers.

II

THE INNOVATION of the Dickensian novel in numbers in April 1836 is wonderfully sudden. The *Pickwick Papers* emerged, fully formed, apparently from nowhere. Chapman & Hall (perhaps prodded by Robert Seymour, perhaps inspired by Jorrocks) had the idea in February. By the last day of March, the first serial part was on the bookstands. After a little tinkering with length and number of illustrations, by midsummer *Pickwick* had found the form that was to remain standard for the next 35 years.

Conventionally, the genesis of *Pickwick* has been seen as a kind of book-trade miracle, 'phenomenon' or, as Robert Patten puts it, an 'accident'.[2] But one can demystify its birth a little by uncovering precedents and possible inspirations. There was, of course, nothing new about the part issue of books. The practice (particularly with non-fiction and less than new works) goes back to the seventeenth century. Dickens himself remembered from his boyhood, 'certain interminable novels in [serial] form which used . . . to be carried about the country by pedlars'.[3] And there was a more chic nineteenth-century precursor in Pierce Egan's *Life in London* (see Plate 1). Carrying 36 illustrations by Robert, Isaac and George Cruikshank, this 'Original Work' came out in 12, 32-page monthly numbers, costing three shillings each, October 1820–July 1821 (published by Sherwood, Neeley and Jones).

Egan's ramble through the metropolis was a hit with the reading public. But its form of issue doesn't seem to have been much imitated in its own day, and the revival by Chapman & Hall of *Life in London*'s style of serialization after 15 years of disuse is surprising.

There were other possible precursors which merit a little digression. Harriet Martineau's *Illustrations of Political Economy* had appeared in 1832, in 25 numbers. The *Illustrations* were essentially 25 improving tracts (around 125 small octavo pages each) bundled into a series, rather than a serial novel. But there are interesting connections with *Pickwick*. Having failed to interest the Society for the Diffusion of Useful Knowledge and other publishers in the venture, Martineau was prevailed on by Charles Fox to coat her two dozen instructive pills with fiction and to issue them monthly (in which form they cost one shilling and sixpence). A thousand was the maximum sale hoped for. In fact, ten times that number were snapped up.

In Martineau's case, monthly serialization originated in the desire to spread purchasing cost, and to ease the effort of reading for readers of a distinctly lower class than the author. The *Illustrations* breathe a condescension typical of Victorian philanthropy doing its duty to the poor. The essence of the Dickensian novel in numbers is quite different. It addresses the reader in a spirit of manly equality; a sentiment confirmed in the author's habitual prefatory addresses to his reader.

With their *Pickwick* innovation of April 1836, it is more likely that the partners were inspired by the recent striking use which John Macrone had made of George Cruikshank in collaboration with Harrison Ainsworth and later 'Boz'.[4] This teaming must have revived recollections of Cruikshank's earlier liaison with Egan. There is also an interesting connection to be found with the ubiquitous publishing rogue, Henry Colburn. In late 1835–early 1836, the Prince of Puffers was down on his luck. His disastrous break-up with Bentley in 1833 left him short of both capital and literary property. To raise cash, he ingeniously worked the copyrights which remained his (principally those of Bulwer-Lytton). In January 1836, Colburn was offering *Pelham* and *The Disowned* for sale in six, one-shilling, weekly parts. (Effectively, these were Standard Novels, broken up and paper wrapped for faster sale, and to expand the look of Colburn's list.) In the same month, the first instalment of Marryat's *Frank Mildmay* was also on offer in what was grandly called 'The Novelist's Library'.

Colburn's wheeze created some stir in the book trade, at the exact period when Chapman & Hall were sorting out their problems with Dickens and Seymour as how best to proceed with *Pickwick*. The

Literary Gazette, for instance, called the Novelist's Library: 'A truly popular undertaking. The series so got up and embellished, and so cheap, must extend the fame even of the Author of *Pelham.*'[5] (This was four months before the publication of *Pickwick.*) In 14 May 1836, in allusion to Colburn, the *Athenaeum* wrote: 'It is a new feature of the literary character of the age, that publishers can find a remunerating sale when they offer works of imagination and established character in shilling numbers.' (At this period, although the *Athenaeum* was apparently unaware of its existence, *Pickwick* was languishing in an extremely unremunerative condition.)

Colburn's bright idea was latched on to by his competitors. In March 1836, Baldwin & Cradock brought out a 'fourth edition' of *Traits and Stories of The Irish Peasantry* by William Carleton, in 25 one-shilling parts, at fortnightly intervals (the work was ultimately designed to be bound up in five volumes). In February 1836, Saunders & Otley issued Bulwer-Lytton's *Pilgrims of the Rhine* in half-crown monthly parts, illustrated by Maclise, among others. This work is harshly dismissed by Michael Sadleir as 'fondant fiction at its worst'. But it was newish if not brand-new fiction (the work was first published in 1834), and it was part issued. None of these can claim unchallenged precedence over *Pickwick Papers.* But they confirm that the idea of novels in numbers, illustrated and costing one shilling a part was in the air in April 1836.

III

AFTER ITS deadly slow start (sinking as low as 400 monthly sales) *Pickwick* took off meteorically, soaring past Martineau's mark to some 40,000 a number. And with hindsight one can plausibly reconstruct why the serial succeeded as it did in drumming up what was effectively a whole new reading public. The devastating slump of the early 1830s had stripped out the English bookselling network, particularly its softest sectors, the outlying distribution and retailing agencies. The novel in numbers, by using the railroad routes opened (by W. H. Smith notably) for newspapers and magazines enjoyed countrywide distribution. In numbers, the novel could sell independently of the bookshops like the newspaper, at a time when newspapers were becoming a national medium. This extension of supply across England is evident if one looks at the self-advertising in, for instance, the second number of the Mayhews' *The Greatest Plague of Life* (February 1847). The advertiser carries eulogies on the current serial from: the

Bedford *Mercury*, the Berkshire *Chronicle*, the Brighton *Herald*, the Bristol *Gazette*, the Cheltenham *Examiner*, the Hull *Advertiser*, the Leeds *Intelligencer*, the Liverpool *Mail*, the Macclesfield *Chronicle*, the Nottingham *Journal*, the Northampton *Mercury*, the Plymouth *Herald*, the Somerset County *Gazette*, the Bath *Chronicle*, the Kent *Herald* and the Sheffield *Iris*. It would have been difficult to get three-volume editions of the new novel into the bookshops and circulating libraries of all these provincial towns. And to have supplied reorders while the demand whipped up by good notices was still warm would have been frankly impossible. How to cater adequately from London for the reader in Macclesfield or Sheffield is, it may be noted, a problem which the British booktrade has still not satisfactorily solved.

Dickens followed *Pickwick* with *Oliver Twist* in *Bentley's Miscellany* and in 1839 produced *Nicholas Nickleby*, whose sales soared to 50,000 a monthly part.[6] These figures were unprecedented. Never too proud to share in somebody else's good thing, the British book trade was quick to jump on the Dickens bandwagon. Charles Lever, for instance, whose *Harry Lorrequer* had been quite serenely and haphazardly running in the *Dublin University Magazine* since February 1837 had the work reissued by his publisher (Curry) in 11 monthly parts, with illustrations by Phiz, a bright idea which was fatally damaging to what little structure the narrative possesses. Ainsworth's *Jack Sheppard*, running in *Bentley's Miscellany* from January 1839, was simultaneously issued in weekly parts: an experiment in tandem publication that does not seem to have suited anyone.

There being no copyright in ideas (or much else in the 1830s), there was a rather desperate attempt to crack the formula and identify the active ingredients in Boz's appeal. The result over the period 1839–40 was a shambling parade of novels in numbers, most marked by some particular emphasis which was hoped to be the key to Dickensian success. Mrs Trollope (Anthony's mother) and Colburn, for instance, thought the Boz secret to be the display of social conscience in fiction. Although neither had any love of numbers (women, incidentally, used the form very seldom) they together concocted a topical bleeding heart tale for monthly issue: *Michael Armstrong, the Factory Boy* (1839–40). This homage to *Oliver Twist* was promptly answered in numbers by Frederic Montagu's *Mrs Trollope Refuted: Mary Ashley or Facts Upon Factories* (published by a Manchester bookseller, the work was planned in ten monthly parts from August 1839, but collapsed after its second instalment). Frederick Marryat also played the *Oliver Twist* card in his *Poor Jack* (1840). This tale of Jack Saunders, a

Thameside waif was published by another unlikely firm, Longman.
They were clearly uncomfortable with the vulgar associations of
monthly serialization and produced a cover (and internal illustrations
by Clarkson Stanfield) of remarkable stuffiness (see Plate 2). Even
less likely a Dickensian-style serialist than Marryat was the historical
romancer, G. P. R. James. He brought out his sole experiment in the
form with *The Commissioner* (1841–2), published racily enough (but
without any great success) by Lever's Irish publisher, William Curry
with Lever's normal illustrator, Phiz (see Plate 3).

   Other would-be Dickenses assumed that the spluttering consonantal
alliteration in the titles of *Pickwick Papers* and *Nicholas Nickleby*
were the easy way to public favour. So, in March 1839, the consumer
could have chosen among: *Valentine Vox, the Ventriloquist*; *Will's
Whim, Consisting of Characteristic Curiosities*; *Charley Chalk*; *David
Dreamy* (illustrated by 'Peter Pallette') and *Paul Periwinkle or the
Pressgang*.

   This last was illustrated by Phiz (i.e. Hablôt K. Browne). Phiz
himself was thought by many to hold the secret and he was showered
with more commissions than he could conscientiously fulfil. He, like
Boz, had the sincere flattery of imitation in such serials as *Heads of
the People* (1838–9), where J. Kenny Meadows pseudonymized himself
as 'Quizzfizzz'. ('Heads' serials—of characters in *Nicholas Nickleby*,
for example—were an established line of trade at this period, and
witness to a pervasive desire to visualize popular fiction. As J. R.
Harvey has surmised, the ravenous appetite for visual stimulation
probably explains at least part of the mania fuelling novels in numbers
in the late 1830s.[7] Meadows's serial, published by Tyas, was the most
popular work he ever produced.)

   A main point of interest in the cascade of 1839–40 serials and their
clumsy attempts to reconstitute Dickens's recipe is the unconscious
evidence they supply on how the contemporary book trade construed
the Boz phenomenon. Take, for instance, the barrage of pseudo-
Dickensian elements in the following offering: *The Rector's Progress,
or the Veritable amusing and interesting History of the Family
Connexions, Characters, Doings and Delinquencies of Dr Daniel
Tithegripe, by Clericus*. (The tale was illustrated by the ubiquitous
Phiz, and issued from 1 November 1839 by the obscure publishers
Grattan & Gilbert. How many instalments it achieved before expiring
I don't know.) Still others, such as G. W. M. Reynolds with *Pickwick
Abroad* (1838–9, published by Sherwood, illustrated by A. Crowquill)
banked on unvarnished plagiarism to suborn the Dickens public.

Probably, he succeeded better than most pretenders to Bozian fame. Altogether, in 1839–40, the addict could have spent 15 shillings to a pound a month on novels in parts. This was far more than the market could bear. More so as the publishers of most of these serials embarked with unrealistically high hopes. The prospective advertisers of *Effingham Hazard* (1839) were informed by the publisher (Edward Ravenscroft) that the serial was 'an entirely original Work the same size as *Nicholas Nickleby* and similarly illustrated [and] A Circulation of 20,000 is guaranteed for the first part'. In fact, it sank without trace. For Marryat's *Poor Jack*, Longman demanded 10,000 bills from prospective advertisers. What it sold is unrecorded. But the serial run was cut back from an announced 20 to 12. And Longman took care not to publish Marryat in this form again. The author's next foray into the novel in numbers (in 1847, with Hurst) didn't make it past the first instalment.

Alas, soundalike names and lookalike plots were easier to simulate than Boz and Phiz's sales figures. Most of the imitative serials slumped badly and a number went bust. *Paul Periwinkle*, for instance, fell into the hands of the ruthless remainderer, Tegg, after its fifth number and the insolvency of its original publisher. *The Comic Novel, or Downing Street in the Days of Victoria* by 'Lynx' (published by Bailliere, 'with illustrations in many styles') was promised in 20 monthly parts, but collapsed after four in May 1840. *Will's Whim* collapsed after three.

It was not entirely a lottery in which Dickens alone held the winning tickets. Cockton's *Valentine Vox* (published by H. Lea, illustrated by T. Onwhyn) prospered and made its author temporarily a rich man. But he promptly lost his windfall speculating in the East Anglian barley trade. His subsequent five exercises in serialized fiction were as ill-fated as his business speculations.

IV

AFTER THE free-for-all of 1839–40 (resembling nothing so much as the contemporary railway manias), the business of novels in numbers was prosecuted with more sobriety. The smaller publishers learned the hard way that (for the middle-class, shilling-paying public, at least) this kind of serialization was a rich man's game. For success it required an expensive 'name' author working in liaison with an expensive 'name' illustrator; lavish advertising; heavy and awkwardly recurrent production costs (up to £600 a month for a Dickens serial); and efficient kingdom-wide agency and co-publishing relations.[8] Most publishers of new fiction were safer staying with the three-decker with its low capital cost and direct, secured line of supply to the library. As a regular thing, the novel in numbers was left as the near-exclusive preserve of the new giants of the trade, Bradbury & Evans and Chapman & Hall.

Originally partners (Bradbury & Evans were Chapman & Hall's printers for *Pickwick*), by the mid-1840s the two firms had become rivals. In a sense, Bradbury & Evans had greatness thrust upon them when Dickens defected from Chapman & Hall in 1846, on the grounds that: 'A printer is better than a bookseller.'[9] By 'better' he meant 'more ductile'. But as printers (very reluctantly) turned publishers, Bradbury & Evans had other valuable qualifications. They were particularly expert in illustration, pioneering among other things colour reproduction of plates in England. As a firm based in Fleet Street, they suffered none of Paternoster Row's traditional inhibitions about dabbling with newspapers. Thus, in 1842 Bradbury & Evans acquired *Punch*. Under the convivial management of Mark Lemon this weekly paper had made itself by 1846 a national institution, the official comic organ of the English middle classes.

For Dickens (who evidently disliked *Punch*'s 'eternal guffaw'), Bradbury & Evans retained the form of serial issue devised in 1836 by Chapman & Hall. But for the gifted coterie of writers and illustrators from their *Punch* stable, they allowed a significantly modified style of part issue to evolve. Its characteristics were an easy ironic address, a loose-knit essayistic format, a central stress on illustration in the currently modish pictorial style (including colour plates) and plentiful use of the incidental woodcuts *Punch* specialized in. (Dickensian serialization rationed itself to two full-plate etchings, placed separately at the head of the text as a detachable unit.)

The first serial in shilling monthly numbers published 'at the *Punch* Office, 65 Fleet Street'[10] was the *Table Book*, edited by G. A. A'Beckett. This work was published in 12 monthly parts, January–December 1845, with 12 steel etchings and 116 woodcuts, all by George Cruikshank. It was followed by Cruikshank's *Our Own Times*. This monthly serial began on 1 April 1846, but petered out in July after four numbers. Why is not clear, but since Cruikshank transferred his (highly profitable) business to Bogue at this time he probably fell out with Bradbury & Evans, as he usually fell out with everyone eventually. *Our Own Times* was followed on 1 July by Gilbert A'Beckett's Macaulayan spoof, *The Comic History of England* which had better fortunes. Advertisements promised that this serial would

DEDICATED TO THE KING.

No. I.

OF

AN ORIGINAL WORK,

ENTITLED

Life in London;

OR, THE

DAY AND NIGHT SCENES

OF

JERRY HAWTHORN, ESQ.

AND HIS ELEGANT FRIEND,

CORINTHIAN TOM,

IN

Their Rambles and Sprees

THROUGH THE

METROPOLIS.

BY PIERCE EGAN,

Author of "Sporting Anecdotes," &c.

London:

PRINTED FOR SHERWOOD, NEELY, AND JONES,
PATERNOSTER-ROW.

Price 3s.

1 The wrapper of the opening number of *Life in London* (October 1820).

No. I.   PRICE 1s.

POOR JACK.

BY

CAPTAIN MARRYAT, C.B.

WITH

ILLUSTRATIONS

BY CLARKSON STANFIELD, R.A.

LONDON:

LONGMAN, ORME, BROWN, GREEN, AND LONGMANS,
PATERNOSTER-ROW.

1840.

2 Longman's conservative cover for the part-issue of *Poor Jack* (January 1840).

3 Curry's cover-design for the part-issue of G. P. R. James's *The Commissioner*. Note the lack of the author's or illustrator's name (Phiz).

4 The last double number of *The Knight of Gwynne* (July 1847).

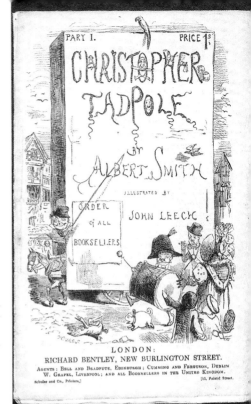

5 Leech's cover for *Christopher Tadpole* (September 1846). Bentley chose an unusual printer (Schulze). Presumably he was expert in reproducing illustrations.

6 The cover-design for *The Greatest Plague of Life* (February 1847). Notice that the authors' names (Henry and Augustus Mayhew) have been suppressed in order to highlight Cruikshank's.

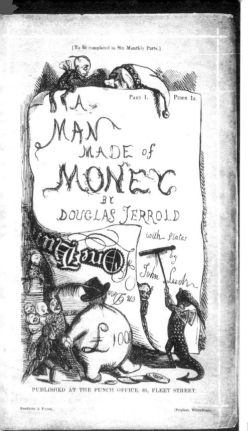

PART I. PRICE 1s.

A
MAN
MADE of
MONEY
BY
DOUGLAS JERROLD

with Plates

by

John Leech

£100

PUBLISHED AT THE PUNCH OFFICE, 85, FLEET STREET.

Bradbury & Evans. [Printers, Whitefriars.

7   The first part of *A Man Made of Money* (October 1849).

8   The first number of *Mr Romford's Hounds* (May 1865).

9   Cruikshank's cover for *1851* (February 1851).

10 The first number of *Frank Fairlegh* (January 1849). Cruikshank's name dominates.

11 The first number of the illustrated *The Gordian Knot*. Tenniel's design for the cover is very fine (January 1858).

12 The last double number of Lever's last novel in numbers (February 1865).

13 Luard's crude design was used prominently in the advertising campaign for *The Headless Horseman* (1865–6).

PART I.   APRIL.   ONE SHILLING.

SUNRISE

A Story of These Times

by

WILLIAM BLACK

Author of "A Daughter of Heth"

&c. &c.

LONDON

SAMPSON LOW · MARSTON · SEARLE · & RIVINGTON

1880

14   The last novel in monthly 1s. numbers (1880).

run 'from twelve to twenty' one-shilling monthly parts. Each part
contained one large coloured etching and up to a dozen interspersed
woodcuts by John Leech. The trade were informed that the *Comic
History*,'will appear regularly with the monthly magazines' and copies
were presumably bundled up on magazine day (the last of the month)
with *Douglas Jerrold's Shilling Magazine* and the two-shilling parts
of *Punch.*

A'Beckett's serial evidently caught on. In October 1847, it was
announced that it would, after all, run to the maximum 20 numbers.
The *Comic History* also served as pilot for another *Punch* writer's
'Pen and Pencil Sketches of English Society'. This story later retitled
itself as 'A Novel without a Hero', and finally emerged as *Vanity Fair.*
Thackeray's great work began publication inauspiciously in January
1847, having been held back a year. The number to which it was to
run was not initially specified by Bradbury & Evans, either in the
contract or the advertisement. And, as is legendary, *Vanity Fair* did
not immediately succeed with the reading public. There was a serious
danger that it might terminate after particularly disappointing sales
for the third instalment in March 1847, and as late as the fourteenth,
Bradbury & Evans were advertising the work as running to 'eighteen
or twenty numbers'.[11]

A number of reasons can be advanced for the precarious start
of *Vanity Fair.* Thackeray (who had written for ten years under
a pseudonym) was unknown. The opening chapters of the work
(which was originally intended for another publisher) were probably
something of a surprise for the *Punch* subscribers. Thackeray was
technically inferior to Leech, currently the fashionable serial illustrator. There was a sharp trade depression in early 1847 which hit all
periodical publications hard.

But the most plausible explanation for *Vanity Fair*'s initial inability
to catch on was the state of the market. Despite being considerably
thinned from five years earlier, it was still overcrowded with monthly
serials. In January 1847, for example, the bookstands carried the
thirteenth number of Lever's *Knight of Gwynne* (Plate 4). This was
Chapman & Hall's lead title. Heavily advertised and illustrated by
Phiz it was devised to fill the gap left by Dickens. There was intramural
competition from the seventh number of A'Beckett's *Comic History*
with its attractive Leech designs. Leech also illustrated Albert Smith's
The Struggles and Adventures of Christopher Tadpole (see Plate 5).
In January this was in its fifth number out of a promised 12. But
Bentley was pleased with the work (which had a definite *Punchified*

air to it), and persuaded the author (who was as new to serialization as Thackeray) to extend to 16 numbers. At a somewhat lower level a new series of Reynolds's *Mysteries of London* in monthly sixpenny parts had begun another of its interminable issues in September 1846 (published by G. Vickers). G. Herbert Rodwell's *Woman's Love* had opened in monthly parts on 1 February 1846, illustrated by Alfred Crowquill. According to its publisher's (W. R. Sams) schedule it should have been in its last double number in January 1847. *Rowland Bradshaw, or the Way to Fame* ('by the author of *Raby Rattler*', published by Sherwood, Gilbert and Piper) began on 1 November 1846, illustrated (unmemorably) by S. P. Fletcher. A month later, on 1 December 1846 there was launched *The Miser's Will*, by Percy B. St John, promised by its publisher (Hurst) in 20 monthly one-shilling numbers. And in mid-January 1847 there was announced *The Greatest Plague of Life*, in six numbers, illustrated by George Cruikshank (see Plate 6). Subtitled 'The Adventures of a Lady in search of a good servant' this was another *Punch*-inspired venture (authored by the brothers Mayhew and published by Bogue), drawing on the paper's standing jokes about 'servantgalism'.

A field of half-a-dozen strong runners and as many stragglers was bound to produce also-rans. *Woman's Love* ended up in 1847 the property of another publisher, and almost certainly did not get through its monthly run. St John's *The Miser's Will* immediately dropped out of sight, reappearing as a serial in the *Mirror*, in January 1848. It too seems unlikely to have made it beyond a couple of numbers. *The Greatest Plague of Life* was held back two months, until March (although dated February). *The Knight of Gwynne* had slumped disastrously and was proving a loss to Chapman & Hall by January 1847. They none the less kept it going (although Lever's reputation was irreparably damaged). Hurst, publisher of Marryat's *The Children of the New Forest* had no such compunctions. The first monthly issue appeared in April 1847 and was promptly killed. (The work appeared in complete volume form in October 1847. In the long run it went on to be Marryat's most reprinted work.)

Amid this carnage *Dombey* was enjoying the usual Dickens triumph. And trailing by five months, Thackeray had ground to make up, if he was not to close down or limp ingloriously to a dozen or less instalments. But, famously, *Vanity Fair* came from behind to contest (as Thackeray fondly thought) the leadership with Dickens. *Vanity Fair* was also a triumph for the *Punch* enclave with Bradbury & Evans. They followed up with an immediate contract for *Pendennis*, which hiked Thackeray's monthly stipend from £60 to £100. A major departure was the extension of the run, during the novel's publication, to 24 numbers. It would seem that although Thackeray's appeal was not massive (just over 9,000 copies of *Pendennis* were sold in parts and first book edition), he none the less had an extraordinarily faithful public, who would stick with him for ever, apparently.

The *Punch* office put out another successful, but much less ambitious novel in numbers at this period. In October 1848 there appeared the first number of a monthly serial by Douglas Jerrold, *A Man Made of Money* (see Plate 7). The work (handsomely illustrated by Leech) ran to six parts, until March 1849, by which time it was completely overshadowed by the early numbers of *Pendennis*. The story remains Jerrold's best effort in fiction (which was never, of course, his first interest in writing).[12]

After *Pendennis*, Thackeray broke with *Punch*, rarely contributing again to the paper. He also broke with Bradbury & Evans, transferring his services to George Smith, for *Henry Esmond* (three volumes, 1852). But Thackeray had helped find a successor to himself before leaving his friends in Bouverie Street. In May 1849, Robert Smith Surtees had approached him to illustrate the reissue of *Mr Sponge's Sporting Tour*, then running as a serial in Ainsworth's *New Monthly Magazine*. The suggestion was highly presumptuous. Surtees was at this stage far from famous, and Thackeray was now the second greatest author in England. More to the point, as he tactfully pointed out, Thackeray was incapable of drawing horses. He courteously referred Surtees to his *Punch* confrère Leech, who *could* draw horses; none better. Leech was very enthusiastic about Mr Sponge, and in turn suggested Bradbury & Evans as publishers for the novel in volume form. Evans on his part liked the work. And he eventually suggested that it might be reissued in a dozen monthly numbers, with coloured plates and woodcuts by Leech. In this form, he was 'sure we shall have a hit'.[13] So, in 1852, they did. And the partnership between John Leech and Surtees went on to become one of the glories of the mid-Victorian serial novel (see Plate 8).

Thackeray came back to his 'old friends' with *The Newcomes* (1853–5). Although he no longer wrote for the magazine, a definite *Punch* link was formed by recruiting Richard Doyle as his assistant illustrator. *The Newcomes* was followed by *The Virginians* (1857–9) which (to their cost) Bradbury & Evans also serialized in the now standard 24 numbers. The venture was a costly failure, and Thackeray recoiled to George Smith again. Thereafter, Bradbury & Evans largely restricted their interest in fiction to Dickens (whom they had until the mid-1860s) and to their lavishly illustrated magazine *Once a Week.* But on losing Dickens, they tried a novel in numbers with another *Punch* stalwart, Shirley Brooks. *Sooner or Later*, ran for 14 monthly issues from November 1866. The work was not much of a hit, but it remains attractive for its 17 fine illustrations by George du Maurier.

The *Punch* variant on the novel in numbers has various achievements to its credit. It loosened up the tight authorial dominance of the Dickensian style, allowing a free interchange between pen and pencil. Its form was more elastic, moving easily from six to 24 numbers. Like everything to do with the magazine, the *Punch*ified novel in numbers was democratic, good natured, and tolerantly ironic of the foibles of life. More significantly, it introduced a far wider range of unfettered pictorial talent into the genre than Dickens would ever have permitted.

V

GEORGE CRUIKSHANK's influence is everywhere encountered in the origins and progress of the Victorian part-issued novel. As a junior illustrator on *Life in London*, he embodied a direct link with *Pickwick*'s closest ancestor. And in so far as the novel in numbers meant a new liaison between narrative and pictorial art, Cruikshank was scarcely less important than Dickens in its development.

Cruikshank's first extended work with English fiction was as illustrator for the eighteenth-century texts in Roscoe's 'Novelist's Library', 1831-3. The Library was published by James Cochrane, who later went into partnership with the brilliant but ill-fated John Macrone. After the partnership broke up in 1834, Macrone had the inspiration to use Cruikshank to embellish the fiction of a living novelist. The resulting illustrated fourth edition of *Rookwood* (whose copyright Macrone had acquired from Bentley) was a brilliant success. Momentously, Macrone also teamed Cruikshank with the young Dickens for the first series of *Sketches by Boz* (1836). And in November 1836, Macrone planned a monthly serial in one-shilling numbers, *The Lions of London*: the text to be provided by Ainsworth, the illustrations by Leech and Cruikshank.[14]

Macrone's chronic financial crisis sank *The Lions of London* venture (although Cruikshank's title-page survives). Cruikshank was snapped up by the better-heeled Bentley to illustrate *Oliver Twist*, which began its run with the *Miscellany* in January 1837. This was followed in the magazine by *Jack Sheppard*, in which Cruikshank was again partnered with Ainsworth, this time on a new novel. Ainsworth's Newgate romance was sensationally popular, and Bentley published a concurrent issue in numbers. And this in turn was successful enough to warrant a new, and lavishly-produced, independent work in numbers, *The Tower of London* (1840).

The Tower of London was the most luxurious novel in numbers yet produced. It was beautifully printed (Bentley's speciality). It carried three full-plate designs on steel in each instalment, and a total of 58 topographic woodcuts. In fact, the work is so heavily illustrated that Ainsworth's story has trouble trickling through Cruikshank's pictorial undergrowth. But the venture was much to the public taste. Bentley paid Ainsworth handsomely (£2,000, it has been suggested), and the work was launched with a party at which all the literary luminaries of London attended.

As an illustrator, Cruikshank had the advantage of his pre-eminent name and reputation. But he did not come cheap. Whereas illustrators like Phiz or Leech made do with as little as £6 per etching, Cruikshank demanded a share commensurate with his name. Thus, for *The Tower of London*, he was paid as an equal partner in the profits with Ainsworth and Bentley (an agreement which yielded him £517).[15]

In addition to a fair share of the revenue, Cruikshank also demanded an equal hand in composition. His egalitarian method of working with Ainsworth is recorded by the author: 'I used to spend a day with the artist at the beginning of the month in the Tower itself; and since every facility was afforded to us by the authorities, we left no part of the old fortress unexplored.'[16] Notoriously, in old age, Cruikshank exaggerated his contributions (unusual as they were) claiming, for instance, that 'The original idea of [*The Tower of London*] was suggested by me . . . in this work Mr Ainsworth and I were *partners*, holding equal shares'.[17] Cruikshank's claim to have invented Ainsworth's novels (and *Oliver Twist* to boot) was stoutly denied. But undeniable was the aesthetic dominance of his illustrations. As Thackeray put it (in his *Essay on the Genius of George Cruikshank*, 1840), think of Ainsworth's fiction, and what do you remember? 'George Cruikshank's pictures, always George Cruikshank's pictures'.[18] A writer as strong minded as Dickens simply could not pull in harness with Cruikshank over a long period. And it is a tribute to Ainsworth, that he managed to wring so much good work out of the artist in their tempestuous collaboration on six novels (most of them published in the novelist's *Ainsworth's Magazine*).

During his intermittent spats and after his final bad-tempered break with Ainsworth (in 1844), Cruikshank devoted himself to his *Omnibus* and *Comic Almanacks*, published in monthly serial form by David Bogue (successor to Tilt and Bogue). And it was Bogue who also published a dried-out Cruikshank's Hogarthian serial, *The Bottle* (1847) and *The Drunkard's Children* (1848). Everything with Cruikshank's name on it was popular, particularly *The Bottle* which on publication sold 100,000 copies at a shilling for the eight-picture set.

With this kind of tribute to his independent genius, Cruikshank may well have felt collaboration with mere novelists unnecessary. None the less, he made a number of subsequent, highly characteristic contributions to novels in numbers. Of these, his longest relationship was with the Mayhew brothers, Augustus and Henry. With them he brought out *The Greatest Plague of Life* (published by Bogue, 1847). The cover design is remarkable for the prominence given to Cruikshank's name, and the invisibility of the authors of the 48 pages of text contained therein (see Plate 6). This initial venture was followed by the similarly conceived *Whom to Marry and How to get Married* (Bogue, six parts, 1847–8). The finest fruit of the collaboration, however, was *The World's Show: 1851, or, The Adventures of Mr and Mrs Sandboys and family, who came up to London to 'enjoy themselves' and to see the Great Exhibition* (Bogue, eight parts, February–October 1851) (see Plate 9). No less than Dickens, Cruikshank was excited by a crowd. And the milling hordes of tourists in London in the Exhibition festive year fairly set his imagination ablaze. For Mayhew's mild comedy he supplied a series of double-paged panoramic illustrations, culminating in 'All the World Going to See the Great Exhibition of 1851'. Reaching for the modern term 'logo', the *Athenaeum* (8 February 1851) called this picture 'The sign of the show . . . the popular record to be painted on crockery and printed on calico'. Although Henry Mayhew now gets a small billing on the cover, the work clearly demonstrates Cruikshank's autocratic habit of reducing his fellow writer to a mere provider of letterpress for his designs.[19]

For Bogue, Cruikshank also illustrated Angus Reach's promising *Clement Lorimer, or the Book with Iron Clasps* (six parts, 1848–9). Possibly he might have done more with Reach had the unlucky young author lived longer. More probably, he would have crushed him into a poor second place, as he did the Mayhews. Otherwise, Cruikshank did a handful of other novels in numbers, apparently as random acts of personal friendship or to pick up a little easy income. Least interesting are the plates (shared with his brother) for the 12 monthly parts of M. H. Barker's ultra-nautical *The Old Sailor's Jolly Boat Laden with Tales, Yarns, Scraps, Fragments, etc.* (published by W. Strange, 1843). Even less successful was Cruikshank's collaboration with another sailor, Francis Higginson RN's *The Brighton Lodging House* (published by J. How). This monthly serial lapsed in 1849 after only two numbers.

More substantial was Cruikshank's collaboration with Frank Smedley. The two were brought together professionally on *Sharpe's Magazine*, which Smedley edited and where the early (and by far the best) chapters of his tale, *Frank Fairlegh*, were published. The story, as expanded, was very popular. And since its school and college chapters chimed nicely with *Pendennis* and *Copperfield*, Hall & Virtue (publishers of *Sharpe's Magazine*) brought out an issue in 15 numbers from January 1849 (see Plate 10). The publisher specialized in illustrated books, and their treatment of Smedley's text was barbarous. The pre-existing volume edition was simply chopped into 32-page sections, the first six numbers breaking halfway between sentences. But the work was none the less a bestseller, largely due to Cruikshank's vigorous illustrations. His name alone appears on the cover. On the strength of Cruikshank's contribution, *Frank Fairlegh* went on to become one of the most reprinted of Victorian illustrated novels. Future collaboration seemed likely when the two men at last met and evidently hit it off. Smedley took up the post of editor on *George Cruikshank's Magazine* in January 1854. But the venture only lasted two issues. Smedley's subsequent two novels in numbers were illustrated by Phiz, and failed lamentably.

These novelists (the Mayhews, Reach, Smedley, Barker) have one thing in common. They are unredeemably second rate. As Dickens's artistic sovereignty seems to have led him to select the less than best illustrator for his serials, so Cruikshank's *amour propre* seems to have led him to work with (not for) writers far inferior to himself in ability. Dickens progressively suppressed his illustrators (as evident from the billing Phiz received over 25 years). In the same spirit, Cruikshank actually obliterated his collaborators from the title page. One of the great might-have-beens of Victorian fiction is what would have happened, had these two majestic egos been able to continue the relationship so profitably begun in 1836.

VI

IN THE LATE 1850s and 1860s there emerged a new generation of publishers (George Bentley, John Maxwell, William Tinsley, Hurst and Blackett) and novelists (Meredith, Reade, Collins, Ouida, Braddon) for whom serialization in monthly numbers was as antediluvian as the powdered wig or the buckled shoe. Generally speaking, it remained a viable option only for a nucleus of male authors born in the same decade as Dickens and swept along, willy-nilly, in the turbulence of his success. From these sub-Dickensian authors' attempts at fiction in numbers one can assemble an impressive catalogue of 1850s failure. One of the more spectacular was Shirley Brooks's *The Gordian Knot* (published by Bentley, illustrated by Tenniel). This serial began in January 1858, suspended publication for almost a year, and limped to an ignominious conclusion in December 1859 (see Plate 11). Ainsworth's *Mervyn Clitheroe* (published by Chapman & Hall, illustrated by Phiz) collapsed after four numbers out of a scheduled 20, in March 1852. (Extraordinarily, the serial was completed in 12 numbers by Routledge, 1857–8.) Lever, who published more novels in numbers than any of his contemporaries (16), finally gave the form up in 1865 as a non-paying proposition with *Luttrell of Arran* (published by Chapman & Hall, illustrated by Phiz) (see Plate 12). Thackeray dropped out in 1859 with *The Virginians* (published by Bradbury & Evans, illustrated by the author), a serial on which the publishers made a loss of over £3,000. Bradbury & Evans also lost heavily on Surtees's and Leech's *Handley Cross* which finished an interrupted run of 17 numbers in October 1854.

It was not so much the case that occasional success could not be achieved by the novel in numbers, but that this success could not be consistently maintained. Thus Frank Smedley had a huge hit in 1849–50 with *Frank Fairlegh* (published by Hall & Virtue, illustrated by Cruikshank). But its successors *Lewis Arundel* (1850–2) and *Harry Coverdale's Courtship* (1854–6) flopped. Captain Mayne Reid seemed to have found a winning new formula with *The Headless Horseman* (published by Chapman & Hall, illustrated by L. Huard) in March 1865. This novel came out in sixpenny as opposed to shilling numbers and, aided by a high-pressure advertising campaign, became a famous bestseller (see Plate 13). But when Trollope latched on to the sixpenny instalment with *The Last Chronicle of Barset* (published by Smith Elder, illustrated by G. H. Thomas) 'the enterprise was not altogether successful'.[20] And when Trollope induced James Virtue to repeat the sixpenny experiment in 1868–9 with *He Knew He Was Right* (published by Virtue, illustrated by M. Stone), the publisher promptly slid into insolvency.

Logically the mid-1860s should have seen the end of the novel in numbers. It was an idea whose time had gone. The form had served a valuable transitional function in mobilizing a nation-wide reading public before the full evolution of the fiction-carrying periodical. But now its natural span was over. There was nothing it could do that the novel in magazines could not do better and cheaper. Dickens must have read the signs as clearly as anyone. After *Little Dorrit* finished in July 1857 he turned his novelistic energy to setting up *All the Year Round. A Tale of Two Cities* boosted the early numbers of that twopenny journal to unprecedented figures of 100,000 or more. But a concurrent issue of the novel in eight monthly numbers (by Chapman & Hall) slumped disappointingly, finishing on a mere 5,000 sales a month—disgraceful by Dickens's standards. His next novel, *Great Expectations*, was his first full-length novel for 20 years not to be published in monthly numbers. It was run through *All the Year Round* and reprinted as a hugely successful three-decker. (This was the sequence pioneered by Dickens's most gifted protégé, Wilkie Collins.)

Then, for mysterious reasons, Dickens chose to ignore the clear signs of the times. He wrote to Frederic Chapman proposing 'a new work in twenty monthly numbers, as of old'.[21] It is quite clear that Dickens made the necessary publishing decision about what was to be *Our Mutual Friend*'s form of issue. And equally clear that it was in the circumstances a somewhat obstinate decision to have made.

Dickens's exercise in nostalgia justified itself. Although it sold around 5,000 copies less a month than *Little Dorrit*, *Our Mutual Friend* was highly profitable for all parties. And five years later, *The Mystery of Edwin Drood* (scheduled for a curtailed 12-issue run) notched up record sales, stimulated for the first three numbers by the excitement of a new Dickens novel, and for the next three by the morbid attraction of the work now being posthumous; Dickens writing from the grave. And the last three numbers of *Edwin Drood* find Dickens eerily by himself in the field. After the ignominious petering out of Trollope's *The Vicar of Bullhampton* in May 1870,[22] there was no further competition in monthly numbers. The mêlée of 1839–40 had finally dwindled to one victorious survivor.

VII

AS A MEMORIAL to Dickens, the novel in numbers enjoyed an odd afterlife. Despite her nervousness about serialization, George Eliot allowed *Middlemarch* to be published in parts from December 1871 to December 1872. The form she, Lewes and John Blackwood chose was strategically modified from the Dickensian norm. The novel was issued as eight five-shilling 'books', appearing at first bi-monthly, then monthly. Each book was the equivalent of four Dickensian numbers, but unillustrated. Something under 6,000 copies were sold in this form; a figure which was respectable but nothing wonderful. And at a 40 per cent author's royalty, there was not much profit for Blackwoods. Nevertheless *Daniel Deronda* was published on the same pattern and with much the same initial sales, January–September 1876. Apart from these two experiments (together with a half-hearted stab by Trollope with *The Prime Minister*), there was no general interest in the novel in oversize numbers. It yielded too little for the publisher. When they made their stocktaking in 1879, Blackwood's reckoned Eliot's copyrights to be valueless to them, the novels having cost so much to produce.

Ever hopeful, Trollope returned to the novel in 20 numbers with *The Way we Live Now* (1874–5). He was at this stage of his career on the board of Chapman & Hall, and presumably dictated the choice of form. Why he returned to the novel in numbers is not clear. Perhaps since *The Way we Live Now* was an old man's satire on modern ways he felt an old-fashioned style of publication was fitting. But the experiment failed. Having paid the author a large sum (£3,000), Frederic Chapman economized on the artist and the work is execrably illustrated. *The Way we Live Now* was not well received, apparently did not sell well and the copyright was sold off at a tenth of what Chapman had given to Andrew Chatto, even before the end of the serial run. The contract for Trollope's next novel (drawn up in April, 1874) indicates that he originally expected this too might come out in monthly numbers. But after their experience with *The Way we Live Now*, Chapman and Trollope decided to try *The Prime Minister* in eight of George Eliot's (unillustrated) five-shilling parts. These duly appeared monthly, November 1875–June 1876 and signally failed to interest the reading public. Trollope published no more novels in numbers during the five writing years that remained to him.

In 1877–9 Blackwood's attempted yet another revival with the so-called 'Cheveley' novels by Valentine Durrant. Durrant is an obscure author.[23] The impecunious son of a Brighton baker, he worked on boys' periodicals in the early 1870s. Little else is known about Durrant. His proletarian origins may have led Blackwood's into thinking him another Dickens. If so, they were sadly mistaken. The first of the Cheveley series, *A Modern Minister*, appeared in 12 parts, from June 1877. It was followed in June 1878 by a second Cheveley novel, *Saul Weir*, designed for a similar 12-month run (which it seems not to have completed). Durrant was an appallingly bad novelist and the serials attracted reviews of bloodcurdling severity. According to the *Athenaeum* (15 May 1878): 'Durrant's style, when not a ridiculous reproduction of Dickens's worst is very ponderous. His humour is clumsy in the extreme; his incidents are melodramatic; his characters caricatures drawn with an unintelligent hand. It is sincerely to be hoped that the series may not be prolonged.' Nor was it. Why Blackwood should have perpetrated this aberration is mysterious.

The latest true novel in monthly numbers that I have seen is William Black's *Sunrise* (see Plate 14). This work was brought out by Sampson Low in 15 one-shilling 64-page parts from April 1880 to June 1881. It was printed in large type, as for a three-decker, whose tripartite pagination it in fact followed. (A case for binding the parts up in three volumes was offered at three shillings and sixpence extra.) The serial was unillustrated, but carried a stunning wrapper design of the sun rising over the ocean. (Vividly described seascapes were a prized feature in Black's fiction.)

The serialization of *Sunrise* was evidently not a success. The book edition of the work appeared prematurely in February 1881, which presumably killed any subsequent sale in parts. But otherwise the novel was warmly received. Subtitled 'A Story of These Times', the plot involves secret society adventures, and was found exciting. Critics generally thought *Sunrise* refreshingly different from Black's earlier novels. ('No yachting, no highland lochs' as the *Athenaeum* reviewer noted in some surprise.) In volume form it was something of a bestseller, running to at least six editions in the first multi-volume form.

Sunrise brings one to the setting of the novel in numbers. That it lasted 40 years is a striking tribute to the force of the Dickens mystique; a mystique that induced in imitators a blind willingness to flog away at what was for them often an extremely dead horse.

What is more interesting, perhaps, is why Dickens himself continued to use what as early as September 1841 he called 'the old form'.[24] He was not temperamentally conservative and no novelist had greater freedom to choose how his books appeared. The standard explanation is that the novel in monthly numbers gave him a sense of intimate contact with his public. This is undoubtedly true. But there were probably more material factors determining his preference. As an economic strategy, the novel in numbers spread payment at all levels of production and consumption, allowing a larger investment in time and money by the involved parties. Over 18 months, the reader could afford by hire purchase a total outlay of a pound—a huge sum for a single novel. And on his side, the publisher was allowed to pay his serialist on a stipendiary basis, month by month. Since these stipends could come out of monthly receipts (from readers and advertisers), it allowed ever higher scales of remuneration. Thackeray, Trollope, Ainsworth and Lever had the greatest rewards of their writing lives from their novels in numbers.

Like the bidding in a poker game, the novel in numbers tended to force out players as the stakes got higher. Ainsworth dropped out of the big game at around £2,000 (with *The Tower of London*) and Lever at £2,400 (with *The Knight of Gwynne*). Trollope dropped out at £3,200 (with *He Knew He Was Right*), Thackeray at £6,000 (with *The Virginians*). And this thinning of ranks finally left Dickens as the only player, earning £10,000 a novel.

Dickens evidently liked vast payments as much as the next novelist. But as important, I suspect, was the proven fact that only he could handle the novel in numbers to its full potential. The failure of others certified his success. It seems, on the face of it another example of Dickens's will to uniqueness, his burning need to be among, yet finally transcend the crowd.

CHAPTER FIVE

Eliot, Lytton, and the Zelig Effect

WOODY ALLEN's movie *Zelig* (1984) depends on a single extended joke. The eponymous hero (played manically by Allen himself) is omnipresent at all the great events of twentieth-century history: with Lenin before the storming of the Winter Palace, on the podium at the Nüremberg rally with Hitler, with Freud behind the couch as he makes his great discovery about psychoanalysis. But, mysteriously, history (outside the film) has never recorded Zelig's existence. Posterity gives its due to Lenin, Hitler, and Freud and consigns Zelig to oblivion. The deliciousness of the joke is that the film declines to make the obvious deduction that Zelig is a victim of gross megalomaniac delusion—a version of the stereotypical maniac who thinks he is Napoleon.

It is an apt analogy for the case of Edward George Earle Lytton [Lord] Bulwer-Lytton (to give his full list of names and titles in his maturity). Lytton can claim to have fathered any number of genres and styles in which other novelists gained immortal fame. Think of a great moment in the evolution of Victorian fiction and Lytton was there. None the less, Lytton is comprehensively forgotten. Other Victorians have made it to the canonical core of Victorian novels which have 'lasted'; he, notably, has not. While the British reading classes of the mid-1990s are drowning in reprints of Trollope, Dickens, Brontë, Eliot, and Hardy, not a single title of Lytton's is available in World's Classics, Penguin Classics, Everyman, or Wordsworth Classics. To all intents and purposes, Lytton has been neglected out of literary history.

The vainest of men, it is not a verdict he himself would have taken equably. Nor is the neglect fair. To the objective eye Lytton has a remarkable list of literary achievements to his credit and (unlike Zelig) he really was in at the foundation of any number of major styles and genres in Victorian fiction. As 'the author of *Pelham*' (1828), he founded the dandy fashionable novel which was to reach its apogee in Disraeli's 'Young England' trilogy. *Pelham* can also claim to be the greatest of the 'silver fork' novels and the narrative's ironic mockery of its own conventions (not least in the anti-heroic hero) anticipates Thackeray's 'Novel without a Hero', *Vanity Fair*.

Lytton's Queen Anne historical romance, *Devereux* (1829), is a clear source for *Henry Esmond*. Lytton founded the 'Newgate Novel' with *Paul Clifford* (1830), a genre whose works descend through Harrison Ainsworth (notably *Rookwood*, 1834) to *Oliver Twist* (1837). *Eugene Aram* (1832) has been plausibly put forward as the first detective novel proper in English. As we have seen, Lytton pioneered the monthly serial some months before *Pickwick* came along and took all the credit.[1] In 1834, he published the first successful historical romance of the classical era—*The Last Days of Pompeii*—a work which led, in course of time, to *Quo Vadis, Ben Hur, Spartacus* and the toga-melodramas of Cecil B. de Mille. With *Zanoni* (1842), Lytton gave Dickens the basic idea for *A Tale of Two Cities* (a Hoffmanesque, 'elixir of life', mystical tale, *Zanoni* is the work of Lytton's that has most currency today through the network of American 'New Age' bookstores). Lytton's *The Caxtons; a Family Picture* (1848–9) was immensely influential. The 'Shandyan' mode of autobiographical narration clearly inspired Thackeray's *Pendennis* (1850) and Dickens's *David Copperfield* (1850). The idea of having the narrator-hero carry over into a following work (*My Novel*, 1853) was picked up by Thackeray (who does the same with Arthur Pendennis in *The Newcomes*, 1855). The mild comedy of *The Caxtons* was the clear forerunner of Trollope's 'domestic' vein of fiction which was to become very popular in the 1860s and after. With *The Coming Race* (1871)— a stunningly original conception—Lytton arguably created the first true work of science fiction in English, some twenty years before H. G. Wells. But for every hundred modern readers conversant with the major works of Thackeray, Dickens, Trollope, Wells, there will hardly be one who has read any of the seminal works of Lytton. Nor would his string of names be recognized by the millions who participated in the '*Middlemarch* frenzy' of 1994, when—amazingly—the novel reached the top of the paperback bestseller list. Yet, Zelig-like, Lytton can be found popping up in front of George Eliot's masterpiece as well, exasperatedly claiming that he was there first, dammit!

The authoritative account of the writing and publication of *Middlemarch* is to be found in David Carroll's meticulous introduction to the 1986 'Clarendon' edition of the novel. Carroll concurs with earlier scholars (notably Jerome Beaty in *Middlemarch, from Notebook to Novel* and Eliot's biographer, G. S. Haight) in finding the form in which *Middlemarch* was published to be 'ingenious' (which it certainly was) and entirely 'new'.[2] As these critics present it, the exotic serialization of *Middlemarch* in eight, bimonthly 'Books' at 5*s*.

each was the sole brainwave of G. H. Lewes. The Blackwood Papers at the National Library of Scotland indicate at least two other parties who might legitimately have claimed to have originated the form of *Middlemarch*'s serialization: John Blackwood (the novel's publisher) and—inevitably—Lytton.

Lytton became a 'Blackwood's author' in the late 1840s. His first novel for the house, *The Caxtons*, was somewhat slow to take off and in November 1849 he wrote (as an author who had been at the top of the tree for twenty years) to John Blackwood to reassure him:

Sometimes I find my novels hang fire at first and recover afterwards. This was the case with *Eugene Aram* for which I remember the subscription was only 1000 copies—but it sold 3000—of the 3 volume form.[3]

After this consolation Lytton went on to speculate about the current modes of publication for fiction:

I own, however, that I am more and more inclined to think that for great sales the usual 3 volume form is wearing out and think something great might be done by a popular book in a new shape—avoiding what has been done before in mere form whether by Dickens etc. or the orthodox Circulating Library Editions. Tristram Shandy and Clarissa Harlowe came out volume by volume—Don Quixote was published in portions.

Lytton in fact had a likely novel in mind for this new form of issue (it later became *My Novel*). The work would, he predicted, be 'thoroughly English in Country Life' and would occupy a large canvas. (This, recall, was 1849.)

What Blackwood replied to this tentative overture from Lytton is not known. But he was clearly interested. In his next letter the novelist, apparently encouraged, elaborated his scheme for a new mode of serialization which would emulate the achievements of Thackeray and Dickens in the serial field—but without descending to the level of what Lytton liked in his lordly way to call 'the common herd'[4] of readers:

a literary friend of mine informed me that a publisher whom he was connected with, was extremely anxious to engage me to write a serial work—that might deal with manners etc.—in what is called genteel life— distinguished from the classes Dickens has so popularly illustrated—and afterwards wrote me word that his publisher would give me 2000*l* for such a work, and make up for any loss the serial form might entail . . . I have tried to consider well your idea of the 5 shilling parts—I own I have great doubts therein it seems to me that there are 2 classes of readers—the one who like the serial form the other who prefer waiting till the whole is completed.[5]

At this stage three forms of sequential publication for *My Novel* were being appraised: serialization in 'Maga' (i.e. *Blackwood's Magazine*), intermediate issue in made-up numbers of as yet undetermined size or price and conventional three-volume publication. Lytton, in the same letter, went on to outline his view of the market and the chances of the 5*s*. numbers Blackwood had proposed:

Now the first [class of readers] will be taken off by the Magazine—and the last will still wait till the whole is out—On the other hand it is true that such subdivision lightens the cost to the purchasers. Many will pay 5*s*. at a time who will not pay 30*s*. at once. And the attempt may create a 3rd. class of readers and purchasers not now existing here, but which does exist for the French novels—first published in newspapers and then in *livraisons*—before final completion. And lastly even if not very successful such an intermediary form might still take off from 5 to 700 copies—besides the ultimate reissue of the work completed and that would be all the difference between loss and gain—Thus looking on both sides I am puzzled and require a little more time to consider the question . . . At the present I have arranged it for 15 parts—longer on an average than the earlier numbers of the Caxtons—but it would easily bear lengthening if necessary—I have done, or rather sketched 5—I propose larger subdivisions in Books—with introductory chapters like Fielding's to his Books.[6]

At this period of the novel's composition the situation between Blackwood and Lytton was still very undecided. So it remained for a number of months, although new ideas continued to be exchanged between the two men. In the new year John Forster (who as Chapman & Hall's literary adviser was probably the 'friend' referred to earlier) contributed his ideas on how *My Novel* should come out. Why not have intermediate reissue in shilling volumes, he asked (his ideas are reported by Lytton):

which might be so arranged as to complete the novel in about 12 volumes, and to admit of a rearrangement at its close, bringing it into either 6 vols. or 4 as may be thought best . . . the form (as I have the notion of it) would be perfectly original—unlike Dickens etc. (something like the Brussels Edition of French novels which have astonishing sales here).[7]

The proposal of 2*s*. numbers, each comprising two of the magazine instalments, seems to have found favour with Blackwood. In February Lytton went on to organize the composition of his novel accordingly: 'I propose to make my divisions in 12 books so that each florin number shall contain a book and am now rearranging the work in that form'.[8] By this time he had, as he reckoned, finished almost half the novel. In

June Lytton sent Blackwood the first four numbers together with the work's proposed title: 'My Novel, or Varieties in English Life'. The intermediate reissue was, however, giving him some anxiety:

I own I entertain great doubts of the efficacy of a serial at 2s.—containing the 2 numbers, already just read by so many thousands in the Magazine—I almost doubt whether your first idea of 5s. parts be not better. But this must be well weighed and deliberately considered after you have read the specimens sent—In your present idea the 4 numbers comprise 2 parts at 2s. each. There will be 12 parts in all—It may therefore be a doubt (returning to the old idea) whether the present specimens should form rather one part at 4s. Being 6 parts in all instead of 12. But you will think over this.[9]

Blackwood was delighted with the sample of the novel which Lytton enclosed, so much so that he offered £2,000 for magazine publication and republication 'in some form and for such price as may be agreed on between us'. But what exactly this form was to be was still, apparently, difficult to agree on. Lytton hankered after 'small pocket livraisons like the French novels [in their] Belgium Edition'. Blackwood's 'five-shilling numbers' seem increasingly to have appealed to him; on 4 August he returned to the theme again:

4 Numbers would make a pretty little volume, and with woodcuts might well sell for 5s. this—in 6 appearances—would produce 30s. for the whole complete and be a cheap book.[10]

In September, with the proof for the first numbers corrected, he once more went over the arguments in favour of the new form of serialization, but as usual could not firmly make up his mind as to what would be best: either the two-number livraison at a florin or half-a-crown or 'making the reissue consist of 4 numbers—appearing as small vols—and selling at 4 or 5s. . . . But I suspect that more wd. buy at 2s. or 2/6 than would buy the longer portion at 4 or 5s.'[11]

As it turned out all Lytton's speculation and worry were superfluous. Blackwood was, eventually, too prudent to risk the experiment. In December the novelist wrote: 'Have you thought anything more about the plan of reissue[?] It seems that we should now decide that point'.[12] Later in the same month he warned against delay. Thereafter the project seems to have been quietly shelved. *My Novel* was run through the magazine and then published in four volumes. Just over 2,000 were sold in the four-volume form and a similar number two years later in two volumes at 21s. Both editions were promptly sold out and Blackwood may well have regretted not trying the experimental form of issue.

Turn now to *Middlemarch*, twenty years later. Blackwood had known about George Eliot's 'English novel' for some time, although he had not secured it for his house, when G. H. Lewes wrote to him on 7 May 1871 with a letter of proposal:

here is something for you to turn over in your mind, and come prepared to discuss. Mrs. Lewes [i.e. George Eliot] finds that she will require 4 volumes for her story, not 3. I winced at the idea at first, but the story must not be spoiled for want of space, and as you have more than once spoken of the desirability of inventing some mode of circumventing the Libraries and making the public buy instead of borrowing I have devised the following scheme, suggested by the plan Victor Hugo followed with his long *Misérables*—namely to publish it in half-volume parts either at intervals of one, or as I think better, two months. The eight parts at 5/- could yield the £2 for the four volumes, and at two month intervals would not be dearer than Maga [i.e. *Blackwood's Magazine*, which cost half-a-crown a monthly issue] . . . *Tristram Shandy* you may remember was published at irregular intervals; and great was the desire for the continuation. Considering how slowly the public mind is brought into motion, this spreading of the publication over 16 months would be a decided advantage to the sale— especially as each part would contain as much as one ought to read at a time. Ponder this; or suggest a better plan![13]

What is striking about this letter is that although Lewes calls the scheme something 'I have devised' it contains remarkable similarities with what had been discussed between Lytton and Blackwood in 1850. Again one finds initial embarrassment at a four-volume novel, the comparison with *Tristram Shandy*, the argument by reference to French *livraisons*, the 5*s*. price, two-monthly intervals (i.e. the length of four instalments in the magazine), the division into books which make up into volumes. It can hardly be entirely coincidental. Presumably in one of the conversations about library monopoly Blackwood had mentioned his scheme for the 5*s*. numbers and Lewes is here either playing up to the publisher by feeding him one of his own bright ideas—or perhaps it had simply slipped Blackwood's mind who had thought of the new form of serialization first.

It had not slipped Lytton's mind. When Blackwood (who accepted Lewes's proposals in their entirety) advertised *Middlemarch* as forthcoming the other novelist despatched a very sharp letter to Edinburgh:

My dear Sir,—I observe in the Paper an advertisement that you are bringing out a new novel by George Eliot in single volumes—If this be true, it occasions me, naturally, much chagrin—for you will probably remember that I was very desirous of bringing out 'My Novel' and 'What will he do with it' in that form—but after consideration you were against it. Still I always cherished the idea and had intended so to bring out the next novel published in my own name.

Of course, therefore, it is annoying to see the design I had conceived to be my own forestalled by another Novelist. The chance of success in such an experiment is in favour of the author who first starts it—those who may follow the example are looked upon as imitators—And of course it would not become me to imitate any other writer.

Possibly, however the statement in the Newspaper may not be correct.[14]

But it was correct and Blackwood was not to be bullied into giving way by some high-handed lord of an ex-author whose books were no longer selling all that wonderfully. He replied:

I shall be very sorry if the form of George Eliot's Novel should have forestalled any plan of yours but I do not think it can. I remember often discussing with you the very unsatisfactory form of the novel which limited the sale and my impression was that I had always been rather in favour of bringing the French form [*sic*]. In this case the proposition came entirely from Mr. and Mrs. Lewes and the adventure is more theirs than mine.[15]

The extant correspondence bears Blackwood out in this: the 5*s*. design had been as much his as Lytton's—although the novelist gradually came to appropriate the idea as his own. Equally the proposal in the *Middlemarch* case had come from Lewes. None the less one may sympathize with Zelig-Lytton's sense of grievance, however arrogantly he saw fit to present it. The resemblances between what he had projected for *My Novel* and what took shape in *Middlemarch* are so close as to make one suspicious that there was some, perhaps unconscious, cross-fertilization of ideas. However it came about, it must have vexed Lytton's last years. He was eclipsed, while George Eliot, with *his* idea, had consolidated her position as the undisputed great novelist of the day.

CHAPTER SIX

Trollope at Work on The Way We Live Now

TWO FACTS are universally known about Trollope: that he invented the pillar-box and that he wrote his novels 'mechanically'. Both pieces of knowledge require modification.[1] By examination of the manuscript material of *The Way We Live Now* this chapter aims to revise the vulgar misconception (to some extent projected by the author himself) of Trollope's working methods.[2] In the model which emerges, Trollope would seem faithfully to have observed his own maxim that 'to think of a novel is much harder than to write it'. His fiction typically began with a commercial transaction and precise, contractual specification. The first stage of subsequent creative work involved intense imaginative construction ('thinking'). In the *Autobiography*, Trollope describes this phase as 'castle-building' or cohabitation with those 'old friends' his characters.[3] He gives a vivid account of this preliminary absorption in his unwritten novel in the essay 'A Walk in a Wood'.[4] Although this activity was pre-eminently mental, it would appear from *The Way We Live Now* that some unsystematic note-making might accompany it.

The second stage ('writing') was strictly secretarial. The scrappy *aides-mémoire* made at the thinking stage are entirely different from the fetishistically complete calendars of work rate and schedules of length which Trollope compiled for himself and filled in before, during, and after composition. The manuscript itself was written fluently and with no major revisions. Composition was carefully timed to be finished by contract-delivery date and well before publication. For Trollope the subsequent chore of proof-reading was just that—reading. Trollope, this is to assert, did not, like Dickens or Thackeray, take methodical advantage of this last opportunity to improve his work. Unlike these more hand-to-mouth practitioners, he was customarily onto thinking about or even writing the next novel by the time the proofs for the last came along.

The Way We Live Now, although only one novel out of forty-seven, is attractive to generalize from. It was written at the time when Trollope was formulating his views on the art of writing fiction for the *Autobiography*. If chapter 12 represents theory, then *The Way We Live Now* can be taken as corresponding practice. It is a work as massive in conception as in physical size: at something over 1,200 manuscript pages and more than 380,000 words, it is the longest in the Trollope corpus. The novelist had a high price for it—£3,000— and he would have wanted to give full value for money. He was in a position to do so. Although in his late fifties, he was fresh, having just returned from an invigorating trip round the world. Finally, *The Way We Live Now* has the largest mass of pre-publication materials which have survived to us from the writing of the major novels.[5] In what follows, I intend to follow the progress of the work as it can be reconstructed from this evidence.

The contract for an as yet unnamed work was made between Trollope and Chapman & Hall on 28 March 1873. It specifies publication in twenty monthly parts, on the lines of the firm's earlier *Orley Farm*. The dates fixed are from 1 January 1874 to 1 August 1875. (In fact, *The Way We Live Now* came out from February 1874 to September 1875, a month later than agreed.) The first half of the work was to be with the publisher by the end of October 1873. It was evidently understood by both parties that the work (as was normal with this form of serialization) was to cost one shilling for a 32-page number, was to carry two full-plate illustrations, and was to be reissued in two volumes at the end of the monthly run. Trollope, as he generally preferred, made over the copyright entirely on his principle that a 'lump sum' was more useful than a 'deferred annuity' of royalty or half-profit payments. The publishers gave £3,000 for the property, payable at £150 a month over the course of publication.

As has often been noted, this kind of serialization was antique in 1873 and was associated with the bygone glories of the now dead Dickens and Thackeray. The publishers may have been disposed to revive it for *The Way We Live Now* by the extraordinary sales clocked up by the early numbers of *Edwin Drood* (which they had also published) and by the eight-part publication of *Middlemarch* in bimonthly five-shilling installments (Trollope's next novel, *The Prime Minister*, was published by Chapman & Hall in this form). But whatever the motives and sales hopes, it was evident that from the first *The Way We Live Now* was forecast in the exact divisions of the fixed-size, fixed-term monthly part.

Trollope had not done a twenty-part novel since *Can You Forgive Her?* (January 1864–August 1865) and had therefore to lengthen his sights. His working calendar begins with the calculation:

1873. Carbury novel. 20 Numbers. 64 pages each number. 260 words each page. 40 pages a week. To be completed in 32 weeks.

(As in the contract, Trollope uses the blank specification 'Carbury novel'; titling of both chapter and work was a late act in his procedure of composition.)

In the above schedule Trollope reckons in manuscript pages. It is evident that one reason for the striking cleanliness of his manuscript was the overriding need to keep strict metrical order if he was to write fast, in one uninterrupted draft, and fit the procrustean requirements of the 32-page printed number. Crossing out, interlineation, and superaddition were luxuries his timetable did not afford him. There was another control, not apparent in this initial calculation. Unlike Dickens and Thackeray, Trollope measured his monthly part into an invariable five chapters. The result in *The Way We Live Now* is uniquely symmetrical: 100 chapters in the novel, 50 per volume, 5 per number.

Trollope made another forecast calculation at the head of the Dramatis Personae plan. This ran: 'Novel in 20 parts. 32 pages. 520 words = 5 volumes.' Trollope is here thinking in terms of printed pages. The monthly serial on the Dickensian–Thackerayan pattern used larger octavo pages than the conventional three-decker. At a rough 260 words per quarto of manuscript page, Trollope could aim at a 64-page MS number (a target he in fact held to exactly). He also reminds himself here that the whole length of this new (as yet immaterial) novel will be two-fifths longer than the three-decker to which he had recently become habituated. He was, to all intents and purposes, writing a five-decker. It was a challenge to his stamina, and, as we shall see, Trollope did in fact run into problems around the 12–14 number area.

As usual, Trollope made a writing calendar, to be filled in as he went along. According to it, he began his 'Carbury novel' on 1 May 1873 and by the end of the month had completed three numbers (fifteen chapters). He then broke off to write *Harry Heathcote of Gangoil*, which was completed by July 1873. The novelist immediately picked up *The Way We Live Now* and wrote numbers 4–6 between 3 July and 30 July. From the end of July to 11 August he took a short rest. This prepared him for a major effort, the writing of numbers 7–14 from 11 August to 19 September. There followed another short rest until 10 October, a period in which he records 'reading my own manuscript' (the first half of which was due Chapman & Hall). In the period from 11 October to 22 December Trollope polished off the remaining chapters while nursing a bad foot. At the end of his calendar he summarizes:

Completed in 34 weeks (instead of 32)—but five weeks were occupied on Harry Heathcote and therefore this novel 'The Way We Live Now' has been done in 29 weeks. Dec. 22 1873.

There are points of interest in this record other than the impressive rapidity of the performance. One notes that Trollope did not begin writing immediately on signing the contract. It is likely that the interval was occupied with the kind of 'thinking' described in 'A Walk in a Wood'. It is also noteworthy that Trollope, according to his own account, wrote *The Way We Live Now* sequentially, from chapter 1 to 100. (One needs to bear this in mind when examining the 'Chapter plans for the second volume,' which propose a different order of events from that in the printed novel.) It is also likely, from the evidence of these plans and the MS, that Trollope needed an additional period of 'thinking' (19 September–11 October) to resolve the conclusion of the novel—whether or not, for instance, to put Melmotte on trial or have him commit suicide.

In spite of the forecast calculations, which offered no pause, Trollope worked on *The Way We Live Now* in a series of bursts, or spells of composition. Especially in the first half of the novel, each of these bursts is devoted to a different aspect of the plotwork. The first extends over May and the first fifteen chapters (it is evident, incidentally, that there were no starting pangs; Trollope kicked off writing very briskly). In this opening spell (particularly in chapters 1–2) Trollope drew closely on the first entries in the Dramatis Personae plan. These opening chapters are, perforce, expository ('Let the reader be introduced to Lady Carbury' runs the first line of the novel), and lay out the sets of characters and social settings which are to figure centrally. In this first conception Trollope evidently foresaw three more or less equivalent nuclei: (1) Lady Carbury's West End milieu, with its literary salon and club life (2) Squirearchical Suffolk, where Roger Carbury wrestles with his Tory principles and religious doubts (3) Melmotte's city world of dubious finance and his campaign to 'buy' English society. In the novel as it was actually written, this three-yoked conception was altered. Lady Carbury's literary career (and the literary-critical racket) was down-played, and Roger's religious crisis all but disappeared. Melmotte, correspondingly, outgrew the first frame and came to dominate the narrative. It was quite proper that when Trollope came to commission a design for the monthly cover, it should have featured exclusively the Great Financier's rise and fall in vignette.

Harry Heathcote was completed by July, and Trollope resumed the larger novel. Chapter 16 begins with some redundant recapitulation as Trollope evidently got the story straight in his mind. Then, between 3 and 30 July, he wrote chapters 16–30. His pace had kept up with the breakneck composition of the first burst. In number 4 all of the five chapters are set in Suffolk and represent a coming to grips with the theme prefigured in the Dramatis Personae plan:

[under the Roger Carbury entry] Life at Carbury Hall with neighbours the bishop—RC priest—big squire in next parish who has large income and is in debt. Doubts about his [i.e., Roger's] religion.

Chapter 16 gives us 'The Bishop and the Priest' and a spiritually restless Carbury squire as the easy-going Anglican primate and fanatic Roman Catholic quarrel across him. The 'big squire' in the next parish is Adolphus Longestaffe Sr., whose debts have enforced an intimacy with the sordid (but wealthy) Melmotte—eventually this intimacy is to result in the sale of the family's other estate in Sussex. But even at this stage one can see strains developing. It is difficult to get Melmotte into East Anglia and the Whitsun excursion is implausible. Even more difficult is to retain for the vacuous Roger the role of 'hero.' During this period of composition Trollope must have decided to relegate him.

The third spell of writing took in the bulk of the novel, numbers 7–14 (11 August–19 September). During this burst Trollope exploits the tangles of Paul Montague's love life and his promotion to the main role vacated by Roger. Winifred may well have been an afterthought. Her existence is inserted into the margin of the Dramatis Personae, apparently answering the admonition about scrapes which must be devised for Paul. The first mention of her, which we find in a tailpiece to chapter 6 of the printed text, was a superaddition, the manuscript reveals. If Trollope can be said to have problems in the writing of *The Way We Live Now*, they can be located in this spell, as I shall argue later. It was, even by Trollope's standards, hard going: forty chapters in under six weeks. After his rest, Trollope concluded the novel at a comparatively leisured pace.

Trollope's main surviving planning document for *The Way We*

Live Now (what I have termed the Dramatis Personae plan) is
rather misleadingly called an 'advance layout' in Sadleir's *Trollope:
A Commentary*, where it is reproduced typographically with more
regularity than it actually possesses. This is how I read it:

Novel in 20 parts. 32 pages. 520 words = 5 volumes
<u>Lady Carbury.</u> widow of late General Sir Michael C. Bart. (dead in India)
left with £1000 a year—had left her husband, but not in adultery, (from his
hard temper & her impetuosity) had gone back and been forgiven—but the
evil report remained. living in ~~Bryanston~~ Square Welbeck Street—with son
& daughter—spoiling the son & helping to pay his debts—clever impetuous.
Thoroughly unprincipled from want of knowledge of honesty, an authoress,
very handsome, ~~46~~ 43[6]—trying all schemes with Editors &c. to get puffed
infinitely energetic. bad to her daughter from want of sympathy flirts as a
matter of taste, but never goes wrong; capable of great sacrifice for her son.
The chief character
<u>Sir Felix Carbury.</u> Bart. 25. been in the Guards—sold out (enquire about
this). Magnificently beautiful. dark, with perfect features. brown eyes.
utterly selfish. reckless from utter thoughtlessness. debts paid by mother,
by sisters lover, by the lady who loves him;—but all is hopeless. His father
had left him £1000 a year—He and his sister to divide the mother's £1000
at her death. Dies.[7]
<u>Henrietta Carbury</u>—Hetty by some. Harry by her brother:—almost as
handsome as her brother, but thoroughly strong and good—antagonistic to
her mothers dodges courted by her cousin Roger Carbury the head of the
family, a man of wealth and position, considerably older than herself—she
~~23~~21. But in love with Paul Montagu. She almost yields when she is made
to believe that Paul is bad, but never quite does so. is entitled to £6000,
on her marriage with the consent of either her mother or her cousin, who
is executor under her father's will. Loves her brother.
<u>Roger Carbury</u>, of Carbury Hall, in Norfolk, ~~40~~38—straightforward about
£2000 a year—ready money,—very good. horribly in love with his cousin
hero of the book. property will go to the other Carburys—takes Paul
Montagu by the hand, and sacrifices himself at last.
Life at Carbury Hall with neighbours;—the bishop—R. C. priest—big squire
in next parish, who has large income & is in debt. Doubts about his
religion;—finds it easier to love his neighbours than his God. staunch old
Tory.
<u>Paul Montagu</u>—Hetty's lover. Gets into some scrapes which must be
devised. Marries at last under the auspices of Roger—quite true in his
living, but a scapegrace; has glimmerings of radical policy for the good of
the people, and disgusts Roger Carbury—lives at last at Carbury Hall and
marries Hetta—Suffolk Street

Bishop of Elmham—old Longley, Yelgnol. Yeld.[8]
Father John Barham—Pervert. Waltham priest. very poor.[9]
Hepworths of Eardly rich £7000. Primeros Spaniards by descent.
Adolphus Longestaffe Esq. squire of Caversham in Norfolk neighbour of Roger Carbury with Lady ~~Diana Caversham~~ Pomona Longstaffe and young Dolly the heir—large property much involved. hot tempered & cross grained. Country going to the dogs. All of them spending too much money.
Sophia (Mrs George Whitstable)—
Georgiana—
Toodlam
Mr Nicholas ~~Balfe~~ Broune—Editor
of the '~~weekly Literary Chronicle Gazette~~ Morning Breakfast Table. Pall Mall—office in Trafalgar Square. Fond of ladies.
Mr Booker editor of the '~~Morning Breakfast Table~~ Literary Chronicle,—a supposed writer of criticism. very poor.
Mr Ferdinand Alf. Editor of the evening 'Pulpit.' great swell
~~Latham~~ Leadham & Loiter—publishers
~~Marianna Treegrene~~ Marie Melmotte, the heiress, daughter of ~~Samuel Emanuel~~ Augustus ~~S. Treegrene~~ Melmotte the ~~great American~~ French swindler
Madame Melmotte—fat Jewess.
Herr Vossner, purveyor to the Bear Garden
Duchess of Stevenage. Castle Abbey. Grendalls.
Lord Alfred.
Miles Grendall second son [illegible] ~~Gustavus Grendall in the city~~[10]
Ruby Ruggles 23—Daniel Ruggles of Sheepsacre—John Crumb.

In the course of making this plan, Trollope had some afterthoughts, corrections, and additions, which he inserted into the margins, left and right. In the margins alongside his initial calculations as to length, he inserted: 'Presumed period 1873' and 'Begins ~~Jan.~~ 25 Feb 1873'. Alongside Lady Carbury's entry he added the Christian name 'Matilda' and the cryptic note, 'every Tuesday', indicating her habit of entertaining on that day. Trollope also added a detail of her past life, 'Lady Carbury had run away'. Alongside Felix's entry, he added 'Felix a coward'. Also at this point he reiterated '[the action] opens 25 ~~January~~ February'. At the end of Felix's entry, Trollope added in the margin, 'Todd Breghert and Goldsheiner', indicating Felix's imprudent dealings with moneylenders. In the margins opposite Paul Montagu's 'scrapes which must be devised' Trollope elaborated: 'Mrs Hurtle Winifred lodges in Suffolk Street'[11] and 'Caradoc Carson Hurtle'. Opposite the Longestaffe entry, Trollope added '& Pickering

Park' and 'Squercum lawyer'. Opposite his trio of vulgar journalists (Broune, Booker, Alf), whom he linked with a large marginal bracket, Trollope wrote 'Alfred Shand'. It has been conjectured that the novelist may have based his caricature of 'higher journalism' on the actual journalist Alexander Innes Shand (1832–1907), associated with the *Saturday Review* which had, in the 1860s, been very hard on the works of Anthony Trollope. The crossed out 'weekly Literary Chronicle' may have been originally intended as a hit against the 'Saturday'.

The framing of this plan with its prominent declarations 'presumed period 1873' and 'The chief character', indicate that Trollope drew it up for guidance, before starting to write. The 'Suffolk' (i.e., Carbury) group of characters were firmly drawn. Paul Montague was a less clearly focused element. The London plot, centered on Melmotte, was hazier still. Indeed, Melmotte himself was at this stage a provisional character, ambiguously Jewish, French, or American. Some instrumental figures, like Squercum and Brehgert, were marginal additions and probably afterthoughts. Fisker is altogether absent. There are large changes of emphasis in the novel as written. Melmotte eventually ranks as 'chief character'. Felix is not loved by his sister, nor does he die (if it is he, not Lady Carbury, who is intended to expire). Roger and his theological qualms were neglected. So too was Paul's political fanaticism.

The function of this plan was to act as a trigger, releasing characters into an existence whose full complications could later emerge more or less spontaneously. The relevant passages in the *Autobiography* are familiar:

At . . . times I have been able to imbue myself thoroughly with the characters I have had in hand. I have wandered alone among the rocks and woods, crying at their grief, laughing at their absurdities, and thoroughly enjoying their joy. I have been impregnated with my own creations till it has been my only excitement to sit with the pen in my hand . . . [The author's characters] must be with him as he lies down to sleep, and as he wakes from his dreams. He must learn to hate them and to love them. He must argue with them, quarrel with them, forgive them, and even submit to them.[12]

Trollope wrote the Dramatis Personae plan on a piece of quarto paper folded so as to give four writing surfaces. On the last side he jotted down some random notes relative to a later period of composition:

Dinner at club 18 April. Fisker started Saturday 19th.
Samuel Cohenlupe.
Roger's married sister in California—had befriended Montague.
Hamilton K. Fisker. Montague and Montague (Paul £720 per an. or $3600)
Fiskerville
at Liverpool. 4 March. Board meets on Thursday.
Mrs Hurtle lives with Mrs Pipkin. 5 children. A widower
['South Central and Mexican Railway' at bottom of sheet]
['Montague's pledge. No 5. p.20' along right-hand edge]

The bulk of entries here feeds chapters 9 and 10 ('The Great Railway
to Vera Cruz' and 'Mr Fisker's Success'). Since Paul's pledge is indeed
mentioned on MS page 20 of the fifth number, Trollope must have kept
this plan by him until well into his second spell of composition. At
this stage the commercial plot seems to have established itself more
firmly than it first did.

II

THE EXPOSITORY Dramatis Personae plan served Trollope for the first
volume. For the complications and resolution of the plot in the second
volume he evidently needed something different. The following chapter
plan was most likely drawn up ʼs he embarked on the narrative's last
fifty chapters. Its foresight is remarkable, even if, as we shall see,
Trollope was obliged to reorder the sequence of events and alter the
climax. With this plan in mind, it is hard to take at face value his
assertion in the *Autobiography*, 'I never could arrange a set of events
before me.'[13] For *The Way We Live Now* he obviously could.

In reading the plan the following key is necessary: in general, entries
summarize the main elements of chapters. The number preceding the
entry is that of the chapter as it appears in the ultimately printed
text. The number following the entry is that of the chapter as Trollope
preconceived the sequence of narrative before writing. It is clear that
Trollope eventually did a good deal of rearranging. The last number,
in parentheses, records the MS pages written for the chapter. For
chapters 51–56, Trollope also entered the part number (11).

No 10
Chapt. 46 Lowestoffe 12
47 Montague at Carbury 16
48 Ruby and Mrs Pipkin 8
49 Marie and Felix in the Square 12 Felix and his mother

50 Marie is off but Felix does not go

[These five entries take up a whole side. They are widely spaced out and Trollope was evidently concerned with totting up MS pages. At the foot of the page is a calculation: 20 x 64 = 1280. This represents the total number of pages to be written. The remainder of the plan which follows is written neatly, in a much smaller hand, on the other side of the paper. '1A' and '19A' are mysterious.]

51 11–2 Paul and Mrs Hurtle lA (12)
52 11 Sir Felix after his misfortune 1 (10)
53 11-3 His interview with Melmotte 2 (14)
54 11-4 Melmotte's Election   ? Roman Catholicism 3 (16)
55 11-5 Roger and the Bishop at Carbury 4 (8)
56 11-5 Roger and the priest 5 (12)
57 ~~Melmotte Returned 6~~ Nidderdale 6 (12)
64 Alf's speeches. Lady Carbury's doubts. Threats of libel 7 (12)
65 Miss Longestaffe at Lady Monogram's 8 (12)
68 Marie's anger at Sir Felix 9 (10)
63 Melmotte ~~returned~~ as candidate. ln the city as MP 10 (12)
[Trollope later circled this entry and indicated that it was to come between the later entries 60/14 and 66/15.]
59 The Dinner 11 (12)
62 The Party 12 (17)
61 Lady Monogram at the party 13 (7)
60 Miss Longestaffe's lover 14 (12)
66 Hetta accepts Paul Montague 15 (12)
69 Marie agrees to marry Nidderdale in her despair 16 (16)
73 Marie and Nidderdale. he is [illegible—'willing'?] 17 (10)
58 Dolly and his father—Dolly and Squercum 18 (12)
70 Felix at Mrs Pipkin's. Felix and Ruby 19 (12)
Mrs Hurtle comes 19A
75 Squercum [?] attacks Melmotte for the money 20 (12)
Marie endeavours to get Felix back 21
67 Felix tells his sister of Mrs Hurtle 22 (10)
Lady Carbury and her books 23
78 Lady Pomona's despair at the ~~trial~~ marriage 24 (10) ['marriage' is added in what looks like a later ink]
72 Hetta again refuses ~~Paul~~ Roger and tells him 25 (14)
76 Hetta renounces Paul 26 (13)
74 Scene at the Beargarden 27 (12)
77 Melmotte ~~at the trial~~ with Marie 28 (13) ['with Marie' is added in what looks like a later ink]
Nidderdale at last will not marry 29
Longestaffe's despair about his money 30

79 Miss Longestaffe's lover. She is taken home 31 (14)
Miles and Felix both expelled 32
Roger Carbury and the bishop about Westminster 33
80 Felix and Ruby 36 (10)
Mrs Hurtle and Paul 37
She sends the letter 38
71 Crumb comes and ~~hits~~[?] Felix 39(12)
71 ~~Sir Felix dies [?] 40~~
Fisker reappears about the Railway 41
Scene in Grosvenor Square 42
~~The trial 43~~ Melmotte dead 43 [added in an apparently later ink]
~~The trial [?] 44~~
~~Delay [?] 45~~
Lady Carbury's despair 46
~~Melmotte to be imprisoned[?] 47~~
~~Alf's triumph about the trial 48~~
Hetta forgives Paul 49
Roger's behaviour 50

Apart from chapters 46–50 the whole plan was written neatly in one draft. The printed text chapter numbers are, however, added later. So too are the manuscript quantity numbers in parentheses (they tally exactly with what we find in the manuscript). The numbers 1–50 (which represent the original order of chapters that Trollope anticipated) were written at the same time as the plan. All the lead entries up to the second 71/40 ('Sir Felix dies') are ticked off— presumably as the chapter was written. After 71/40 Trollope crosses out items which were clearly at odds with the novel as it was actually emerging on the printed and published page.

The plan gives us insight into Trollope's extraordinary flexibility. Weaving these elements into an entirely new sequence must have been a complex business. Yet so thrifty was he that practically nothing was discarded. Up to 57/6 the entries keep an accurate and parallel record (was it during the eleventh number, one wonders, that he wrote the plan?). At 57/6 Trollope was forced to desert the order of events laid down, because of problems with Melmotte. Originally he was to be 'returned' (i.e., to parliament) at this point. But the event was postponed to 63/10, and then a long loop carries it forward to between 60/14 and 66/15. (In the printed novel Melmotte wins Westminster in chapter 64.)

After 57/6 Trollope's order of composition and narrative arrangement diverged broadly from the plan. But the content of chapters, wherever they eventually came out, diverged remarkably little. Admittedly, in chapter 47 there is only half a terminal page of Paul at Carbury and in chapter 69/16 Marie's agreement figures only very briefly. In 53/2 'his' must be taken to refer to Broune or Nidderdale, not Felix, as Trollope may originally have intended. In 56/5 we encounter not Roger and the priest but Melmotte and the priest. In 79/33 'Roger and the bishop about Westminster' is lost altogether; it was presumably part of the religious subplot which Trollope largely discarded. The second element of 79/32 also disappears; Miles and Felix are not expelled from the Bear Garden, whose committee is in no state to expel anyone after Vossner decamps. In 77/29 'Nidderdale at last will not marry' is postponed to chapter 83 of the printed text, and 'Longestaffe's despair about his money' to 88.

Most interesting are those elements which Trollope, finding he could not weave them into his new pattern, discarded or changed utterly. Melmotte originally was to have gone on trial for forgery. The trial is first mentioned in 78/24 where it was to have caused Lady Pomona despair. Trollope kept the despair but gave it a new source. In the printed chapter 78 it is the prospect of Brehgert as son-in-law that sinks hearts at Caversham. The trial next came up at 77/28 where the scene of Melmotte at the Old Bailey (presumably) was substituted by the argument with Marie which we find in the published novel. In 71/39 Trollope (if my reading is correct) was to have Crumb kill Felix (who 'dies' in the Dramatis Personae plan, it will be remembered). There would thus have been another trial. In 43 and 44 the trial figures again—although Trollope crossed out the entries and put in the alternative conclusion 'Melmotte dead'. If I read 47 correctly, Melmotte was to go to prison and the odious Alf was to triumph over his opponent.

In an article published in 1963, P. D. Edwards points to Trollope's two minds over how to dispose of Melmotte.[14] But what has not been noted is how the manner of the financier's downfall was kept open to the last minute of composition. In the printed text his death comes in chapter 83 ('Melmotte Again at the House'). Having disgraced himself in parliament, Melmotte retires to his study to drink. This is how the chapter originally concluded in the MS:

He was habitually left there at night, and the servant as usual went to his bed. But at nine o'clock on the following morning the maid-servant found him asleep.

In a later hand and ink Trollope crossed out 'asleep' and replaced it with 'dead' and squeezed in the continuation:

Drunk as he had been, more drunk as he probably became during the night, still he was able to deliver himself from the indignities and penalties to which the law might have subjected him by a dose of prussic acid.

A sleeping Melmotte would have awakened to face immediate arrest and Alf's jubilation at his fall. Trollope evidently kept this option open for as long as he possibly could.

III

THE MANUSCRIPT of *The Way We Live Now* conforms to Trollope's practice at this mature stage of his career. He writes on both sides of quarto sheets, in regular script, to predetermined length and with remarkably few alterations. He maintains a consistent 28–31 lines and around 250 words per page. On the left-hand margin there are three numerical entries which indicate the part-number, the chapter, and the manuscript page within the number. Trollope wrote to a normal number length of 64 of his manuscript pages. Following every completed number in the MS there is a sum whose significance eludes me. But since the first part is always '64' (e.g., 64 x 96, 64–167) I assume it has to do with fixing an exact number of lines in the printed work.

At times the appearance of the MS is so perfect as to give rise to the suspicion that Trollope may have supplied the printer with fair copy. In the second number, for instance, there is a run of twelve MS pages, blemished only by twenty-one synonym corrections (e.g., 'recommend' for 'advise') and tiny deletions. But the likelihood that Trollope made a fair copy is almost nil. For one thing, to do so would have been against his usual practice; moreover, he had little time to do so. If he produced numbers 7–14 in just under six weeks, it is unlikely that he could have allowed himself the luxury of redrafting. And from the MS itself there is ocular evidence as to spontaneity. One of the more frequent of Trollope's corrections is that in which his mind momentarily runs ahead of itself and has to be reined in. Thus:

'You and Grasslough were never ~~very~~ pals' (1/32, p. 24; Trollope was about to write 'very friendly').

he took her in his arms, and ~~embraced~~ kissed her lips as well as her cheeks (9/20, p. 341; Trollope here gives Paul Montague a little more lover's daring).[15]

This kind of scribal error typically happens when a writer is composing. In copying, words tend to be dropped or repeated; such slips are not found in *The Way We Live Now* manuscript.

Reading the manuscript is somewhat frustrating for anyone hoping to make startling discoveries. There are, however, small illustrations of Trollope's liveliness to be found. These are no less impressive for being extremely economical. For example, at their first tense meeting in England, Winifred asks the backsliding Paul: 'Well, speak out. Is there another woman that you love?' To this outright question, Trollope first had the wretched young man reply: 'I do love another.' This, however, was crossed out and replaced by 'There is another' (6/11, pp. 212–13). The weak ambiguity and passive grammatical form are entirely in character. It leaves sufficient aperture for Winifred to insert cunning levers and prise Paul away from his firm intention to be true to Hetta.

There is no reason to suppose that Trollope could not have been an extensively revising writer, had he so wished. In the massive length of *The Way We Live Now*'s manuscript there is just one major scene revision. But it is so effective as to make one wonder if he would not have done well to give himself more scope for this kind of improvement. The revision is found at 5/47 (p. 196). Felix is at the Bear Garden and determined to get his IOUs paid by Miles Grendall. Miles of course has no intention of ever paying any gambling debt. In the MS, Trollope first pictured his shiftiness thus:

Miles took three or four long puffs of smoke, so as to give himself time for thought. Then he heaved himself forward and whispered into the ear of his companion. 'You come to me tomorrow in the city and I'll tell you about it all.' Then he threw himself back in his chair, and smoked away with infectious complacency. 'What time?' asked Sir Felix. 'Any time Two.' It need hardly be said that Mr. Miles Grendall had already made up his mind that he need not attend in Abchurch Lane the following day.

Having written this, Trollope crossed it out, and wrote into the margin of the page the following altered version:

'Will any fellow come up-stairs and play a game of billiards?' said Miles Grendall rising from his chair. Then he walked slowly out of the room, leaving Sir Felix to take what revenge he pleased. For a moment, Sir Felix thought that he would expose the transaction to the whole room; but he was afraid, thinking that Miles Grendall was a more popular man than himself.

Miles coolly cuts an impotent and outfaced Felix. It is a striking improvement on the sly Miles of the first passage. Clearly, too, if Trollope could do it so felicitously here he could have done it elsewhere in the manuscript. But it would have meant frittering away time that his schedule simple did not allow.

It would appear that Trollope found the third spell of composition (11 August–19 September) most problematic. He wrote extraordinarily fast at this stage: eight numbers (7–14) in under six weeks. The plot of the novel was at its most tricky; there is the elopement, the crisis of Paul and Winifred's affair, the visit of the Emperor of China, Melmotte's rise and fall. Things were also complicated for Trollope by the fact that he was more used to writing at three-volume length. This meant that he would normally finish a novel around what was the fourteenth part of *The Way We Live Now*. For this work he had to spin out another thirty chapters.

There are two main sources of evidence to support the contention that Trollope wrote this section of the novel (and particularly numbers 11–14) under some strain. The first which will strike any reader is the congestion and in some places the awkwardness of the plot. The other evidence is the greater than usual amount of surgery which Trollope was obliged to perform on the MS. Like a bowler in cricket he began to lose control of his length, overpitching and underpitching.

Trollope's adjustments to this stretch of the manuscript novel can be briefly summarized. Originally he intended chapter 39 to end with a nice surprise. Paul Montague goes to Islington to visit Mrs. Hurtle, and the door is opened by, guess who? Ruby Ruggles. Chapter 40 was intended to open with Ruby's alarmed 'Oh laws, Mr. Montague, is that you?' Trollope, however, sacrificed this nice bridge between chapters and grafted what was intended to be the opening of chapter 40 back onto the end of the old chapter 39. This left a new chapter 40, centered on Melmotte. ('Unanimity is the very soul of these things.')

At the end of the ninth number Trollope was forced into more tinkering. There was evidently overmatter in the copy supplied to the printer, and at 9/55 (p. 366) he removed, in proof presumably, some fifty words descriptive of Paul's fear that Felix will blab about Mrs Hurtle to his sister. At the end of the number, over one hundred words were cut (like the previous passage, they stand unobliterated in the

MS) describing Mr. Longestaffe's 'heavy heart' about the developing battle between Squercum and Melmotte. Neither of these passages contains information essential to the plot. But neither is redundant, and in normal circumstances Trollope would have preferred them to stand.

In number 11 the carpentry is harder to uncover. The MS reveals that chapter 53 was originally intended to begin at what is now its fourth paragraph. Trollope evidently latched on some five hundred words concerned with the aftermath of the elopement. With number 12, he plunged into the complexities of the Pickering forgery, whose details he may not have sufficiently pondered in advance. In the margin of 12/29 (p. 469) he inserted the information that '[Dolly's] father, some time since, had put before him, for his signature, a letter, prepared in Mr. Bideawhile's office, which Dolly said that he had refused even to read, and certainly had not signed.' This is the first introduction of what is to cause Melmotte's downfall and it could usefully have been prepared for earlier than this in the narrative. In the same twelfth number Brehgert is abruptly introduced, a figure who is hereafter to have principal status in the action. Again in this number, Trollope had difficulty in getting length right. Two long sentences had to be added to the ends of chapters 58 and 60.

Length was again a problem in number 13. Trollope found it necessary to add some 750 words to the end of chapter 64, 'The Election' (pp. 520–22, from 'It was very much to be member for Westminster'). This addition is not to be found in the MS, and was probably made in proof. As it happens, the reader can be extremely grateful for the emergency that provoked the supplementation. Trollope devised a superb passage describing Melmotte's sombre jubilation as he simultaneously contemplates his parliamentary grandeur and his commercial doom:

Whatever they might do, quick as they might be, they could hardly prevent his taking his seat in the House of Commons. Then if they sent him to penal servitude for life, they would have to say that they had so treated the member for Westminster! (p. 521)

There are other indicators of strain around numbers 13–14. Chapter lengths, for instance, begin to vary from the normal 12 MS pages. Thus chapter 61 is unusually short at 7 MS pages while chapter 62 is unusually long at 17 MS pages. The chronological organization of events around Melmotte's imperial dinner, party, and election is somewhat incoherent. The account of the dinner and the after-dinner party is awkwardly interrupted by chapter 60 which introduces the long previous business of Brehgert's wooing Georgiana. Trollope fits it in by using such unsettling conjunctions as 'A few days before that period in our story which we have now reached, Miss Longestaffe was seated in Lady Monogram's back drawing-room' (p. 482). There are other niggling features of the narrative at this stage. Trollope for the first time introduces the business of the shared house and desk in Bruton Street. It helps explain the otherwise improbable forgery business but it makes implausible scenes such as that in number 9, where Longestaffe Sr. cannot get hold of Melmotte and is forced to cool his heels in Abchurch Lane. Logically he could have bearded Melmotte at any time he wanted, using his own key and the privilege of entry to his own home. The whole machinery of the shared house (and even more so the shared desk) is a forced contrivance. Nor is it worked out consistently. We are told at the beginning of chapter 55 'a fortnight before the election' (i.e., the last week in June) that Melmotte has taken the Longestaffes' Bruton Street house for a month. The reason is that his Grosvenor Square mansion has to be fitted out for the great dinner. But in chapter 49 (30 June, by the novel's calendar) Marie is still living at Grosvenor Square. And in chapter 50 (July 4) it is evidently to Grosvenor Square and her indignant family that Marie is returned after the elopement fiasco. On July 5 (chapter 56), however, we understand that Grosvenor Square is suddenly uninhabitable from workmen being employed there. As with the uncertain chronology, this confusion does not break the plot down. But it creates areas of vagueness. And I would suggest that Trollope may have pushed himself too hard at this phase of composition. After his rest in September Trollope returned apparently refreshed to the novel. He wrote the concluding numbers more slowly and to judge by the MS without any of the earlier strain.

IV

THE TIME-SCHEME of *The Way We Live Now* is very close and somewhat controversial. As Bert Hornback has pointed out, 98 of the novel's 100 chapters occupy February–September 1872 and 'forty-five days account for sixty-six of the novel's chapters.' Hornback goes on to argue that Trollope must have guided himself through the tangle of his multiplot novel by constant reference to an 1872 calendar.[16] In an answering article P. D. Edwards refuted this alleged recourse to a mechanical aid. Trollope, he pointed out, made up his own calendar for the novel's main events and incorporated it into his list of chapter titles for the novel.[17] Since one knows that titling was one of the last of Trollope's acts of composition, it is certain that he made this list (which again seems to have been written at one sitting) after the novel was complete. From the way the dates are cramped in alongside the chapter titles, however, it is evident that he must have inserted them later presumably while he was checking the novel and weeding out errors before dispatching it to Chapman & Hall. It is worth noting that the list of chapter titles is still headed 'Carbury Novel' with a trial title off to one side of 'The life we live now.'

It would seem that Trollope made more or less rough calculations as he went along. His calendar for the novel's action was at points fairly elastic. Thus against chapter 43, 'The City Road', he writes, 'say Wednesday 26.' Nor is he punctilious where he doesn't have to be. For the last number he gives only one time marker, specifying the collapse of the Bear Garden as occurring on 10 August. On the back of this chapter and date list Trollope made out a day-by-day table from Wednesday July 17 to Tuesday September 16. In it he inserted a few plot events but apparently gave up using it almost immediately. There also survives one substantial set of pencilled jottings in a spare column of the ink-written chapter and date list:

Lady Carbury's elopement
Melmotte had arrived within the last 12 months.
page 21 ? can this be altered?
12 months? 24
Melmotte's house south side of the square
Melmotte has been in prison at Hamburgh.

The reference is obviously to chapters 2 and 4. Lady Carbury's possible adultery was a delicate matter for Trollope. He brings it up in the text, but after airing the possibility of infidelity, concludes that it is none of the reader's business to know. In chapter 4 we learn that Melmotte's house is on the south side of Grosvenor Square (in later sections of the novel Trollope forgets himself and makes it Portman Square). Melmotte's adventures in Hamburg are withheld until much later in the novel—but clearly Trollope wanted a criminal aura to be present from the first.

One can decipher the meaning of the date-memoranda by reference to 1/38 (p. 28) of the MS, where Trollope wrote:

The giver of the ball was Augustus Melmotte, Esq., the father of the girl whom Sir Felix Carbury desired to marry and the husband of the lady who was said to have been [an Italian] [crossed out, 'a Bohemian' added] Jewess. It was thus that the gentleman chose to have himself designated, though within the last twelvemonth he had arrived in London from Paris.

In the printed version of the novel the last sentence reads: 'though within the last two years.' It must have struck Trollope while reading the proofs (when these notes were made) that even Melmotte could not have won over English society in twelve months. It is probable that Trollope made many such fugitive notes on these lines at every stage of composition and revision. This survives only because it is attached to a more substantial working paper.

On the folder in which he kept the papers for his novel Trollope wrote: 'Commenced 1 May 1873. Finished 22 Dec. 1873.' For Trollope, then, the work was effectively finished when he sent the MS off to the publisher, not when he had corrected proofs. The proofs of *The Way We Live Now* have not (as far as I know) survived. And it is unlikely that they would be very informative if they had. As has been said, he did not take this opportunity to improve his novel. And in this forbearance he is very different from his idol Thackeray. The novel did not apparently sell well.[18] There were subsequent cheap editions during the few years of life that remained to Trollope, but he did not apparently revise the novel for reissue (as he did earlier with *The Three Clerks*, for instance).

The conclusion one draws is obvious enough. Trollope's secretarial exactitude and the aggressive account he gives of it in the *Autobiography* have masked the substantial creative effort which went into his fiction. And on the evidence of the plans which have survived one needs perhaps to be sceptical of the novelist's own protestations of unpreparedness. Trollope's self-deprecating description of himself charging at his plot like a horseman at a fence he cannot see does not stand up in the light of the working materials which have survived for *The Way We Live Now*.

CHAPTER SEVEN

Miss Bretherton, Miss Brown, and Miss Rooth

ACCORDING to the trumpeter Miles Davis, reflecting on his career shortly before his death, 'it takes a long time before you can play like yourself'. All artists, it is safe to say, start by imitation. Most never break through the initial bondage to the style of others. Mary Ward (*née* Arnold, better known to posterity as Mrs Humphry Ward)— the niece of Matthew Arnold and the aunt of Aldous Huxley—knew, almost from her earliest conscious moment, that she was born to be a writer. From her earliest stages of childhood literacy she also apprehended that she was to be a writer of fiction.[1] But as with many writers, the urge to write was accompanied by an uncertainty of how she should write. Whom should she imitate in order to become, eventually, herself? The answer came when she and her husband (the thoroughly eclipsed Humphry) moved to London from Oxford in 1881. London was a larger world where they enjoyed a vastly expanded social life and cultural stimulus. More particularly, Ward's discovery of what her bearings should be in fiction came with her introduction to Henry James. He became her master. Her eventual liberation into the kind of fiction with which she was to become the bestselling author of her day came with her subsequent (and commendably pragmatic) repudiation of the Jamesian model.

Mary Ward first met 'beloved Henry James' at a dinner party given by the man of letters, Andrew Lang, in 1882. The novelist was in his early forties and *The Portrait of a Lady* had recently finished its run in *Macmillan's Magazine*. They took to each other and embarked on what was to be a lifelong friendship (palpably warmer on her side than his). Almost immediately, James began to influence Ward's ideas on literature. There survives in one of Ward's early notebooks (which also contains the opening chapters of *Miss Bretherton*) the 'sketch of an article' outlining Ward's views on the art of fiction in 1883. The draft essay hails the 'rise of a new school of fiction' in America. James is 'the head of the school' and W. D. Howells its 'most characteristic representative'. Ward had evidently recently saturated herself in the novels of the 'young nation', devouring the works of Hawthorne, Thoreau (whom she seems to have considered a novelist, interestingly enough), Harte and Cable. She claimed in her enthusiasm for things transatlantic to relish even the works of the new world's 'bad' and 'second-rate' writers. American writers, in mass, were more 'joyous' that the Russians, she discovered, and more palatable (i.e. moral) than the French. 'How different', she asserted, 'are the works of James and his fellow-Americans from French realism which [is] like a last despairing effort to feel [and] to get sensation at any cost—the art of the decadence one feels with no promise in it. Whereas this American art has the promise of the morning in it.'[2] *Miss Bretherton*—Ward's 'first serious attempt at a novel'—was to be a homage to James and his 'art of the morning'.

On his side, James got slightly less from the relationship (although *Miss Bretherton* was to provoke one of his finest mid-career works, *The Tragic Muse*). James looms as the tutelary spirit in Ward's autobiographical *Recollections*.[3] His relationship with the Wards supplies only a few footnotes and a couple of incidental pages in Leon Edel's massive biography.[4] It was not an overwhelmingly important aspect of his life. He evidently enjoyed visiting 61 Russell Square, where the Wards lived in the 1880s, and where Mrs Humphry Ward held her famous Thursday afternoon tea-salons. James took an avuncular interest in the early authorial strivings of his young friend, and encouraged her. She was, she claimed, twelve years his junior (in fact it was nearer eight years), and eagerly accepted the pupil's role as she had earlier at Oxford with the charismatic don, Mark Pattison. What James principally got from the Wards in the 1880s was some good food, some good dinner conversation, distinguished company, and useful material for his fiction. It was at the Wards' table, for instance, that he first met Matthew Arnold socially. Privately, he was often mystified by Mary Ward and hints in his letters suggest he may have had some doubts about her intelligence. When, within two years of being his devoted pupil, she had bounded to the class of the £10,000 a year novelists, he may even have felt some twinges of envy.[5]

II

THE DIRECT INSPIRATION for *Miss Bretherton* was the sensation caused by the 23-year-old American actress, Mary Anderson, with her first English season at Henry Irving's Lyceum theatre, in September 1883. Anderson's father had been killed in the Civil War when she was eight. As a convent schoolgirl she had conceived a burning desire to be an actress which overrode all opposition from her family and guardians. Her debut, aged 16, in the part of Juliet in her home town of Louisville, was judged sensational. Having conquered New York, in spring 1883 she set off (her mother and stepfather in attendance) for the old world. Anderson was stunningly beautiful but as English reviewers complained, a very limited actress—at least by European standards. Her opening performance as the female lead in *Ingomar* was virtually inaudible and physically clumsy. But the theatre was packed nightly by audiences happy just to see the American girl with the lovely face and figure.

Ward leaves a precise recollection of the *donnée* for *Miss Bretherton*. She and her husband (together with James and Ward's companion, Gertrude Bell) had entertained Anderson (now the toast of the town) at Russell Square, on 30 January 1884. They found her a charming guest. Afterwards, at the actress's particular invitation, they had gone to see her perform in W. S. Gilbert's *Comedy and Tragedy*, at the Lyceum. The part had originally been for the more accomplished Kate Terry. Gilbert's play was a costume melodrama, similar in most points to 'The White Lady', which Ward invents in chapter 3 of her novel.

In her diary, Gertrude Bell records the party's disappointment: 'We all agreed that her part was grievously overdone; too excited, too loud, too restless, no self-control, no dignity, no self-expression.' And James, who was also in the box provided by the luckless actress, 'raved over what he called Miss Anderson's "hysterics".'[6] A couple of days afterwards, in Tottenham Court Road, Ward informed Bell that the occasion had furnished her with the idea for a novel—her first novel, as it would be. Appropriately for a first work, it would be a study of artistic apprenticeship reflecting—it is plausible to assume—the complex mixture of inspirations she had experienced from the American *ingénue*, Anderson, and the American *maître*, James. At this stage, Ward evidently expected to publish it as a serial in *Macmillan's Magazine*, a journal which had published many of her non-fictional essays. She selected the same name for her heroine as James in *The Portrait of a Lady* (also a *Macmillan's* serial)—Isabel. It is a touching piece of authorial *naïveté*.

The Ward-James party's perplexed reaction to Anderson's acting was not unique. Anticipating the idea of *Miss Bretherton*'s plot with uncanny exactness, the *Athenaeum* reviewer of *Comedy and Tragedy* observed that:

Pleasing as it is Miss Anderson's art has always had a certain crudeness . . .

Matters are now changed . . . Her histrionic gait is, so to speak, unsteady, and her method scarcely formed. The power is, however, genuine, and the capacity to grip an audience, to stir it with emotion, and melt it into pathos, is established. What now seems necessary to make an excellent Parthenia, and a delightful Galatea, a Juliet, a Phèdre, a Hecuba, is that ripening influence of passion and suffering which, even in the interest of art, it would be cruel to wish an actress. (2 February 1884)

It is noteworthy that between September 1883 and February 1884 Anderson had advanced in her craft from sheer, inaudible, incompetence. The sense of an actress struggling painfully to emerge from the awkwardness of the merely beautiful girl struck Ward. In her novel, she supplies the 'necessary . . . ripening influence of passion and suffering'.

Ward evidently let her idea ripen and discussed it in conversations with James. There is an entry in his notebook for 19 June 1884, which indicates that at the pre-composition stage, the main structure of *Miss Bretherton* was in place:

Mrs H. Ward mentioned the other day an idea of hers for a story which might be made interesting—as a study of histrionic character. A young actress is an object of much attention and a great deal of criticism from a man who loves the stage (he oughtn't to be a *professional* critic) and finally, though she doesn't satisfy him at all, artistically, loves the girl herself. He thinks something may be made of her, though he doesn't quite see what: he works over her, gives her ideas, etc. Finally (she is slow in developing, though full of ambition), she takes one, and begins to mount, to become a celebrity. She goes beyond him, she leaves him looking after her and wondering. She begins where he ends—soars away and is lost to him. The interest, I say, would be as a study of a certain *nature d'actrice*: a very curious sort of nature to reproduce. The girl I see to be very crude, etc. The thing a confirmation of Mrs Kemble's theory that the dramatic gift is a thing by itself—implying of necessity no *general* superiority of mind. The strong nature, the personal quality, vanity, etc., of the girl: her artistic being, so vivid, yet so purely instinctive. Ignorant, illiterate. Rachel.[7]

It is clear that James had been more than a mere sounding board for Mrs Ward's idea. He had let his own imagination loose on the project, doubtless communicating a sense to her of how her story should be developed—how one should, in his phrase, 'do the actress'. And, in light of later developments, it is worth highlighting the poignant conclusion James foresaw—'she goes beyond him, she leaves him looking after her and wondering. She begins where he ends—soars away and is lost to him.' As in *Portrait of a Lady*, the reader was to be left with an *amari aliquid*, a touch of bitterness, something 'tragic'. Having nurtured the plot in her mind for six months, Ward wrote *Miss Bretherton* in a creative rush in August and early September 1884. According to Gertrude Bell, composition lasted:

about six weeks. She used to lie or sit out of doors at Borough Farm [in Surrey, where the Ward family adjourned to in the heat of the London summer] with a notebook and pencil, and scrawl down what she could with her left hand [although she had chronic writer's cramp, most of the notebook draft is in fact written with Ward's right hand, Bell is evidently embroidering] then she would come in about twelve and dictate to me at great rage for an hour or more. In the afternoon and evening she would look over and correct what was done, and I copied out the whole. The scene of Marie and Kendal in his rooms [at the end of chapter 7] was dictated in her bedroom; she lay on her bed, and I sat by the window behind a screen.[8]

Bell's fair copy of *Miss Bretherton* was first submitted to John Morley for consideration as a serial for *Macmillan's Magazine*. He returned it on 10 October observing that 'as a study it is a success; it is the analysis of an interesting and attractive character . . . But there is not story enough.' It would not do for the magazine. But while rejecting *Miss Bretherton* as too eventless for a serial, Morley endorsed it as a candidate for volume publication. It was duly passed on to another Macmillan's editor, Henry Craik. Having read the work, Craik accepted *Miss Bretherton* on 12 October, offering half-profits and adding, 'whether there is profit or not we shall pay you £50.'[9] The work should be published in one volume, running to 310 pages.

Macmillan's terms were not obviously munificent. But they indicated considerable trust on the publisher's part. Ward had earlier received from them an advance of £250 for a work of criticism on French literature not yet started and an advance of £50 for a translation of Amiel's *Journal* as yet incomplete. Enthusiastically proposed works on English poetry and Spanish literature had fallen by the wayside. She had produced one volume of children's stories which had been published but was a long way from recovering its costs. In the circumstances, Macmillan's offer was generous.

Miss Bretherton went speedily into print (Victorian production timetables would make a modern author green with envy). On 4 November 1884 (less than three weeks after acceptance) Ward approved the binding and sent back the finally corrected proofs, over which the author had laboured less than was to be her subsequent practice. There was, in fact, some minor panic over the cover. On 21 November Frederick Macmillan wrote that 'I have heard on very good authority what I did not know before viz. that Mudie [the 'leviathan' of the London circulating libraries] has a very strong objection to books lettered in black and as he is a rather crotchety person he is just as likely as not to buy as few as possible of *Miss Bretherton* if we stick to the black letters.'[10] This captiousness doubtless fortified Ward in her efforts, ten years later, to break Mudie's monopoly with *Marcella.*[11]

Ward was eager to hurry on to publication and meaningfully informed Macmillan that 'between ourselves—a review in the *Times* would be much more probable this month than next.'[12] Humphry Ward was, of course, a senior journalist on *The Times* and had the ear of the literary editor. Macmillan assured her that 'not a moment of needless delay will take place'. He was as good as his word and the novel was published in the last days of November. 'I wish we could have got the book out sooner,' Craik wrote, 'but we tried our best.'[13] Six weeks from still-to-be-accepted manuscript to publication day was considered foot-dragging in 1884. Macmillan gave the novel top billing in their Christmas advertisements.

Even to the most sympathetic reader, *Miss Bretherton*, as Morley objected, has too little story and too much of the would-be Jamesian *étude*. It opens, effectively enough, at the Royal Academy private view of May 1883. The cosmopolitan *littérateur*, Eustace Kendal, is struck by the beauty of a young woman in one of the crowded galleries. Forbes, an artist friend, tells him it is an actress newly arrived from the West Indies, Isabel Bretherton, the current toast of the English stage. Kendal subsequently contrives to meet Isabel at an afternoon party given by the American hostess, Mrs Stuart. He joins the Stuarts in a box at the 'Calliope' theatre where Isabel is playing the lead in *The White Lady*. It is a sad let-down. As an actress Miss Bretherton has 'physical charm' but no expertise, nor any intellectual awareness of dramatic tradition. Isabel also as yet has no sense of her inadequacy and offers herself for the main part in *Elvira* which Kendal's friend Wallace (clearly based on Henry James) has just written. Kendal undertakes to dissuade her from requesting the part at Oxford, where she has come for the day. Isabel, who whatever her dramaturgical inadequacies is not lacking in sensitivity off-stage, sees through Kendal's delicate insinuations. She forces him to pronounce his true critical opinion of her talent. 'What is it I want? What is it that seems to be threatening me with failure as an artist?'

'What you want,' he said slowly, as if the words were forced from him, 'is *knowledge!* London has taught you much, and that is why you are dissatisfied with your work—it is the beginning of all real success. But you want positive knowledge—the knowledge you could get from books, and the knowledge other people could teach you. You want a true sense of what has been done and what can be done with your art, and you want an insight into the world of ideas lying round it and about it. You are very young, and you have had to train yourself. But every human art nowadays is so complicated that none of us can get on without using the great stores of experience others have laid up for us.'[14]

In passing, one should note that Ward was addicted to introducing her mentors into her fiction, thinly disguised and with the utterances they had actually made in response to her dutiful requests for advice. (See, for instance, Mark Pattison and the philosopher, T. H. Green, who appear as Roger Wendover and Professor Grey respectively in *Robert Elsmere*.) It is very likely that the encounter of Kendal and Isabel at Oxford, and his wise but bracing counsel, records actual exchanges with James and his verdict on her early efforts in fiction and her ardent wish to succeed in it. I would guess that it was James's advice that launched her on the orgy of reading American, French, and Russian fiction of which the residue is the uncompleted article described above.

Kendal's honesty is a death sentence to any hopes of winning Isabel's heart. But his duty as a critic is imperative. At the end of the season, the now unvalued applause of the English philistines ringing in her ears, Isabel leaves for the Continent. There she is taken up by Eustace Kendal's sister, Madame Marie de Chateauvieux. Under this good and cultivated woman's guidance, Isabel learns French and laboriously trains herself in that culture's superior acting techniques (this section of the story is awkwardly narrated by letters). In six months she returns to London, and wins a triumph in Wallace's play for which she is now genuinely equipped. It is not merely the multitude but the connoisseurs who applaud:

She had passed the barrier which once existed between her and the world which knows and thinks, and been drawn within that circle of individualities which, however undefined, is still the vital circle of any time or society, for it is the circle which represents, more or less brilliantly and efficiently, the intellectual life of a generation.[15]

A reconciliation between Kendal and Isabel is effected by Madame de Chateauvieux, dying vaguely of a 'chill', who entrusts her brother with a memento for Isabel. At the necessary meeting, all obstructions melt away and the novel ends with the lovers' embrace. Art and criticism are reconciled in their prospective marriage.

III

Miss Bretherton survives in two versions. The first is the notebook-pencil draft that Bell describes Ward writing out-of-doors at Borough Farm. This, apparently, represents first thoughts and ideas. The second version is the published text which incorporates various revisions and corrections made to Bell as amanuensis. The notebook *Miss Bretherton* is divided into 'parts' rather than the chapters of the printed version (these 'parts' presumably correspond to the serial divisions that Ward foresaw).

The opening scene (which remains the best thing in both versions) is generally identical in both drafts of *Miss Bretherton*. But originally, Isabel was 'American'. It is a telling alteration. The second section of the narrative, which covers the visit to the theatre, is substantially altered. The first version records more honestly the Ward–James party's disgust at Anderson's performance in *Comedy and Tragedy*. The play Isabel stars in is more closely identifiable with Gilbert's piece and she is quite simply inept: 'a half-educated beauty, playing a rôle of which she had no real conception whatever and struggling with an art of which she barely knew the rudiments.' Ward evidently toned this down to spare Anderson's feelings. In the novel as it was published, Isabel shows latent genius, as yet undeveloped. Her performance is by no means a disgrace, merely technically imperfect.

The first *Miss Bretherton* omits entirely the Oxford interlude in which, against the setting of the river at Nuneham, Kendal the critic dashes the hopes of Kendal the lover by exposing Isabel's immaturities to her. In the first version of the novel Isabel's performance in *The White Lady* is her farewell for the season and is followed immediately by 'Part 3'. There were, evidently, to be only four parts, the fourth being made up of Marie's account of Isabel's initiation into the finer points of her profession at Venice. The draft ends abruptly with a torn-out page, just before Isabel's triumphant return to the London boards with *Eloise*.

The expansion of the narrative and the toning down of the awfulness of Isabel's acting style make for a more subtle study of character. But the alteration of her national origin from American to West Indian of Scottish extraction also witnesses to a loss of nerve. It sidesteps what would have been an exploration of James's 'international theme', the collision of American energy and European sophistication. The changes also led to problems of size and proportion. As enlarged, *Miss Bretherton* remains awkwardly poised between inflated short story and novel. How to edit her own fiction was to be a major problem for the rest of Ward's writing career.[16] She was never further from a satisfactory solution than in *Miss Bretherton* which, as published, drags painfully in its later sections, relatively short though the whole thing is.

Miss Bretherton has other faults, some of which Ward candidly admitted in her 1909 preface. It shows, all too clearly, the 'first effect of London on academic inexperience'.[17] The novelist was girlishly dazzled by the new metropolitan world of private views, literary dinners, and first nights. And the whole conception of *Miss Bretherton* is suffused with the Arnoldian snobbishness by which the judgement of the discriminating few (with whom the novelist clearly feels natural kinship) is paramount over the philistine preference of the general population (the readers Ward wished to entice into buying or borrowing her novel). Things French are automatically better than anything that provincial England can supply. There might be some truth in this, but the Great British Public has never cared to hear it.

Like her heroine, Ward always felt herself performing for two audiences; the great mass of novel readers and the 'circle which knows and thinks', represented by the friends to whom she proudly sent pre-publication copies of *Miss Bretherton*. The knowledgeable inner circle of artists, dons, and politicians (James, Walter Pater, Mandell Creighton, John Morley, Sir Henry Taylor, Edmond Scherer) were unanimous in their praise for *Miss Bretherton*. Published reviews of the novel were mixed and in some cases less than gratifying. The *Pall Mall Gazette* was exceptionally hostile. *The Times* loyally declared itself 'impressed throughout by the refinement and the evidence of culture which underlie the book', and the scarcely less friendly *Manchester Guardian* (on which Mary's brother William Arnold was the literary editor) noted that 'into the seductive form of a single-volume novel Mrs Humphry Ward has cleverly thrown a great deal of excellent dramatic criticism'. Both these plaudits were used prominently in Macmillan's subsequent advertising for the book.

Indifference and general neglect were, however, the principal responses to *Miss Bretherton* in the London prints. The unkindest review was in the *Athenaeum* (where unluckily Mary Ward did not have a close relative on the staff), which was curt to the point of insult:

The main interest of Mrs Ward's novel lies in the fact that it is all about Miss Mary Anderson. Whether the picture is true to life or mostly fanciful is a question of no moment. In either case it will satisfy those readers who like prying into the private life of an actress, while those who look for some touch of art in fiction will be disappointed. Though the book is well written and is obviously the work of a woman of much ability and knowledge, it is not in any true sense a novel. It is merely a talk about Miss Anderson and her friends. (20 December 1884)

An infuriated Mary Ward wrote back to the journal a letter for publication on 27 December roundly asserting that 'Miss Bretherton is not a portrait of any living person whatever. She is an attempt to handle an artistic problem.' The slur that *Miss Bretherton* was no more than gossip fictionalized irritated Ward intensely, and she flatly contradicted the allegation for the next quarter of a century. Over and over she insisted in public 'Isabel Bretherton [is] in no sense a portrait of Miss Anderson'.[18] Given the known circumstances of the work's genesis, and her prudent alterations of the heroine's nationality, Ward's protests were disingenuous. Nor was there much doubt on the topic in her own immediate family circle. Writing to her daughter on 14 December 1884 Mary's mother, Julia Arnold, wondered 'what Mary Anderson feels about [*Miss Bretherton*] now that I suppose she has read the book. With the exception of the unfavourable mention of Miss Bretherton's uncle and aunt which I feel sure she will think is meant for her mother and stepfather there is nothing in the book which ought to annoy her at all.'[19] The letter Mary sent in reply has not survived but one doubts it reiterated: 'Isabel Bretherton [is] in no sense a portrait of Miss Anderson.'

In spite of thin reviews, dismissive comment, and sluggish early sales Ward remained optimistic about *Miss Bretherton*'s long-term sales prospects. Macmillan were less sanguine. On 31 January the publisher advertised a 'second edition'. There was no such edition, it was merely a ruse to clear the unsold bulk of the first printing. Thereafter they ceased advertising the work. On 5 February 1885 Ward asked Craik if they were going to reprint (genuinely) and if anything were yet known about the American sale: 'I am very anxious the book should make some impression there,' she told the publisher.[20] In the same letter she outlined her plans for her next work, *Robert Elsmere* as it was to be: 'I open I may be able to send you a story next October which will be better worth people's interest than this one. I have it all planned, and I shall take, all being well, five quiet months in the country to write it. It will be in two volumes.'[21]

Ward was anxious to get on to this new work. On 26 February 1885 she enlarged on it to Macmillan. The story would be 'altogether a longer and more substantial piece of work than *Miss Bretherton* and its subject will be one of general interest.'[22] She was prepared to sell the novel when completed for £250, subject 'to the resumption of my right in it after 2,000 copies have been sold.' In the same letter, Ward confessed that the £250 advanced for the French literature book weighed on her mind. But the weakness of her hand from writer's cramp made 'all minute critical or historical work so difficult to me . . . that I have been indefinitely thrown back.' The prospect of her finishing the study was now 'a remote one'. Where this left the £250 advance was not clear. Presumably it was to be amortized by profits in the as yet unwritten novel.

Macmillan saw little likelihood of any such profit. Craik wrote back an uncompromisingly factual letter, explaining 'exactly' the position of *Miss Bretherton*. 'We printed 2500. We gave away 71. We have sold 1150. We have sent to America 750. We have on hand 521. The book sells at 6*s*. We gave you £50. We are out of pocket £22.'[23] Nevertheless Craik offered £100 for 750 copies of the new two-volume novel (to sell at 21*s*.), with £40 for every 250 printed above 750. He finished his letter with some stern words of encouragement:

I sincerely hope that you will write a book that will be largely and permanently successful that will repay you in every way. I hope our offer will induce you to go on with heart. You should always remember that your first book [he meant *Miss Bretherton*] has been unusually noticed and spoken about but it perhaps did not deal with matters that were of universal interest. If you write a good book with a generally popular subject the results ought to be better.

A distraught Ward replied: 'I was quite dismayed at the results of *Miss Bretherton*. How do books pay at all if what I suppose is a rather more successful book than usual ends with a deficit of £22? I must still hope that the sale will go on long enough to recoup you. Of course, I cannot expect you to risk much on another book.' Would Ward, though, submit to the logic of the ledgers and accept the hack's price of £100? She would not. Her letter continues: 'At the same time I am sure you will understand the importance of the money side to me and will not think ill of me for having carried my proposal to another publisher, also a friend, who accepted it at once.' She added tartly: 'I can only hope that I shall not always be destined to be a loss to somebody.'[24]

Craik sent what was, in the circumstances, a gracious reply, recording his firm's 'disappointment' and their continuing 'personal interest' in her as a writer. He stoically congratulated her on her new friend: 'I am glad you have been able to get better terms than we could give just because you say it is important you should have money.'[25] George Smith, Craik ventured, 'is a capital publisher, and if you are satisfied, so much the better.'[26] On her part, Ward confessed that, 'I feel very flat about the new novel, mostly I think because of the new hands which are to bring it out. But I can only hope to come back to you some day with more assured prospects. It is most distressing to me that you should have lost on *Miss Bretherton*.'

In fact, Macmillan just about broke even. Between early March and the end of April they sold another 70 copies, which lowered the loss to around £10. And their good nature (together with Ward's genuine affection for her first literary employer) laid the way for later partnerships with Colonial and American editions of her subsequent bestsellers. But Macmillan and Craik must have kicked themselves in 1888 when *Robert Elsmere*, which they had let go, went on to become the most successful novel of the decade, and possibly the century. It would have been £250 well spent. To get merely the American rights for Ward's third novel, *The History of David Grieve*, in 1892 they had to pay a record-breaking £7,000.[27]

One has to ask why, given the reception of *Miss Bretherton*, Ward resolved to continue as a novelist. The public had spoken and it did not much care for her work, even enough to return the £50 pittance which Macmillan had given her. Macmillan clearly enough did not like *Miss Bretherton* well enough to bid realistically for its successor. In the past, Ward had readily learned the lessons of literary failure: *Milly and Olly* (1880) did not sell, so she wrote no more children's stories. But she was determined to the point of doggedness where her unwritten two-volume, five-month work was concerned. (Eventually, it would take her a gruelling 27 months, and occupy three, over-packed volumes.) The subsequent months of composition, in which Smith, Elder & Co. gave her scant encouragement, must have been a dark period for her. She did not hear it directly, but Uncle Matt's (Matthew Arnold's) comment about *Miss Bretherton* must have tormented her: 'She cannot write a novel. No Arnold could write one; otherwise I should have done it myself.'

The period 1885–7 more than any other period of Ward's life shows her at her artistic toughest. As she told her contemporary, the feminist Frances Cobbe, the years during which *Robert Elsmere* was written destroyed its author's health for the rest of her life. Isabel Bretherton had it easy by comparison with her creator. Ward had no clear need to make this sacrifice. As the wife of Humphry Ward (rising journalist and art critic), the niece of Matthew Arnold, a respected woman of letters and bluestocking in her own right, and a distinguished London hostess, she led what everyone must have conceded to be a fulfilling and enviable life. But she determined that, cost what it might, she must be a novelist. The cost was to be high.

IV

ONE THING THAT clearly sustained Ward during this grim period was the support of James. He expressed his magisterial approbation in a letter of 9 December 1884, when the fact that *Miss Bretherton* was not, after all, going to set the Thames on fire had finally sunk in. His remarks are wonderfully diplomatic and judicious. Even after a century, one can imagine their soothing balm on the inflamed self-esteem of Mary Ward. The letter evidently followed a conversation on the novel:

Dear Mrs Ward—There was more I wanted to say about *Miss Bretherton*. I read it with much interest and pleasure—it is very refined and *senti* (on your part) and contains a great deal of charming, suggestive writing. Very charming indeed is the scene between Isabel and Kendal on the Oxford excursion, and very touching and human many other passages—especially the description of Mme. de C's death. The whole thing is delicate and distinguished, and the reader has the pleasure and security of feeling that he is with a woman (distinctly with a woman!) who knows how (rare bird!) to write. I think your idea, your situation interesting in a high degree, and

I further think that you have drawn many of the notes of its meaning, its beauty.

From the novelist whom above all others she revered, this was praise worth having. But James—whilst proffering this reassurance that she was indeed a writer with a future—branched meaningfully into how *he* would have dealt with the theme. More particularly, he returned to that all important detail which he had elaborated on in his notebook scenario of June 1884—namely the ending. In James's vision of how the theme should be treated *Miss Bretherton* should have ended with separation, not happy-ever-after reunion:

I am afraid I have a certain reputation for being censorious [he told Mrs Ward]: let me therefore profit by it with you and insist on one or two points in which I should have liked your story to be a little different; or at least upon *one*. I am capable of wishing that the actress might have been carried away from Kendal altogether, carried away by the current of her artistic life, the sudden growth of her power, and the excitement, the ferocity and egotism (those of the artist realizing success, I mean; I allude merely to the natural normal dose of those elements) which the effort to create, to 'arrive' (once one had had a glimpse of her possible successes) would have brought with it. (Excuse that abominable sentence.) Isabel, the Isabel you describe, has too much to spare for Kendal—Kendal being what he is; and one doesn't feel her, see her, enough, as the pushing actress, the *cabotine*. She lapses toward him as if she were a failure, whereas you make her out a great success . . . The granting that she cared to marry Kendal, you overlook too much, I think (but this I said to you), the problem of a union between two such opposed lives, and how her blaze etc., with all its vulgarities, would appear to him, keep him off. Also how the concessions she would have to make to his tone and his *type* would alarm her, hungry for more fame and success. I should have made her pass away from him—with hopes (on his part perhaps) of catching up with her later. I think your end has a little too much of the conventional love-story: though granted your view is very pretty indeed.[28]

The implication here is clear enough; Mrs Ward had made her story a study in too cosy a muse. The notion that one could achieve greatness in one's art and have the consolations of marital love and companionship was 'pretty'—but unreal. It was at this period that James was firmly putting down rumours that he was intending to marry. 'I think I shall take a house,' he told his American friend Elizabeth Boott in December 1883, 'but there is no hurry, and when I do a conjugal Mrs H[enry] is not among the articles that I shall put into it.'[29] His comments in his letter to the author of *Miss Bretherton* might also be construed that no one aggressively titling herself 'Mrs Humphry Ward'—a 'conjugal Mrs H.' if ever there was one—could ever aspire to be a great artist.

Ward regarded James's letter to her as marking 'a white stone . . . the first landmark in our long friendship'. His praise doubtless kept her going through the defeat of her hopes for her first novel and over the next three wretched years as she laboured on her second. But, for all her adulation, Ward had clearly decided that the Jamesian line of high fictional art was not the one that she should follow if she wanted to succeed. Other friends—Craik as we have seen, and the historian Mandell Creighton whom she admired above all men—urged her to try for 'popularity', a more traditional, melodramatic mode of fiction. *Miss Bretherton* was a Jamesian *étude* with some reverential liftings from *The Portrait of a Lady*. For the new novel, Ward turned to a bestseller of 1883, Walter Besant's *All Sorts and Conditions of Men*, a work dedicated to the establishment of a 'People's Palace' for the virtuous recreation of the poor in the East End of London, as *Robert Elsmere* is dedicated to the establishment of a settlement in the same slums. (Both novels succeeded in the establishment of the institutions they outlined, although Elsmere's 'settlement'—the 'Mary Ward Centre' as it now is—set itself up in the slums of St Pancras.) Ward, sensibly enough, decided that her literary future lay not in Jamesian art but in useful romance for the millions. It made her, for a decade, the richest novelist in England. She was never to write a novel that wholly pleased James (to whose judgement she continued to refer her work) but she outsold him ten-to-one.

Oddly enough, at exactly the same period, the last months of 1884, there appeared another novel inspired by Henry James, with remarkable resemblances to *Miss Bretherton*. Vernon Lee (i.e. Violet Paget, 1856–1935) was another self-confessed disciple of the author of *The Portrait of a Lady*. Lee had received encouragement from James, who admired her cosmopolitanism and her writings on Italy. One of Lee's earliest meetings with James was at a soirée given by Mr and Mrs Humphry Ward, in summer 1884—exactly the period when Mrs Ward was meditating her 'first serious attempt at a novel'. (Lee seems to have found the Wards rather dull, and the American novelist entrancing.) The very first meeting of Lee and James may well, it seems, have taken place at the National Gallery, anticipating the opening scenes of both *Miss Bretherton* and *The Tragic Muse*.[30] Lee's novel, *Miss Brown*, like *Miss Bretherton*, was written as a consciously apprentice piece for his masterly approval. The novel (which runs to three volumes) is the story of Anne Brown, an *ingénue* taken up by a bored artist and poet, Walter Hamlin, who sets out to make her his ideal beautiful woman. Miss Brown finally marries Hamlin, with the most dreadful auguries. Against his wishes, Lee dedicated her novel to James, with the flourish, 'TO HENRY JAMES I DEDICATE FOR GOOD LUCK, MY FIRST ATTEMPT AT A NOVEL'.

Although he was courteous to her face when told of the novel's impending publication and his name on its dedication page, James was savage on the subject in a letter of 24 January 1885 to Grace Norton:

Has the fame of the unfortunate *Miss Brown* reached the U.S.A.? Such is the title of a disagreeable and really very unpleasant novel dedicated to me, by Vernon Lee, which appeared here a couple of months since, and about which I haven't yet been able to bring myself to write to the authoress, though my delay, in view of the dedication, and the first copy being sent me, is scandalous. You probably know that Vernon Lee is the pen-name of a certain astounding young woman named Violet Paget, who lives in Florence, spends part of her time here, and has written two or three very imperfect but very able and interesting books on the Italian Renaissance . . . She has not the kind of ability that a novel requires, and *Miss Brown* is a rather serious mistake (I think); still, with an awful want of taste and of tact, you will say of *decency*—it yet has *du bon*, and is an interesting failure, if an unsavoury one.[31]

Miss Brown and *Miss Bretherton* were both, in their ways, interesting failures. And it was a singular coincidence that two fascinating young women (Ward was 33, Lee 28) had written two 'first attempts at novels' about aspirant young women consciously to please James, and with extraordinarily similar titles and themes. James was dissatisfied with both tributes. His mind evidently revolved how these two works might be rewritten, and merged. The fusion seems to have resulted in the Miss Rooth plot of *The Tragic Muse*.

James evidently made his first serious mention of this novel in 1887. It was eventually published as a long serial in the *Atlantic Monthly*, January 1889–March 1890. Even without the *Miss Bretherton–Miss Brown* coincidence, there were other things to keep Miss Anderson in James's mind. During the late 1880s, the actress did—as Mrs Ward had none-too-subtly recommended—study in Europe and had laboured to improve her craft. She was acknowledged to have grown as an artist in the intervening years. But Anderson was evidently torn by the divergent pressures of art and life, her public and private selves. In 1889, she had a nervous breakdown. In 1890, she married a rich friend of James's, Antonio F. de Navarro, and gave up the stage for good. Her professional wardrobe was sold off with great fanfare.

In *The Tragic Muse* James evidently resolved to 'do the actress' and examine the 'histrionic temperament' as had Ward in her first novel. In the Nicholas Dormer–Miriam Rooth subplot (in which she serves as his artist's model) he may well have also intended to 'do' Vernon Lee's theme in *Miss Brown*. It was, however, Ward who preoccupied him more. He valued her higher than Lee as a writer. Moreover, she had—since writing *Miss Bretherton*—risen phenomenally. She was now the best-paid writer in the world. James, meanwhile, was beginning to feel acutely the slimness of his own literary earnings. *The Tragic Muse* is the kind of novel that Ward did not write in *Miss Bretherton* and despite her new riches, *could* never write. Put another way, James may have been consoling himself by showing his superior skills applied to the same materials as in the work of the former apprentice who had—in the world's crass measurement of such things—outstripped him. At crucial points, James's narrative seems almost ostentatiously to allude to Ward's, to pick up her novel and do it differently and better. *The Tragic Muse* opens, like *Miss Bretherton*, with a brilliantly described art exhibition and the dizzying hub-bub of conversation such occasions generate. As in *Miss Bretherton*, the actress Miss Rooth is gauche and possessed of only a 'rude force' and a stunningly beautiful face. She is coached into the higher mysteries of her craft by the veteran French *actrice*, Madame Carré (whose laconic sarcasms on Miriam's amateurism James captures perfectly). This directly parallels Isabel's tuition under Madame de Chateauvieux. The narrative climaxes with a version of the encounter at the Wards with Anderson at Russell Square in September 1884. In the novel, after tea, Miss Rooth insists the company comes to see her perform in Juliet (the part with which the juvenile Anderson was indelibly associated.) Like Isabel in *Elvira*, it is a triumph. But unlike *Miss Bretherton*, with its flawed conclusion, there is no 'pretty' or 'conventional' ending. Miriam, it transpires, has made a marriage of convenience—more in the nature of a partnership—with her fellow-actor and would-be manager, Dashwood.

James's point, and it is not easily grasped, is that in a Faustian fashion actors and actresses have to give up their essential humanity if they are to reach the heights. Or, as James puts it in his 1908 preface to *The Tragic Muse*: 'the trade of the stage-player, and above all of the actress, must have so many detestable sides for the person exercising it that we scarce imagine a full surrender to it without a full surrender, no less, to every immediate compensation, to every freedom.' Among which, presumably, is the freedom to fall in love as does Isabel with Kendal, and as the artistically tougher Miriam declines to do with Peter Sherringham.

There is no question that *The Tragic Muse* is by far a better novel than those that it seems to be answering, and censuring. Taking the three works together offers a glimpse into the master–apprentice relationships underlying the production of Victorian novels (relationships in which, for complex reasons, masters could be provoked into rivalrous reaction). The three texts also offer an insight into the ways in which Victorian novels conversed with each other. Miss Rooth is a richer and more interesting creation in company with her generally disregarded predecessors, Miss Bretherton and Miss Brown, but they are all three sisters under the skin.

CHAPTER EIGHT

The Victorian Novelists: Who were they?

AWARENESS of Victorian fiction as an industry is uncommon, even at the level of parenthesis or historical backing to scholarly discussion of canonical texts. And generalizations about 'the Victorian novel' (which are common enough) are often hobbled by their being restricted in range of reference to the dozen writers designated as 'major' by the *New Cambridge Bibliography of English Literature*—writers whose extraordinary literary distinction renders them necessarily unrepresentative. Despite fifty years of intense, academically-sponsored research into the form, we still make do with only the sketchiest sense of the infrastructure of Victorian fiction—how the bulk of it was produced; who originated, reproduced, distributed and consumed the product. For most critics, commentators and readers, the Victorian novel is something that appears quite magically on the library shelf, or in the 'Literary Classics' section of the bookshop, found, as it were, under the gooseberry bush, the fruit of Dickens's 'genius' or George Eliot's 'moral sensibility' or Thackeray's 'satire' or Henry James's 'art'.

Statistics are an initial area of vagueness. In his monumental *Nineteenth-Century Fiction, A Bibliographical Catalogue* (5 vols, 1982–86), R. L. Wolff estimates that there are some 42,000 published Victorian novels of which—aiming at completeness—he contrived to collect 7,000. The annual statistics of the trade journal the *Publisher's Circular*, 1837–1901, suggest that total book production rose annually from 2,000 to 8,000 new titles over the Victorian period, and that the proportion of fiction concurrently rose from around 12 per cent to about 25 per cent (the increase being largely explained by the recruitment of new reading publics, particularly after the Education Act of 1870). Assuming exponential progressions for both figures over the 64 years, one arrives at a probable total output of around 50,000 novels. But exactness is impossible, given the fuzzy borders of fiction where it shades into religious-tract, educational and ephemeral periodical reading matter. Around 50,000 is, however, at this stage, a good ball-park figure to start from. When the promised 'History of the Book in Britain' project has done its work we shall know more precisely.[1]

This chapter is concerned less with bibliometrics than with the human infrastructure of Victorian fiction, namely the novelists, those largely invisible masses that Dickens called 'my fellow labourers'. Given an average output of 17 novels per novelist (for the justification of this figure, see below), a work-force of around 3,500 may be hazarded. Given an average working life for novelists of around 32 years (see below again), and the fact that many novelists qualify with only work of fiction, it is a fair guess that two such working forces would populate the period, with the necessary chronological overlaps and a progressive upward scaling to take account of the production increase over the 64 years. At the end of the century, Walter Besant (in his capacity as founder of the Society of Authors) reckoned that there were some 1,200 novelists at work, of whom 200 were entirely self-supporting by their writing. This seems somewhat on the low side and may be biased (especially as regards the self-supporting figure) by Besant's ineradicable gloom about the treatment of the creative writer by philistine English culture. But it is roughly in line with my estimates if one adds the amateurs and one-novel wonders who would have been beneath Besant's notice.

Most of these estimated 3,500 Victorian novelists will never emerge from the obscurity of the statistical mass. Even the most exhaustive investigations can turn up no worthwhile biographical (or sometimes even reliable bibliographical) data. The cult of anonymous authorship which persisted well into the late Victorian period is an often impenetrable screen. Another source of obscurity is the sheer human insignificance of the very minor Victorian novelist. In personal terms, they were of no more consequence than the cabby who drove Dickens to the *All the Year Round* office, or the chambermaid who cleaned the room at the 'Priory', where George Eliot wrote *Felix Holt, the Radical.*

I would guess that some bio-bibliographical profile (dates of birth, death, career details, marital status, total number of novels published) can be readily retrieved for about 1,200 Victorian novelists. For another purpose than this chapter, I have gathered such material on some 878 of them. These represent authors whose records lie close enough to the surface for one to discover salient facts using the resources of the British Library.[2] It is, I think, probably the largest database yet assembled. (The *New Cambridge Bibliography of English Literature*, for instance, has entries on under 200; this will probably be rectified in the third *Cambridge Bibliography*, currently in production.) A lifetime's work could probably turn up a few hundred more, but the majority of Victorian novelists have, I suspect, sunk for ever without trace.

As a sample, 878 cases out of 3,500 is more than substantial enough for statistical analysis, if the sample is not too skewed. But, one must assume, it is manifestly skewed in favour of the 'noteworthy' writer. To have left any record is, in itself, a mark of egregiousness. If the condition of the Victorian novelist is obscurity, to be known is to be in some degree exceptional and to be at all famous (either to one's contemporaries or posterity) is to be a very rare bird indeed. Nevertheless, with the necessary qualifications, 878 novelists is a solid starting point. What I intend to do here is make some preliminary interrogation of this data with the hope of arriving at a set of initially serviceable generalization about the Victorian novelist, *en masse.*

II

CLOSE UP, the corps of Victorian novelists is bewildering in its variety and diversity. All Victorian life seems to be there: from servants, errand-boys and criminals to High-Court judges, generals, admirals, bishops, prime ministers and marquises. In the general catalogue they may, like Macbeth's dogs, be cleped novelists, but what rational points of congruence can one find, say, between the following pair?

LENNOX, Lord William [Pitt] (1799–1881). Born at Winestead Abbey in Yorkshire, Lennox was the fourth son of the fourth Duke of Richmond. His godfather was William Pitt and one of his cousins was Charles James Fox. While still a thirteen-year-old boy at Westminster school, he was gazetted to a cornetcy. He then joined Wellington's staff as an aide-de-camp, remaining in the post until three years after Waterloo. He missed the battle itself, though in Brussels his mother threw the ball for him which is commemorated in Thackeray's *Vanity Fair*, Byron's *Childe Harold* and Charles Lever's *Charles O'Malley*. If not the author of good literature himself, Lennox was the cause of good literature in others. Lennox sold his commission in 1829, and served as a Whig MP from 1832 to 1834. He was, however, more interested in sport (particularly flat racing) and literature than in public service. The young lord went on to write extensively for the journals and was the author of fashionable novels, which hit the taste of the day but which look very feeble to the modern eye. In his later years, he was a sadly broken-down figure willing to hire himself out for lectures on the theme of 'Celebrities I have known'. Nonetheless his volumes of reminiscences, published in the late 1870s, are lively. His fiction includes:

Compton Audley (1841), *The Tuft Hunter* (1843), *Percy Hamilton* (1851), *Philip Courtenay* (1855), *The Adventures of a Man of Family* (1864). There are thirteen novels by Lennox deposited in the British Library.

LEVY, Amy (1861–89). Levy was born at Clapham into a cultured and orthodox Jewish family who actively encouraged her literary talents. She was educated at Brighton, and at Newnham College Cambridge, where she was the first Jewish girl to matriculate. At university in 1881 Levy's first volume of poems was published. Entitled *Xantippe* (after Socrates' fabled shrew of a wife) the work indicated her feminist sentiments. The details of Levy's subsequent life are tantalisingly mysterious. She may have taught, or even have worked in a factory from idealistic motives. She was a friend of Olive Schreiner and of the socialist novelist Clementina Black. Her novel *Reuben Sachs* (1888) is the story of a sexually unscrupulous politician. Its depiction of Jewish life in London as grossly materialistic caused a furore, and was widely taken as a race libel, as was Julia Frankau's similarly anti-Semitic *Dr Philips* (1887). Levy's subsequent novel, *Miss Meredith* (1889) was less tendentious. It is the story of an English Governess, who falls in love with the son of the Italian household where she is employed. Its lightness of tone suggests that it may have been written some time before actual publication. Levy also wrote the shorter fiction *The Romance Of A Shop* (1888), in which four sisters set up their own business. A prey to melancholy, Levy committed suicide by suffocating herself with charcoal fumes shortly after correcting her fifth and last volume of poems for the press. There are three novels of Levy's deposited in the British Library.[3]

Both these are, in their ways (more particularly in their failures), fascinating and instructive cases. Lennox, if we confuse fact and fiction, was actually *there* when George Osborne made his reckless proposal to Becky Sharp on the night before Waterloo. In fact, as the central figure of that actual ball, he survives for posterity only as one of the far background props in its most famous fictional representations. The pathos of his hawking himself around London as a kind of raree show or literary Prufrock is a parable on the treacherous evanescence of fame. And his career is a powerful reminder of the rule that interesting lives do not, inevitably, make for interesting novels. Lennox's is not, of course, a harrowing end, as is Levy's, even in the starkly skeletal form of a dictionary entry. Her Roman death (accompanied by the final act of literary duty) is an almost unbearably poignant indictment of the cruelty of the sensitive Victorian novelist's lot.

Regarding Levy and Lennox as co-professional writers ('two Victorian novelists'), what can one reasonably claim that they had in common, other than that both lived in nineteenth-century England and wrote what the generic record calls fiction? Clearly, the differences make more sense than the similarities. And the main difference I would draw attention to is that Levy began writing early in life as a direct (almost reflexive) career option. Lennox, by contrast, came to novel writing late and indirectly. He ricocheted into it from an earlier, more promising career in the military (cut short by an inconvenient declaration of peace) and from his clear incompetence in fulfilling his expected class destinies in Parliament (possibly due to the equally inconvenient Reform Bill of 1832). This ricochet route into novel writing is, I suggest, a typical male pattern. The direct route into authorship that Levy followed is, by contrast, typically female. In many ways, the archetypal female novelist is Daisy Ashford (1881–1972), who began writing at the age of nine and had four novels complete by the age of thirteen, when she was packed off to convent school, never to write fiction again. The archetypal male novelist, by contrast, would be William de Morgan (1839–1917) who began life as an art student, worked with William Morris, rediscovered medieval techniques for staining glass, set up a successful ceramics factory at Fulham and retired in 1905. In his retirement, aged 65, he began a successful career writing Victorian (in all but date) novels with *Joseph Vance* (1906). He was initially encouraged to write by his wife, who was worried by his depressed state of mind. De Morgan followed this bestseller with five more, and left two works of fiction incomplete at the time of his death. At its bluntest, one may say that men tended to have lived, loved and worked before writing fiction, women often the other way round.

This is not to say that women could not turn their hand to fiction late in life, if they had to; more particularly if it was the only way they could put bread on the family table. One can cite, for instance, the case of Mrs Trollope (1779–1863) who, finding herself let down by her bankrupt husband in the early 1830s, set to at the age of 55 and wrote 35 sprightly works of fiction to keep the Trollopes in middle-class respectability. As resourceful was Amelia Barr (1831–1919), whose husband dragged her off to America and then died of yellow fever (together with three of his daughters), leaving the widow Barr on the streets of New York with $5 in her purse and three surviving daughters to support. At the age of 54, Mrs Barr set to and went on to write 64 popular novels (among them *Remember The Alamo*, 1888, elements of which resurfaced in the 1960s John Wayne movie). A sizeable band of these resourceful ladies can be assembled who, had the wolf not been at the door, would never have put pen to paper, and certainly not in their grandmotherhood.

Something that one may deduce as having been shared professionally by Amy Levy and William Lennox is a sense of guilt and shame. It must have been wormwood for Lennox to pocket his paltry guineas for lecturing on the celebrities he, anything but a celebrity, had known. What the guilt was that drove Levy to suicide one can only guess. But clearly the male, Lennox, was more able to survive than was the female, Levy. This is a pattern one sees elsewhere in the ranks of the profession. Suicide is uncommon, but pseudonyms and anonymity, for instance, were often used to mask shame at being a novelist. Thus Julia Wedgwood (1833–1914, an offspring of the Wedgwood–Darwin dynasty) wrote one of her two novels anonymously and one pseudonymously (as 'Florence Dawson'). Evidently her first (*Framleigh Hall*, 1858) was written without her father's knowledge; her second (*An Old Debt*, 1859) was published only after he gave her his patriarchal imprimatur, having read and censored the manuscript. Thereafter, parental disapproval inhibited Julia Wedgwood from writing fiction altogether. Hugh Stowell Scott (1862–1903) ran into similar paternal opposition. His father, a prosperous shipowner in Newcastle upon Tyne, decreed that his son should follow the family business. Ostensibly dutiful, young Hugh complied. But secretly he began writing and publishing novels, at first anonymously, then under the pseudonym 'Henry Seton Merriman' (the overtones of hedonistic release implicit in this pen name—'the merry man'—are striking). The difference between Scott and Wedgwood is that he did not finally crumple into filial silence. He went on to write 18 bestselling works of fiction. (He also turned his duplicity to good effect in later life by serving as one of the early clandestine agents of the British secret service.) This greater resolution and independence of the male novelist in the face of the stigma attached to writing fiction is generally borne out by mass survey.

Skimming the bio-bibliographies of 878 Victorian novelists yields any number of suggestive primary observations. Not least, the inadequacy of the term 'novelist', implying as it does both someone who merely wrote a novel and someone who devoted their life to (and won their bread by) fiction. It is said that the Eskimo has twenty words for snow. It would be useful to have a similarly discriminating sub-vocabulary for 'Victorian novelist'. As it is loosely applied, the term can legitimately cover someone like Grace Kimmins ('Sister Grace of the Bermondsey Settlement', 1870–1954), whose philanthropy expressed itself primarily in charitable work in the East End, and who in furtherance of that work wrote one successful novel with a purpose, *Polly Of Parker's Rents* (1899). 'Victorian novelist' equally covers the similarly philanthropic, but exclusively literary Miss Evelyn Everett-Green (1856-1932) who has no less than 254 works of fiction deposited in the British Library (many written for the Religious Tract Society). It is hard to imagine that given a 24-hour day and an 76-year life-span Everett-Green ever had time to do anything but write fiction. If quantity means anything, she was a novelist of a quite different stamp from one-shot Grace Kimmins.

A feature that stands out from a cursory scanning of the 878 bio-bibliographical capsules is the clear link between novel writing and certain historical conjunctions. Sea captains in the 1830s, for instance, were recruited in large numbers into the profession (the names of Marryat, Howard, Chamier, Barker, Glascock, and Neale come to mind). Clearly peace, half-pay, and national nostalgia for the Great Victorious War all played a part. But so too did the training and discipline of the officer's life at sea, which was quite different from that of the land-based soldier. Naval service in the early nineteenth century entailed long periods of boredom unmitigated by drink or women. And, unlike their military counterparts, naval commanders were expected to write as a central part of their duty, keeping the log-book being a daily ritual (soldiers, by contrast, were notoriously illiterate). This state of affairs holds up only to the mid-1850s after which (following Crimean reforms) soldiers became better penmen (and more of them wrote novels). With the advent of steam, sailors had less time to spin yarns, in both senses of the term. Apart from the 1830s and 1840s, sea captains rarely feature as active novelists.

Another fact that strikes the casually enquiring eye is the dynastic effect of the great Victorian novelist on those around him/her, particularly close relatives. Thus, for instance, Thackeray had one daughter, Anne Thackeray Ritchie, who went on to be a considerable novelist in her own right. His other daughter was the first wife of

Leslie Stephen, father of Virginia Woolf. The woman with whom Thackeray had his (possibly) adulterous love affair in 1851, Jane Octavia Brookfield, went on after 1868 (Thackeray dying in 1863) to write 4 novels. And her son, Arthur Brookfield, went on in his turn to write 5 novels. A Thackeray cousin, Blanche Ritchie, wrote a novel and so did her husband, Francis Warre Cornish (both narratives were pseudo-Thackerayan in tone). To have 6 novelists clustered so closely around a major novelist is a much higher than chance rate. The same clustering phenomenon is found among the Trollopes. There is Anthony, who wrote 47 novels, his mother Frances Milton who wrote 35, his sister Cecilia who before dying of consumption wrote one, a couple of cousins who wrote about a dozen between them. Finally there was Anthony's brother Thomas Adolphus, who wrote 20 novels, and Thomas's second wife, Frances Eleanor Trollope, who wrote 60-odd. Altogether, Trollopes accounted for some 170 Victorian novels, or 0.3 per cent of the Victorian total. Add his present-day descendant, Joanna Trollope, and the total on the dynastic scoreboard soars out of sight.

Frances Eleanor Trollope's maiden name was Ternan, and she was the sister of Dickens's mistress, Ellen Ternan. Dickens's son Charles Jr did not write novels (although he commissioned many, as the editor in succession to his father on *All The Year Round*). But Angela Dickens, Charles Jr's daughter (1863–1946), went on to write nine novels (all noticeably morbid in tone) and she was aunt (I believe) to the twentieth-century novelist, Monica Dickens. Dickens's daughter Kate married Charles Allston Collins, author of two novels and brother of Wilkie, author of 30. Altogether, this Dickens constellation accounts for some 60 Victorian novels.

Charles Kingsley wrote 10 novels of the first rank. Only slightly less far behind in critical standing was his brother Henry Kingsley, with 20. A daughter of Charles, Mary St Leger, whose married name was Harrison and whose pen-name was 'Lucas Malet', wrote 12 novels. A younger sister, Charlotte (married name 'Chanter') wrote a bestseller, *Over The Cliffs*, in 1860. Altogether, this Kingsley constellation accounts for 45 works of Victorian fiction, all of very high literary quality. Of the 11 children of Frederick Marryat, 4 daughters and one son wrote Victorian novels, running up a family score of around 100 titles.

One could follow these genealogical, or free-masonic, connections much further than I have done here. But it is clear that one of the main predisposing factors to writing Victorian novels was to have a close relative, or intimate acquaintance, who wrote Victorian novels.

III

LOOKING AT individual cases is delightful, yielding the same kind of pleasure as turning over the pages of old photograph albums. And clearly enough it is instructive as well as perplexing to get to know the personnel behind the novels. But I want now to move to quantitative and more systematic analysis of my 878 cases. The questions to which initial answers are sought are: (1) How many Victorian novelists were seriously professional, and how many were amateur or sideline novelists? (2) Given the fact that Victorian fiction was unique in being a profession/industry/hobby in which males and females took part in equal numbers, is there any observable difference in the ways in which men and women were drawn or recruited into writing novels? Put more simply—what made the Victorian a Victorian novelist, and was the process different for men and women?

For multi-factorial research about 40 different fields can be covered by my data, including such factors as class origin, education, religious background, illness or handicap at significant periods of life, career activities, marital status, and so on. For my purposes here, I have collected responses on the following questions: (1) When was s/he born, and when did s/he die? (2) How many novels did s/he write? (3) At what age did s/he start writing? (4) Was there a career previous to writing novels?

Novel writing, I have said, was unique in Victorian society in being a public and professional activity open both to middle-class men and middle-class women on more or less equal terms. Nevertheless, given the social role forced on them, women naturally tended to be more of a modestly submerged component than their male partners. There was clearly more inhibition on women revealing themselves in the public activity of publication, hence they made more use of the pseudonymity and anonymity conventions afforded by the profession. Revealingly enough, their pseudonyms tended to be sexually neutral, or trans-sexual as in the following: 'John Oliver Hobbes' (Pearl M. T. Craigie), 'George Egerton' (Mrs Chavelita Bright), 'G. E. Brunefille' (Lady Colin Campbell), 'Lucas Malet' (Mary St Leger Harrison), 'Lucas

Cleeve' (Adelina Kingscote), 'Cecil Adair' (Evelyn Everett-Green), 'Leslie Keith' (Grace Johnston), 'Michael Fairless' (Margaret Barber), 'Maxwell Gray' (Mary Tuttiett), 'John Law' (Margaret Harkness), and, most famously, Currer, Ellis, and Acton Bell (the Brontë sisters). The process is almost entirely one-way. Although men often used pseudonyms, for a variety of reasons, I have discovered only one male using even a vaguely female pen-name, the obscure nautical novelist Alexander Christie (1841–95), who wrote as 'Lindsay Anderson', an amalgamation of his mother's and his wife's maiden names.

The total of 878 yields 566 men and 312 women. As I suggest above, I imagine this is a function of greater reticence about declaring identity among women writers. Altogether, these 878 authors account for 15,490 fiction titles. At first glance, this looks like an impressively large fraction of the 50,000-or-so hypothetical total. But it needs to be qualified. Given the fact that Victorian authors were, regrettably enough, not all born in 1837 and overlap both ends of the period, the 15,490 figure should in prudence be reduced by as much as a third. The following graph shows the birthdates of the 878 novelists, from 1790 to 1870. Many of those born at the very end of the period continued writing, in some cases up to the mid-twentieth century.

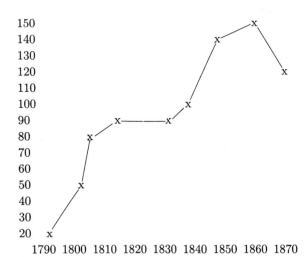

Demographically, the sample reveals no great surprises. The average life expectancy of the male novelist was 66; the female novelist slightly longer, at 68.5 years. The average length of writing career (first novel to death) was 29.9 years for men, and 35.2 years for women. The average age of starting to write was 36 for the male novelist, 33 for the female. (Given the difficulty of determining when a writer actually broke into print, I suspect this figure should be adjusted downwards by about 5 years.) The per-author lifetime total breaks down to 17.6 novels per writer. Sexually, women novelists averaged 21 titles against men's 15.7. This is a high amount in all categories and suggests that the practice of fiction was thoroughly professionalized. At an average payment of around £250, 16–21 novels would make a useful contribution to a life's income and in many circumstances would constitute its bulk. Given the average career lengths, it gives a novel for every 24 months of professional activity. But the per-author output figures rise even higher if one breaks them down. Thus:

878 (100%) wrote 1 novel or more (15,490 titles, or 100%)
553 (63%) wrote 5 novels or more (14,542, or 93%)
400 (45.5%) wrote 10 novels or more (13,352, or 86%)
212 (24%) wrote 20 novels or more (10,651, or 68.7%)
141 (16%) wrote 30 novels or more (8,883, or 57.3%)
95 (10.8%) wrote 40 novels or more (7,277 or 46.9%)
67 (7.6%) wrote 50 novels or more (5,992, or 38.6%)
45 (5%) wrote 60 novels or more (4,159, or 30.7%)
29 (3.3%) wrote 70 novels or more (3,713, or 23.9%)
24 (2.7%) wrote 80 novels or more (3,344, or 21.5%)
19 (12.1%) wrote 90 novels or more (2,932, or 18.9%)
18 (2%) wrote 100 novels or more (2,837, or 18%)

It is evident from this sample that Victorian fiction was largely the product of a relatively small, active component within a fairly large loosely participatory community (i.e. 7 per cent producing a third of all titles). It is evident too that the canonical novelists could make do on smaller than average outputs (Dickens 15, Gaskell 15, Thackeray 9, Eliot 10) because their work was rewarded more highly than average. And Anthony Trollope, with his 47 fiction titles, is not— given the production rates of the profession—as fertile a writer as commonly believed. Almost half of all Victorian novels seem to have been produced by authors clocking up 40 or more titles.

I have not analysed the class backgrounds in the sample, or other predisposing factors such as higher education. But the prior, or concurrent profession field throws up interesting results. Among the male novelists, all but 57 can be allocated at least one (and in many cases more than one) previous or other gainful line of work. In over half the cases, these are lines of work in which the embryo Victorian novelist has not notably succeeded. The principal stepping-stones to a Victorian man's writing fiction were as follows:

Law (predominantly service at the bar) 110
Journalism 82
Business, civil service 75
Church 57
Army 50
Teaching 37
Navy 21
Medicine 21
Manual, menial 17
Book trade 11   Total = 481

The dominance of law as an entry point into novel writing is the striking feature here. Put simply, one in five (male) Victorian novelists was a lawyer, and in the vast majority of cases a failed barrister. 'Called to the Bar but never practised' is thus the commonest prelude to a career in writing novels. And if one adds lawyer fathers (or, for women, lawyer husbands) the coincidence of a training in law with the Victorian novel is even more pronounced. Nor is it just hacks who turned from law to fiction. Among the great novelists one can cite are: Thackeray (failed barrister), Dickens (articled as a solicitor's clerk in Gray's Inn), Blackmore (called to the Bar but never practised), Stevenson (studied law at Edinburgh), Charles Reade (called to the Bar but never practised), Meredith (articled to a solicitor for a while), Wilkie Collins (called to the Bar but never practised), Harrison Ainsworth (studied law at the Inner Temple).

Some reasons for the law-fiction link may be guessed at. To read for the English Bar, it is necessary to have family money, contacts and (usually) an Oxbridge education. To practise at the Bar was, and is, a top job and one from which the working classes are generally excluded. And, for complex reasons, the British aristocracy have never encouraged younger sons to follow law, directing them instead to the army and the Church. None of this is, however, a convincing explanation of the wide bridge connecting Victorian law and Victorian fiction. A more likely factor is the closeness of the Inns of Court to Fleet Street—journalism often being the transitional stage between law and writing novels. But geographically, some of the main teaching hospitals are even nearer Fleet Street. Yet failed doctors did not drift into novel writing in anything like the same numbers as young lawyers.

The critical factor was, presumably, the peculiar nature of legal training. Reading for the Bar centres on two activities: (1) reading, self-evidently; (2) dining; the law, even more than Parliament, being one of the best clubs in London with the difference that taking dinner a certain number of times is obligatory on trainee barristers. Moreover, the study and practice of law is punctuated by absurdly long vacations. Young doctors, especially during internship, are routinely overworked for 50 weeks of the year. And they do not just read up their professional expertise, which is largely a matter of manual and interpersonal skills. Unlike the newly-qualified doctor, the young barrister emerged from his training without any clear next step. He waited, hopefully, for briefs. Often they were slow in coming. Typically, in this awkward interval, the lawyer would marry, incurring new debts. And typically, in this interval, the drift to writing would occur. Finally, although it is a hard link to discern, there is probably an affinity between the mentalities of jurisprudence and Victorian fiction, shaped as both were by the study of individual cases and the canons of (poetic) justice.

Only 32 of the 312 women can be given alternative professional, business or trade activities. Those with no other vocational attribution than 'married woman' or 'spinster' hugely predominate:

Married women 167
Spinsters 113
Journalists 9
Teachers or governesses 8
Actresses or artists 6
Doctors or nurses 4
Book trade 4
Business 1   Total = 312

Not surprisingly, perhaps, the Victorian spinster author was the most productive single category of writer, with an average output of 24 titles.

These findings are very preliminary, and in many cases simply confirm what common sense would anyway suggest. And even where the conclusions are instructive (as in the male-professional and female-amateur finding), they should he treated with some caution. The principal uncertainty can be expressed as a question: do the 878 cases examined mirror the profession, or are they a superstructure of the most successful practitioners self-selected by being that much better than the rest? Granted the sample is probably unrepresentative it is less unrepresentative than the invariable dozen or so novelists who furnish the staple material for the study of 'Victorian fiction' in higher education. Beneath that elite handful my 878 novelists form a reasonably sound and now fairly visible foundation. Beneath these 878 is a still invisible sub-stratum (of several thousands) composed, one suspects, of failures, rank amateurs, third-rate hacks and utter nonentities. Some future literary archaeological tool will have to be devised to investigate these lower reaches.

Plot Summaries

Chapter One

Henry Esmond, William Makepeace Thackeray, 1852, 3 vols, Smith, Elder. (The full title of the work is, *The History Of Henry Esmond, Esq., A Colonel In The Service Of Her Majesty Queen Anne, Written By Himself.*) The work is a third person autobiography with an occasional artful lapse into 'I narration'. Henry is the supposed bastard son of Thomas Esmond. In fact, Thomas married the Flemish girl who was Henry's mother and the boy is legitimate although he is not aware of the fact. Thomas Esmond inherits the estate of Castlewood and is created Viscount. Henry is appointed page to the absurd Lady Isabel Castlewood. At this stage of his life he first encounters the Jesuit Father Holt, a man who profoundly influences Harry's later life. The Castlewoods support the Jacobite uprising, and the Viscount is killed at the battle of the Boyne. The estates and title pass to the good-natured and apolitical Colonel Francis Esmond. Henry attaches himself with what is to be lifelong fidelity to his patron's beautiful young wife, Rachel. As a young man, Henry brings smallpox into the household; Rachel is infected and her looks are damaged. She and her husband are increasingly estranged (his boorishness is partly due to his knowledge that Harry is the true heir). Harry goes to Cambridge, and on his return finds the Viscount has fallen in with the villainous Lord Mohun. An aspersion is made against Rachel's honour, and Castlewood fights a duel with Mohun in which he is killed, but before dying he tells Harry the truth of his birth. Harry is imprisoned for a year for his part in the duel, and Rachel unkindly blames him for her husband's death. Once released, Harry serves as a soldier on the Vigo expedition. On his return, he is reunited with Rachel at Winchester Cathedral, and forgiven by her. He meets her daughter, Beatrix, now full grown, and falls in love. Harry is swept up in the War of the Spanish Succession, and is wounded at Blenheim. After the battle of Wynendael, Harry fights a duel with Mohun in which neither party is killed. Rachel learns of Harry's sacrifice for her family (particularly her son, the present Viscount Frank) and comes to love him even more. Harry, meanwhile, is entranced by the dazzling Beatrix, the toast of fashionable London. But her lover, the Duke of Hamilton, is killed in a duel with the fateful Mohun who also dies of his wounds. Largely to win Beatrix, Esmond engineers a plot to return the Young Pretender to the throne of England. This almost succeeds, but at the last minute fails when the young Prince delays in order to seduce Beatrix. Finally disillusioned,

Harry marries the faithful Rachel and emigrates to Virginia, the scene of *Henry Esmond*'s sequel, *The Virginians* (1858-59).

Pendennis, W. M. Thackeray, 1850, 2 vols, Bradbury and Evans. (Serialized in monthly parts November 1848–December 1850, with illustrations by the author. Full title, *The History Of Pendennis. His Fortunes and Misfortunes. His Friends, And His Greatest Enemy.*) Arthur Pendennis ('Pen') is the son of a snobbish Devonshire apothecary who has prospered in his business. Pen, as the only child, is spoiled, particularly by his indulgent mother Helen. When Pen is sixteen, John Pendennis dies and the hero returns as master to the family home Fairoaks where he falls in love with the tawdry star of a visiting dramatic company, Emily Costigan ('Miss Fotheringay'). She is older than Pen, Irish and in every way unsuitable. As is her habit, Helen Pendennis appeals for help to her worldly brother-in-law, Major Pendennis. The major ingeniously frustrates the rash engagement Arthur has made. The next episode takes Pen to Oxbridge, where he lives the life of a fashionable undergraduate. He duly fails his finals and runs horribly into debt. The Pendennises are saved by the assistance of Laura Bell, an orphan whom Helen has adopted. Pen spends some idle months at Fairoaks, during which time he has a flirtation with Blanche Amory, a young lady attached (in no very clear way) to the neighbouring household of Sir Francis Clavering. At his mother's prompting, he proposes to Laura. But she will not have the immature young man, although she secretly loves him. Pen eventually gains a respectable degree and enrols as a lawyer in London. He shares chambers with George Warrington (a distant descendant of Henry Esmond). Warrington is the epitome of manliness, but has a secret in his past which prevents him from ever being more than a bohemian journalist. (His secret is eventually revealed to be a wretched marriage.) Pen drifts into journalism, and writes for the newly founded *Pall Mall Gazette* (whose imprisoned editor, Captain Shandon, is based on Thackeray's early mentor, William Maginn). He goes on to write a bestselling novel, *Walter Lorraine*. In London high society, he renews his relationship with Blanche. An inveterate coquette, she also captivates the heart of Pen's ingenuous but wealthy friend, Harry Foker. More dangerously, Pen becomes sexually attracted to Fanny Bolton, the daughter of his housekeeper. Pendennis falls dangerously ill (as did Thackeray during the course of the novel). He is nursed by Fanny, who is brutally repulsed by a righteous Mrs Pendennis when she arrives in London. On his recovery, the Pendennises and Warrington go on the Continent to aid his recovery. On their travels, Pen discovers that Helen has held back from him letters from Fanny. Mother and son are hopelessly estranged and only reconciled by Warrington who confides details of his own disastrous marriage to justify Helen's conduct. She dies, at peace with her son. On his return to England Pen comes more and more under the influence of his worldly uncle who has parliamentary ambitions for his nephew. Major Pendennis perceives that Blanche Amory has some hold over the Claverings and urges Pen to marry the girl. Pen, now thoroughly cynical, proposes. In a complicated unravelling, it emerges that the Clavering fortune depends on what may be a bigamous marriage. But finally Pen marries the virtuous and infinitely patient Laura.

Vanity Fair, William Makepeace Thackeray, 1848, 1 vol, Bradbury and Evans. (Serialized in monthly numbers, January 1847–July 1848, with illustrations by the author.) The story begins in 1813 with two young girls of different character leaving Miss Pinkerton's private school in Chiswick. Amelia Sedley is a demure young lady, the virtuous daughter of a City of London merchant. Becky Sharp is the orphaned daughter of a bohemian artist, half-French and totally unscrupulous. Becky goes to spend a short holiday at the Sedley house in Russell Square, before taking up work as a governess. There she tries to entrap Amelia's fat nabob brother Jos into marriage. But the scheme is frustrated (in a notably comic episode at Vauxhall Gardens) by Amelia's lover, Captain George Osborne. Having taken up her position at Queen's Crawley, Becky employs her sexual charms to fascinate the boorish Sir Pitt Crawley who, when his feeble wife dies, proposes to his children's unscrupulous governess. But it is too late, Becky has already secretly married Sir Pitt's raffish dragoon son, Rawdon Crawley. Meanwhile, Amelia's affairs have gone awry. Following Mr Sedley's commercial failure, George's father forbids his son to marry her. Urged by his more honourable friend Captain Dobbin, George (who has few honourable instincts himself) does so. The newly married Osbornes and Crawleys spend their honeymoons together at Brighton, before embarking to Belgium to help the Iron Duke counter Napoleon's threat. In Brussels, Becky entraps George into a foolish offer of elopement. But Waterloo intervenes, and George dies at Quatre Bras. After the battle Amelia and Becky (now mothers) go their separate ways. Becky after some years on the Continent comes to London where, aided by the lecherous Lord Steyne, she conquers English society and is presented to George IV. But she is ruined when her husband (whom she has arranged to have arrested) surprises her in her private apartments with Steyne. They part, he to be governor of Coventry Island, where he dies of fever. Becky takes herself off to the Continent, where she lives a bohemian existence. Amelia has meanwhile suffered increasing poverty living with her parents at Fulham. And, with great suffering and heartsearching, she has entrusted the care of young George to his vulgar but rich grandfather, Mr Osborne. Meanwhile she is faithfully loved by Dobbin. Old Osborne finally dies, leaving Amelia prosperous. Dobbin returns from Indian service with Jos Sedley and they go on a continental tour with Amelia and George. In Pumpernickel (i.e. Weimar) they meet up with Becky. She finally entraps Jos, and with perverse good humour, induces Amelia to give up her worship of the deceased George ('that padded booby!') and accept Dobbin. In an ironic postscript, we learn that Becky poisons Jos and enriched by his life insurance reinstates herself as a respectable lady in Vanity Fair (i.e. middle-class England).

Chapter Two

The Woman In White, Wilkie Collins, 1860, 3 vols, Sampson Low. (Serialized in *All The Year Round*, November 1859–August 1860.) Through the help of an Italian refugee friend, Professor Pesca, the hero Walter Hartright secures a position as drawing master at Limmeridge House in the north of England. Before leaving London, Walter meets a strange woman in white in a lonely part of Hampstead. She is clearly distracted, and seems to have escaped from a lunatic asylum. Ominously, she knows Limmeridge and its occupants and says some mysterious things about the place. On arrival at his new place of work, Walter discovers that his pupils are two half-sisters: the energetic and plain Marian Halcombe and the beautiful Laura Fairlie. Both are in the custody of a hypochondriac uncle, Frederick Fairlie. Laura uncannily resembles the Woman in White (whom he meets again at Limmeridge graveyard). Inevitably, Walter falls in love with Laura. But they cannot marry. She is promised to a blackguardly nobleman, Sir Percival Glyde, of Blackwater Park. Aided by the sinisterly fat Count Fosco (a 'Napoleon of crime') it is Glyde's intention to steal Laura's fortune. Walter goes off to the jungles of Central America to forget Laura. After her marriage to Glyde, an epic duel develops between Marian and Fosco. In a complicated twist of plot, Fosco and Glyde take Laura to London and switch her with the woman in white (in fact Anne Catherick, a half-sister). Anne is dying, and it is their intention to inherit Laura's fortune by thus simulating her death. Marian, who has been ill (the result of a soaking while eavesdropping on the villains outside a window), rescues Laura from the asylum where she is held. In a dramatic encounter, Walter is reunited with his love over what he supposes to be her gravestone. In alliance, Laura, Marian and Walter set out to confound the villains. Glyde is burned to death, trying to falsify the parish records which show him to be illegitimate. Fosco, with the help of Pesca, is betrayed to an Italian secret society which eventually assassinates him in Paris. And, by looking at death certificates, the heroic trio eventually prove that Anne could not have been Laura. At the end of the novel, Laura is an heiress again. She and Walter marry and live happily ever after with Marian as their inseparable companion.

Chapter Three

Cheveley, Lady Rosina Bulwer, 1839, 3 vols, Bull. The opening two volumes concentrate on the unhappy marriage of the Cliffords. Lord De Clifford ('A

Man of Honour') is portrayed as a brute, a fool and the ill-bred son of a vulgar harridan. His wife is pure, long-suffering and quite innocent in the passionate love which springs up between herself and Mowbray (later to be Marquis of Cheveley). De Clifford has a 'predilection for governesses' and spawns a bastard by a village girl on his estate. He frames her father on a charge of stealing to keep him quiet during his election campaign. There is a complicated unravelling of the plot, in which the husband-villain is killed falling from his horse. The novel went through three editions, despite the mortified husband's embarrassed attempts to suppress it.

Hard Cash, Charles Reade, 1863, 3 vols, Sampson Low. (Serialized as *Very Hard Cash* in *All The Year Round*, March–December 1863.) A sequel to *Love Me Little, Love Me Long*. The cash of the title refers to Captain David Dodd's £14,000. These life's earnings are resolutely preserved through all shipwrecks and pirate attacks. But when he returns to England, Dodd entrusts his precious cash to his old rival in love, the banker Richard Hardie. Hardie is a villain. He embezzles Dodd's money, driving the sailor mad. Hardie's son Alfred meanwhile has fallen in love with Dodd's daughter Julia. When he threatens to expose his father, the banker has Alfred confined to a private lunatic asylum. Julia thinks she is deserted. As a patient, Alfred is tortured horribly, even more than the other inmates when he repulses the sexual advances of his gaoler, Mrs Archbold (a physically magnificent figure of a woman). Alfred spends what was to have been his wedding night, strait-jacketed in a cell. Dodd Sr and Hardie Jr make their escape from the asylum during a fire. Dodd, still mad, joins the navy as a common seaman and is (apparently) killed saving a comrade. His body is saved for embalming, and a mosquito bite reveals, at the last minute, that he is not dead after all but in suspended animation. He recovers his senses. Hardie's other victim, Alfred, has reunited himself with Julia, defended himself from criminals employed by his father, taken a first-class degree at Oxford and cleared himself in court. He and Julia marry and retire to their 'happy little villa'. Dodd recovers his cash and he and his wife Lucy are blessed with another infant. Hardie goes senile and ends his days in a lunatic asylum.

Pelham, or Adventures of a Gentleman, Edward Bulwer[-Lytton], 1828, 3 vols, Colburn. The narrative is told autobiographically by a self-confessed puppy, Henry Pelham, a Byronic 'coxcomb'. He is nobly born, and rich and a *connoisseur* of *ton* but consumed with 'ennui' despite his 'liaisons' with beautiful women. The English he believes to be 'demi-barbares'. Pelham's father died early and he has been brought up by his doting (and society-beauty) mother, Lady Frances. After public school and Cambridge (both of which he despises) Henry travels to Paris, where he cultivates his wardrobe and fights a duel. He returns to England and enters parliament. Meanwhile, he has fallen in love with Ellen, the sister of his Eton school-fellow, Reginald

Glanville. Glanville is consumed by a dark secret, which emerges in the course of the action. Getrude, the woman he loved, was seduced and abandoned to a madhouse by a villain called Sir John Tyrrell. Glanville dedicates his life to revenge. Glanville is suspected of murder when Tyrrell is found killed, returning from Newmarket races. The murderer is revealed by Pelham's detective work to be a low-life rogue, Thornton. The reprieved Glanville dies of joy. The novel ends with Pelham happily married and about to re-enter Parliament.

Chapter Five

The Caxtons, A Family Picture, Edward Bulwer [-Lytton], 1849, 3 vols, Blackwoods. (Serialized anonymously in Blackwood's Magazine, April 1848–October 1849.) *The Caxtons* is a small-beer chronicle. For the first half of its narrative, interest centres on family portraits: the father forever preoccupied with his magnum opus (a history of human error); the military uncle Captain Roland de Caxton, the veteran of Waterloo, whose hobby-horse is family honour, the speculator uncle Jack whose 'great anti-booksellers publishing company' nearly ruins his relatives. After leaving school, Pisistratus becomes secretary to a statesman, Mr Trevanion, before going on to Cambridge. Trevanion's wife, it emerges, was loved by Pisistratus's father and uncle Roland when young. Pisistratus himself falls in love with Trevanion's daughter, Fanny. Meanwhile, a Byronic stranger whom Pisistratus has befriended attempts to elope with her. The stranger turns out to be Roland's lost son Vivian (or Herbert) by a Spanish mother. The family misfortunes make university impossible, so Pisistratus and Vivian emigrate to Australia. They return after five years, enriched by sheep farming. Vivian goes off to fight and die for his country in India. Pisistratus marries not Fanny but Blanche, Roland's daughter, completing the family pattern of the work.

The Coming Race, Edward Bulwer [-Lytton], 1871, 1 vol, Blackwood. The hero is a bumptious, ultra-republican American mining engineer who stumbles on a lost underground civilisation. The 'Vril-ya', as they are called, enjoy a utopian, perfectly stable social organisation based on vril, a source of infinitely renewable electrical power. (Commerce promptly invented the brand name 'Bovril', the beef essence drink.) Also present are ray guns, aerial travel, ESP and super-advanced technology. But for all its futurism, the subterra of the Vril-ya has its period charm, conceived as it is as a superior Crystal Palace, glistening with paste jewellery and electroplate. The adventure plot (love between earthling and alien princess) is suspended for many chapters of essayistic digression. There is one fine irony of plot. The hero finds the perfect static utopia of the Vril-ya insufferably boring. He is rescued at the last minute from a death sentence by Princess Zee, who flies him to safety. The novel ends with an ominous prophecy that the superior race will invade upper earth, 'the Darwinian proposition' as Bulwer-Lytton called it.

Eugene Aram, Edward Bulwer [-Lytton], 1832, 3 vols, Colburn. Aram was an actual criminal (1704–59) who has an entry in the *DNB*. A self-taught scholar and schoolmaster, he made some significant contributions to early philology. While in service at a village school at Ramsgill, Aram killed (for gain) one Daniel Clark, hid the body in a cave, and fled, making it look as if he had decamped to escape creditors. He settled in Lyme Regis (deserting his wife and seven children). Fourteen years later, Clark's bones were discovered. Aram was discovered, charged with murder and convicted. Bulwer melodramatically improves on history by making Aram a 'scholar' (not a lowly schoolteacher) and a solitary recluse (there is no family in the background). At 'Grassdale', Aram makes friends with the local squire, Rowland Lester. Lester has two daughters, Madeline and Ellinor. Madeline falls in love with the fascinating scholar jilting the cousin, Walter, who loves her. The heartbroken young man leaves the area. By a series of accidents, Walter subsequently discovers that Aram was the murderer of his (Walter's) father, who—for complicated reasons—took the name Daniel Clark. He returns to Grassdale to have Aram apprehended on the morning of his marriage to Madeline. The novel ends with the hero's long, self-serving testament and his hanging. Madeline dies of a broken heart, and Walter pragmatically marries Ellinor. The novel took Europe by storm.

The Last Days of Pompeii, Edward Bulwer [-Lytton], 1834, 3 vols, Bentley. The novel was inspired by the discovery in 1750 of the ruins of Pompeii, from under the volcanic ash deposited by the eruption of Vesuvius in AD 79. The action is contained in a few days before the destruction of the city. The hero is Glaucus, a young man of fashion (Pelham in a toga). An Athenian by origin, Glaucus is loved by a blind Thessalian flower girl, Nydia, whom he has earlier saved from prostitution to the city's gladiators. On his part, Glaucus falls in love with Ione, another Athenian, from Neapolis. Arbaces, a villainous priest of Isis, also lusts after Ione. Arbaces seduces Ione's brother, Apaecides, to the mysteries of his cult. He also conspires with the witch of Vesuvius to destroy Glaucus (in which attempt he is foiled by Nydia). Eventually, Arbaces has Glaucus arrested for the murder of Apaecides (whom Arbaces himself stabbed to death when the young man turned from Isis to the new creed of Christianity). The narrative climaxes with a great circus in which Glaucus is to be sacrificed to the lions. The execution is interrupted by the eruption, which covers the city in an impenetrable gloom of falling ash. The blind Nydia, who knows the streets without the benefit of sight, leads Glaucus and Ione to safety, dying herself. Ten years on, in Athens, Glaucus and Ione are revealed to have embraced Christianity and Christian marriage.

My Novel, Edward Bulwer [-Lytton], 1853, 4 vols, Blackwoods. (Subtitled 'Or Varieties In English Life'.) The narrative is conducted by Pisistratus, hero of the earlier novel, *The Caxtons*, with frequent interruptions by other family members. The opening setting is the village of Hazeldean and there is some mild comedy on the subject of the squire William Hazeldean's intention of restoring the local stocks. Among others involved in this affair are a local Italian refugee, Dr Riccabocca (who voluntarily shackles himself, as a scientific experiment). The subsequent plot lines centre on the squire and his smoother half-brother, Audley Egerton. There are two spirited election episodes in the narrative and a wily Jewish financier who schemes in the background. But the main strand of the plot follows the career of a young peasant of genius, Leonard Fairfield. Leonard is educated by the perceptive Riccabocca, and after apprenticeship in London is discovered to be the legitimate son of Audley Egerton. By the end of the action he is a famous poet and has been reconciled with his dying politician father. A villain, Randal Leslie (a false friend of Hazeldean's son Frank) schemes to abduct Riccabocca's daughter, Violante, and is foiled. His political ambitions collapse with Egerton's death and he ends the novel a drunken usher in a village school. The Italian is revealed to be the wealthy Duke of Serrano, in the novel's unconvincing denouement.

Paul Clifford, Edward Bulwer [-Lytton], 1830, 3 vols, Colburn. The novel is set in the second decade of the nineteenth century. It opens in a 'flash ken' (a drinking den, habituated by thieves) in Thames Court. A dying woman (apparently well born) leaves her son to be brought up by the den's proprietor, 'Mother' [Mrs Peggy] Lobkins. She names the child after her grandfather, who was three times transported and finally hanged. Observing Paul's love of Newgate chronicles of highwaymen Mother Lobkins puts him under the charge of a dissolute literary editor, Peter MacGrawler of the 'Asinaeum' (i.e. the *Athenaeum*, a journal which had been very hard on Lytton's earlier efforts). Paul is taught how to write slashing reviews, how to tickle, and how to 'plaster' (i.e. flatter outrageously). At 16, he is sent to prison for a pick-pocketing which he did not commit. In reaction to this injustice he becomes an inveterate enemy of society. He turns highwayman, and as 'Paul Lovett' leads a band of like-minded buccaneers of the road. Paul acts from rational revenge against society whose laws are 'hostile to the friendless and the poor'. He enters society as Paul Clifford and falls in love with Lucy, the daughter of squire William Brandon and the niece of the lawyer, William Brandon, who was earlier responsible for sending 'Paul Lobkins' to prison. Lucy is also loved by a degenerate earl, Lord Mauleverer, who has had sinister earlier dealings with William Brandon. Clifford robs

Mauleverer in his capacity as highwayman. He intends to quit the road, but is betrayed by MacGrawler. Paul is judged again by William Brandon. He makes a long speech of self-justification in court, claiming that society has 'made me what I am'. Society condemns him to hang, but he is reprieved when he is revealed to be the son of William Brandon. He is transported to Australia but escapes to be reunited with Lucy in America.

Zanoni, Edward Bulwer [-Lytton], 1842, 3 vols, Saunders and Otley. Drawing on Maturin's *Melmoth The Wanderer* (1820), the hero of this novel, Zanoni, is supposed to have the elixir of life. 'The Stranger', as he is called, first appears in Naples. Rumours follow him. Old men claim to have seen him, decades ago, no different physically from what he now is. Zanoni saves the life of a young Englishman, Clarence Glyndon, but later becomes his rival in love for the opera singer, Viola Pisani. Mysteriously, Zanoni instructs Glyndon to take Viola away from Naples and marry her. But the Englishman renounces his claims on her, in order to learn the secrets of Zanoni from his fellow illuminatus, Mejnour. Zanoni, meanwhile, marries Viola himself and they go off to a Greek isle, where she bears a child. Viola intrudes into her husband's secret chamber, and discovers his awful secret. She runs away with Glyndon to Paris. It is now 1794, and the French capital is in the grip of the Terror. Zanoni, pursuing his loved ones, is captured, and gives up his immortal life on the guillotine to save Viola. The similarity between this novel and Dickens's French Revolution work, *A Tale Of Two Cities*, has often been noted. Bulwer-Lytton (an adept in supernatural lore) claimed that the idea for the novel came to him in a dream.

Chapter Six

The Way We Live Now, Anthony Trollope, 1875, 2 vols, Chapman & Hall. (Serialized in monthly numbers, February 1874–September 1875, with illustrations by L. G. Fawkes.) In its satirical design, the novel attacks an all-pervading 'dishonesty'. The dishonesty of the literary world is shown in Lady Carbury's career in authorship. Good reviews of bad books are paid for with sexual favours, and not worth the paper they are printed on. Dishonesty among the younger set is shown at the Bear Garden Club where Sir Felix Carbury and his cronies pay their gambling debts with worthless paper IOUs. Dishonesty on a grand commercial scale is magnificently portrayed in the career of Augustus Melmotte, the financier. At the suggestion of Hamilton K. Fisker (a sharp American huckster) Melmotte floats a gigantic American railway scheme. The English public, their parliamentary representatives, the City of London and the aristocracy are all taken in by the new Napoleon of commerce (who may be French, Jewish American or stateless) and his paper empire. Melmotte is chosen to host a banquet for the visiting Emperor of China. He is elected MP for

Westminster and as the new Tory member is conducted into the House by Disraeli himself (whom Trollope particularly disliked). The bubble bursts, Melmotte is ruined and commits suicide. Trollope weaves a multiple love plot in with his satire. The caddish Sir Felix is beloved by Melmotte's daughter but drunkenly bungles his elopement with her. His attempts to seduce the country girl, Ruby Ruggles, earn him a deserved beating-up from her aggrieved swain, John Crumb. Felix's amiable sister, Hetta, is torn between the love of her gentlemanly Suffolk cousin Roger (squire of Carbury Manor, and the original hero of the novel, as Trollope designed it) and Paul Montague, a handsome young man dangerously involved with Melmotte. On his part, Paul is entangled with Winifred Hurtle, a 'wild cat' American who has pursued him from San Francisco. In the final working out Paul wins Hetta, and is adopted as heir by Roger. *The Way We Live Now* is one of the longest of Trollope's forty-seven novels, and rich in subplot. Roger is in a religious dilemma between the Catholic and Anglican churches (Trollope originally intended to make more of this). And there is a particularly interesting narrative centred around the courtship of the aristocratic Georgiana Longestaffe by the vulgar (but essentially decent) Jewish financier, Brehgert. Trollope was inspired to write *The Way We Live Now* by the financial scandals which rocked England in the early 1870s.

Chapter Seven

Miss Bretherton, Mrs Humphry [Mary Augusta] Ward, 1884, 1 vol, Macmillan. Ward's heroine, Isabel Bretherton, is an actress (from the colonies) who wins the heart of a fastidious Oxford man of letters, Eustace Kendal. Despite his love for her, Eustace is obliged to tell Isabel that she lacks true dramatic art. Isabel retreats to the Continent where with the help of Eustace's sister, Marie, she learns her craft from European masters. On her return to London, Isabel triumphs in the lead of a new play written for her by Eustace's American friend, Edward Wallace. Marie, dying, effects a reconciliation between the lovers.

Miss Brown, Vernon Lee (i.e. Violet Paget), 1884, 3 vols, Blackwood. Miss Anne Brown is a beautiful girl, working as nursemaid to an artist's family in Italy. She is taken up by another bored artist, the Pre-Raphaelite poet and painter, Walter Hamlin, who settles money on her to allow her to be educated in Germany. Afterwards she may or may not become his wife; it is her 'soul' he is principally interested in. In the event he fails to make her his ideal aesthetic woman. She is radicalized by her Scottish cousin Richard Brown and becomes instead a socialist. But when Hamlin is finally a broken man, Miss Brown relents and in a spirit of self-sacrifice marries him. The last rather ghastly image in the novel is Hamlin's face by gaslight: 'radiant with the triumph of satisfied vanity'. The story's extended satire on the contemporary art world went down well with middlebrow reviewers but the second volume sags badly. Much against his wishes, Paget dedicated this first novel to Henry James.

Robert Elsmere, Mrs Humphry Ward, 1888, 3 vols, Smith, Elder. Robert Elsmere is an excessively earnest young Oxford graduate. A robust younger son of an old established Sussex family, he nevertheless has a strand of feminine weakness in his makeup. Following a good university career ('he was neither dull enough, nor great enough for a striking Oxford success'), he takes up a Church post in the gift of a relative. Meanwhile, visiting at Long Whindale in Westmorland (lovingly described by Ward), he meets and falls in love with Catherine Leyburn, a widow's daughter. Catherine has inherited from her unorthodox father an unusual intellectualism, together with her physical attractions. The two marry and return to Robert's parish. But his religious duties are complicated by doubts sown in his mind by the earnestly philosophical Edward Langham (Robert's Oxford tutor), Professor Grey (based on T. H. Green, the novel's dedicatee) and Squire Roger Wendover (based on Mark Pattison, a man who sacrifices everything to intellect). These worthy sceptics test Robert's faith by exposing it to various forms of rational doubt. To Catherine's distress, he gives up his appointment and goes to the East End of London, where he sets up a commune called the New Brotherhood of Christ. It is massively successful, but Robert finally dies of tubercular disease, exhausted by his missionary efforts among the poor. Catherine is left a widow, worshipping at the Anglican Church and keeping her husband's community going as well. ('The New Brotherhood still exists and grows.')

The Tragic Muse, Henry James, 1890, 3 vols, Macmillan. (Serialized in the *Atlantic* magazine, January 1889–May 1890.) The widowed Lady Agnes Dormer follows her two children to Paris with ambitious plans for them. Nick (who has leanings towards art) she wants to take up a career in English politics. Her daughter Biddy she wants to marry well. In Paris, Nick is urged to follow his artistic inclinations by the aesthete Gabriel Nash. The diplomat Peter Sherringham pulls him in the other direction. Peter's widowed sister, Julia Dallow, is in love with Nick and helps him to win parliamentary election in England. Peter, meanwhile, has fallen in love with a half-Jewish English actress, Miriam Rooth. Miss Rooth has latent talent which is brought on by the Parisian teacher, Mme. Carré. Nick gives up politics for art (throughout much of the action, Miriam is sitting for him as the Tragic Muse). Biddy loves Peter who is increasingly fascinated by Miriam. In a complicated denouement, Miriam surprisingly marries a fellow actor, Basil Dashwood, for the sake of her career. Peter, after a period of despair, marries Biddy. It is possible that Nick will, eventually, marry Julia.

Notes

1. Thackeray's Errors

1. Walter Scott, *The Antiquary*, 'New Abbotsford Edition' (Boston, 1900, ed. A. Lang), pp. 83–4.
2. H. Grierson, *Sir Walter Scott, Bart.* (London, 1930), p. 200.
3. Charles Dickens, 'In Memoriam', *Cornhill Magazine*, IX, Feb. 1864, p. 130.
4. Peter Shillingsburg, *Pegasus in Harness: Victorian Publishing and W. M. Thackeray*, (Charlottesville, 1992), pp. 15–6.
5. *Pegasus in Harness*, p. 16.
6. Three major novels have, at the time of writing, been published in this authoritative edition, under the imprint of Garland Press, New York. They are *Vanity Fair* (1989, ed. P. Shillingsburg), *The History of Henry Esmond* (1989, ed. E. F. Harden), *Pendennis* (1991, ed. P. Shillingsburg).
7. See Gordon N. Ray, *Thackeray: the Uses of Adversity* (New York, 1955), pp. 445–6.
8. See *The Letters and Private Papers of William Makepeace Thackeray*, ed. G. N. Ray, 4 vols (Cambridge: Mass, 1945–8), 2, 383.
9. *Pegasus in Harness*, p. 169.
10. These chronological references, and others which confirm the general argument, will be found in the notes to my edition of *Pendennis* ('Penguin Classics', Harmondsworth, 1994).
11. Gordon N. Ray, *Thackeray: the Age of Wisdom* (New York, 1958), pp. 121–2.
12. See, for example, Elaine Scarry, '*Henry Esmond*, the Rookery at Castlewood', in *Thackeray, Hawthorne, Melville, and Dreiser*, eds, E. Rotsheim and J. A. Wittreich (Wisconsin, 1975); and, J. Hillis Miller, '*Henry Esmond*, Repetition and Irony', in *Fiction and Repetition* (Cambridge: Mass, 1982).
13. Page references are to the 1908 'Oxford' edition, ed. G. Saintsbury.
14. See G. N. Ray, *Thackeray: the Buried Life* (New York, 1952).
15. This letter is in the possession of Trinity College Cambridge, by whose permission I was allowed to read it and the manuscript of the novel.
16. A comprehensive list of authorial corrections to the manuscript of *Henry Esmond* is given by Edgar Harden in the appendices to his 1989 edition of the novel.

17. See *Henry Esmond*, ed. E. Harden, p. 457.

2. Writing *The Woman in White*

1. *Wilkie Collins: the Critical Heritage*, ed. Norman Page (London, 1977), p. 13.
2. *Wilkie Collins: the Critical Heritage*, p. 118.
3. Significantly, the example is taken from the *Annual Register* account of the trial of William Palmer, of which more later.
4. References are to *The Woman in White*, ed. Harvey Peter Sucksmith (London, 1975).
5. Freakish or obscene. When Bulwer made the murderer-hero of *Eugene Aram* (1831) a scholar, there was a furious outcry, and the novelist was obliged to alter his novel. See Michael Sadleir, *Bulwer and his Wife* (London, 1933), pp. 276–7.
6. For a useful account of the emergence of the modern police detective force, and the effect of the 1856 Act, see chapter 9 ('The Police') of Philip Collins's *Dickens and Crime* (London, 1962). One of the main provisions of the 1856 Police Act was to oblige local authorities to establish their own forces.
7. This is very hypothetical since, for his own reasons, Collins chose to conclude *The Woman in White* in 1851, six years before the liberations of the new divorce law.
8. See H. R. Fox Bourne, *English Newspapers* (2 vols, London, 1887), ii, 232.
9. *Wilkie Collins: the Critical Heritage*, p. 122.
10. See Harvey Sucksmith's 'Appendix E' ('The Main Source of *The Woman in White*') to his edition of the novel, pp. 599–600.
11. See Kenneth Robinson, *Wilkie Collins, a Biography* (New York, 1952), p. 98.
12. See Nuel P. Davis, *The Life of Wilkie Collins* (Urbana: Illinois, 1956), p. 211. According to Davis, Collins's statement 'is re-Englished from a direct quotation in in Louis Dépret's *Chez les Anglais* (Paris, 1879).'
13. *The Annual Register* (London, 1857), p. 387.
14. 'The Demeanour of Murderers', *Household Words*, 14 June 1856, pp. 594–8.
15. Graves's book, published a hundred years after Palmer's execution, is written as a vindication of a wrongly-hanged man.
16. See the appendix here, 'Plot Summaries'.
17. A. Trollope, *An Autobiography* (London, 1883, reprinted 1950), p. 257.
18. Letter, 18 August 1859, held in the Pierpont Morgan Library.

19. *The Letters of Charles Dickens*, ed. Walter Dexter (3 vols, London, 1938), iii, 145.
20. The manuscript of the novel, which is autograph and complete, is held in the Pierpont Morgan Library. I am grateful for permission to examine and quote from it.
21. Letters, Pierpont Morgan Library, 11 July 1860 and 'Friday', June 1860.
22. The *All the Year Round* numbers follow Collins's numbering in the manuscript by which No. 1 of the novel = No. 31 of the current issue of the journal. Page numbers in the journal follow, and finally the numbers as in the Sucksmith edition of *The Woman in White*.
23. *Autobiography*, p. 257.
24. Letters, Pierpont Morgan Library, dated 'Friday', June 1860 and 5 July 1860.

3. Dickens, Reade, *Hard Cash*, and Maniac Wives

1. *All the Year Round* letterbook, Huntington Library, HM 17507, 19 May 1859. Wills is writing to T. C. Evans. For a description of the letterbook, see Philip Collins, 'The *All the Year Round* letterbook,' *Victorian Periodicals Newsletter*, 10, November 1970, pp. 23–9.
2. Dickens's phrase. See *The Letters of Charles Dickens*, ed. W. Dexter (3 vols, London, 1939), iii, 131.
3. Dickens to Lytton, *Letters*, iii, 194.
4. F. P. Rolfe, 'Additions to the Nonesuch Edition of Dickens's Letters', *Huntington Library Quarterly*, Vol. 5, No. 1, October 1941, pp. 132–3.
5. *Letters*, iii, 276.
6. Charles L. Reade and Compton Reade, *Charles Reade: a Memoir* (London, 1887). ii, 138.
7. This note is dated 8 January by Dexter (*Letters*, iii, 278).
8. Wills to Reade, *All the Year Round* letterbook, 22 January 1862.
9. Contract for *Hard Cash*, Pierpont Morgan Library.
10. Huntington Library, FI 3635. The year of the letter is catalogued tentatively as 1862. The reference to the Radcliffe Library seems to confirm the date. See *A Memoir*, ii, 143.
11. Letter, 18 November 1862, quoted by L. Rives, *Charles Reade: sa Vie, ses Romans* (Toulouse, 1940), p. 110.
12. *All the Year Round* letterbook, 30 April 1862.
13. *A Memoir*, ii, 142–3.
14. *Letters*, iii, 363.
15. Letter to Wills, in the Huntington, HM 18341. The significance of this communication between the editors—and the identity of John Conolly and A. J. Sutherland as prominent and controversial

psychologists of the period—was uncovered in a revealing article, 'Dickens and Conolly', by Richard A. Hunter and Ida MacAlpine, *TLS*, 11 August, 1961, pp. 534–5. Although I differ with the authors on their friendly evaluation of Conolly, my following remarks are dependent on their essay.

16. For a description and analysis of the Bulwers' marital problems, see Virginia Blain, 'Rosina Bulwer Lytton and the Rage of the Unheard', *Huntington Library Quarterly*, Vol. 53, No. 3, Summer 1990, pp. 211–36. Blain contradicts the view of the marriage to be found in Michael Sadleir, *Bulwer, a Panorama* (London, 1931).

17. *Pelham*, ed. J. J. McGann (Nebraska, 1972), p. 360.

18. Sadleir (*Bulwer, a Panorama*, pp. 399–400) claims that he 'did not look to some other woman for the support and comfort which his official home no longer gave' until 1835. Blain follows Rosina's more recriminatory version.

19. Having voted to reform his seat out of existence, Bulwer re-entered Parliament in April 1832 and represented Lincoln for ten years. After a period in the wilderness, he moved towards the Tories, and represented Hertford, 1852–66.

20. See Thackeray, *Letters*, iv, 456–7.

21. *The Uses of Adversity*, p. 253.

22. Thackeray, *Letters*, i, 473.

23. *The Uses of Adversity*, p. 254.

24. *The Uses of Adversity*, p. 256; Thackeray, *Letters*, i, 474–5.

25. *The Uses of Adversity*, p. 258.

26. Thackeray, *Letters*, ii, 3–5.

27. *The Uses of Adversity*, p. 270.

28. Thackeray, *Letters*, ii, 35.

29. *The Uses of Adversity*, p. 305.

30. Thackeray, *Letters*, ii, 306.

31. Thackeray *Letters*, ii, 341.

32. See *The Letters of Charles Dickens*, eds. Graham Storey, Kathleen Tillotson, and Nina Burgis (Vol 6, Oxford, 1988), pp. 377–80.

33. Rosina Bulwer Lytton, *A Blighted Life* (London, 1880), pp. 28–9.

34. *A Blighted Life*, p. 30.

35. *A Blighted Life*, p. 47.

36. For the best general account of Bell, see Nigel Cross, *The English Common Writer* (Cambridge, 1985), pp. 120–2.

37. See Hunter and MacAlpine, p. 534.

38. Oddly enough, in the early 1830s Conolly settled for a while near Warwick and set up an association to improve the standards of provincial medicine. The young George Eliot (as she was to be) met him socially, and it is conceivable that the charismatic doctor, John Conolly, gave something to the later conception of Lydgate.

39. Elaine C. Showalter, *Female Malady* (London, 1990), p. 42.

40. See the profile of John Conolly given by Andrew Scull in *The Most Solitary of Afflictions* (New Haven, 1993), from which much of the following material is taken.

41. K. J. Fielding, *The Speeches of Charles Dickens* (Oxford, 1960), p. 235.

42. Michael Slater, *Dickens and Women* (London, 1983), usefully prints the whole of The Violated Letter with commentary, pp. 373–5.

43. *Dickens and Women*, p. 146.

44. K. J. Fielding has investigated this mysterious corner of Dickensian scholarship in a number of perceptive articles, notably: 'Dickens to Miss Burdett Coutts', *TLS*, 2 March and 9 March, 1951; 'Charles Dickens to his Wife', *Etudes Anglaises*, 8, No. 6, July–September 1955, 212–7.

45. See K. J. Fielding, 'Dickens and the Hogarth Scandal', *Nineteenth-Century Fiction*, vol. 10, No. 1, June 1955, 64–74.

46. Rosemary Ashton, *Little Germany* (London, 1985), p. 198.

47. Thomas Carlyle, *Reminiscences* (London, 1881), II, 262–3. I am grateful to K. J. Fielding for this reference.

48. See Peter McCandless's essay, 'Liberty and Lunacy: the Victorians and Wrongful Confinement', in *Madhouses, Mad-doctors, and Madmen*, ed. A. Scull (London, 1981).

49. Dickens, *Letters*, iii, 145.

50. Hunter and MacAlpine, p. 535.

4. Dickens's Serializing Imitators

1. From the author's preface to the cheap edition of *The Pickwick Papers* (1847). It is quoted in John Butt and Kathleen Tillotson, *Dickens at Work* (London, 1957) p. 13.

2. R. L. Patten, *Dickens and his Publishers* (Oxford, 1978) p. 46.

3. From the author's preface to the cheap edition of *The Pickwick Papers* (1847).

4. I have examined Macrone's seminal publishing activities in 'John Macrone, Victorian Publisher', *Dickens Studies Annual*, Xlll (1984) pp. 243–59.

5. I have not traced this quotation, which is complacently reprinted in Colburn's advertisements. He was, of course, the erstwhile proprietor of the *Literary Gazette*.

6. In general, I have taken facts about Dickens's publishing history from Patten's invaluable *Dickens and his Publishers*.

7. See J. R. Harvey, *Victorian Novelists and their Illustrators* (London, 1970) pp. 7–18.

8. Usually with Menzies in Edinburgh, Murray in Glasgow, Cumming in Dublin and a host of provincial booksellers and stationers.

9. *The Letters of Charles Dickens*, Pilgrim Edition, eds Madeline House, Graham Storey and Kathleen Tillotson (Oxford, 1974), iii, 517. The letter in question is dated 28 June 1843.

10. Dickens's *Dombey and Son* was identified as published from 'Bradbury and Evans, Whitefriars'. Presumably technical problems in handling woodcut illustrations in the text (together with Dickens's reluctance to have a *Punch* label) was one reason for the different addresses.

11. As Robert Patten and Peter Shillingsburg have pointed out, *Vanity Fair*'s sales even after it caught on were not spectacular and do not justify Thackeray's boast that he was at the 'top of the tree' battling it out with Dickens. *Vanity Fair* (as Shillingsburg calculates) sold 10,500 in its first parts and made-up edition form—about a third of what *Dombey* sold. And Dickens's reprint sales were immensely more. See Peter L. Shillingsburg, 'Twixt *Punch* and *Cornhill*: Thackeray and the Firm of Bradbury and Evans', *Victorian Studies Association Newsletter*, 11 (March 1973) 1–14.

12. The smaller format of the 48-page parts of Jerrold's serial suggest that it may have been devised for *Douglas Jerrold's Shilling Magazine*, which Bradbury and Evans killed in June 1848. The publication of *A Man Made of Money* is often misdated.

13. E. D. Cuming, *Robert Smith Surtees* (Edinburgh, 1924), pp. 252–3.

14. See S. M. Ellis, *William Harrison Ainsworth and his Friends* (2 vols, London, 1911) i, 308–17.

15. See Harvey, *Victorian Novelists and their Illustrators*, p. 188.

16. Ibid., p. 38.

17. Ibid., p. 38.

18. Thackeray may have been motivated at this date by jealousy of Ainsworth. But his observation was an early Victorian commonplace.

19. One regrets that Cruikshank did not illustrate the Mayhews' *Paved with Gold*. This was done in a more extensive 13 numbers by Chapman & Hall, 1857–8, with plates by Phiz at his darkest. The novel (which seems to have been finished by Augustus) is an interesting adaptation of *London Labour and the Poor*.

20. A. Trollope, *An Autobiography*, ed. F. Page (London, 1950), p. 274.

21. The letter is dated 28 September 1863, and is quoted in J. A. Sutherland, *Victorian Novelists and Publishers* (London, 1976) p. 79.

22. Trollope originally expected Bradbury and Evans to serialize *The Vicar of Bullhampton* in their upmarket *Once a Week*. They proposed instead bringing it out in the humbler *Gentleman's Magazine*. As a compromise, it was brought out in a dozen monthly numbers, illustrated by H. Woods, July 1869–May 1870.

23. Robert Lee Wolff mistakenly supposes the name to be a pseudonym. See *Nineteenth-Century Fiction* (5 vols, New York, 1982–8), ii, 41–2.
24. See Butt and Tillotson, *Dickens at Work*, p. 89.

5. Eliot, Lytton, and the Zelig Effect

1. See above, pp. 87–8.
2. See Jerome Beaty, *Middlemarch from Notebook to Novel* (Urbana, 1960), pp. 43–8 and G. S. Haight, *George Eliot, a Biography* (Oxford, 1968), pp. 434–7.
3. Blackwood Papers, MS 4086. Letter dated 12 November 1849, Lytton to John Blackwood. 'Subscription' was the trade practice of buying books at the publisher's specially reduced pre-publication price.
4. Lytton used this injudicious phrase in the preface to the reissue of *Zanoni*, 1845.
5. Blackwood Papers, NLS MS 4086. Undated letter of late 1849, Lytton to J. Blackwood.
6. *Ibid.*
7. Blackwood Papers, NLS MS 4089. Letter dated 30 January 1850, Lytton to J. Blackwood.
8. Blackwood Papers, NLS MS 4089. Letter dated 18 February 1850, Lytton to J. Blackwood.
9. Blackwood Papers, NLS MS 4089. Letter dated 27 June 1859, Lytton to J. Blackwood.
10. Blackwood Papers, NLS MS 4089. Letter postmarked 4 August 1850, Lytton to J. Blackwood.
11. Blackwood Papers, NLS MS 4089. Letter dated 8 September 1850, Lytton to J. Blackwood.
12. Blackwood Papers, NLS MS 4089. Letter dated 6 December 1850, Lytton to J. Blackwood.
13. *The George Eliot Letters*, ed. G. S. Haight (8 vols, Oxford, 1956), v, 145–6.
14. Blackwood Papers, NLS MS 4278. Letter dated 29 October 1871, Lytton to J. Blackwood.
15. Blackwood Papers, NLS Acc. 5643. Letter dated 12 November 1871, J. Blackwood to Lytton.

6. Trollope at Work on *The Way We Live Now*

1. Trollope did not 'invent' the pillar-box (it had been used earlier in France), but he introduced it into Great Britain.
2. The best general account of Trollope's working methods is Mary Hamer's *Writing by Numbers* (Cambridge, 1984). Sympathetic investigation of the subject is to be found in David Skilton, *Anthony*

Trollope and his Contemporaries (London, 1972), pp. 134–7; in Susan L. Humphreys, 'Order-Method: Trollope learns to write', *Dickens Studies Annual*, Vol. 8, 1980, pp. 251–71; and in Andrew Wright's article, 'Trollope revises Trollope' in *Trollope Centenary Articles*, ed. John Halperin (New York, 1982), pp. 109–33.

3. *An Autobiography* (1883, reprinted 1950), pp. 43, 155.

4. 'A Walk in a Wood' was published in the magazine *Good Words*, September 1879, pp. 595–600. The essay derives from the epilogue to Thackeray's novel, *The Newcomes*.

5. The plans and working papers are held by the Bodleian Library under call mark MS Don c10. folios 12–21. The manuscript of the novel is held in the Pierpont Morgan Library.

6. It could be '47' that is crossed out.

7. Sadleir misses 'Dies' out of his transcription. Given the context it could look forward to Lady Carbury's death. But the probability is that it is Felix who is intended to die.

8. Trollope modelled Elmham's Bishop on the former Archbishop of Canterbury Charles Longley, who had taught him at Harrow. He gets the name 'Yeld' by reversing and playing with 'Longley'.

9. In a letter of 26 January 1875, Trollope revealed that he had an original in mind for Barham from his acquaintance at Waltham: 'He was a thoroughly conscientious man, an Oxford man, what we call a pervert and you a convert' (*The Letters of Anthony Trollope*, ed. N. John Hall, 2 vols, Stanford: California, 1983).

10. The early chapters of the manuscript reveal that Trollope at first intended to have another parasitic Grendall offspring in the action.

11. Trollope also has him lodge at Sackville Street in the novel—a small error.

12. *An Autobiography*, pp. 176, 233. But as this plan reveals, it is logically impossible fully to imagine characters without some correlative plot elements. Even at this early stage Trollope saw some interestingly remote complications.

13. *An Autobiography*, p. 320.

14. Peter D. Edwards, 'Trollope changes his Mind: the Death of Melmotte in *The Way We Live Now*,' *Nineteenth-Century Fiction*, 18 (1963), pp. 89–91.

15. References are to be understood as follows: the first numeral is the monthly part number. The second, after the slash, is the page number Trollope gives in the MS. The third number is the page as found in Robert Tracy's edition of *The Way We Live Now* (New York, 1974).

16. Bert G. Hornback, 'Anthony Trollope and the Calendar of 1872: The Chronology of *The Way We Live Now*,' *Notes and Queries*, 208 (1963), pp. 454–7.

17. P. D. Edwards, 'The Chronology of *The Way We Live Now*,' *Notes*

and Queries, 214 (1969), pp. 214–6.

18. See J. A. Sutherland, 'The Commercial Success of *The Way We Live Now*,' *Nineteenth-Century Fiction*, 40 (1986), pp. 460–6.

7. Miss Bretherton, Miss Brown, and Miss Rooth

1. An account of Mary Arnold's juvenilia is given in William Peterson, *Victorian Heretic* (Leicester, 1972), pp. 48–55, and in J. Sutherland, *Mrs Humphry Ward* (Oxford, 1990), pp. 37–42.

2. The notebook, with a mass of other Arnold and Ward families' literary remains, is held at the Honnold Library, Claremont, California.

3. See Mary Ward, *A Writer's Recollections*, 2 vols (London, 1918), *passim*.

4. See Leon Edel, *Henry James: A Life* (New York, 1985).

5. James's literary earnings are analysed by Michael Anesko, *Friction in the Marketplace* (London, 1986).

6. Quoted in Enid Huws Jones, *Mrs Humphry Ward* (London, 1973), p. 63. Jones gives a good account (based on access to Bell's diary) of the composition of *Miss Bretherton*. A comprehensive account of the sensation Anderson caused in London in 1884 is given in D. J. Gordon's and John Stokes's essay on *The Tragic Muse* in *The Air of Reality, New Essays on Henry James*, ed. John Goode (London, 1972).

7. *The Complete Notebooks of Henry James*, eds Leon Edel and Lyall H. Powers (New York, 1987), p. 28. the 'Rachel' referred to is the famous French actress Elisabeth Félix.

8. Janet P. Trevelyan, *The Life of Mrs Humphry Ward* (London, 1923), p. 43.

9. This exchange of letters between Ward and Macmillans is held in the British Library, Macmillan Archive. The novelist's letters are collected in a single volume, Add. MSS. 54928 and the publisher's replies are scattered throughout various of the firm's letterbooks. G. L. Craik to Mary Ward, 12 October 1884, BL Add. MSS. 55418.

10. F. Macmillan to Mary Ward, 21 November 1884, BL Add. MSS. 55418.

11. See J. Sutherland, *Mrs Humphry Ward*, pp. 146–7.

12. Mary Ward to Macmillan, 4 November 1884, BL Add. MSS. 54928.

13. G. L. Craik to Mary Ward, 28 November 1884, BL Add. MSS 55418.

14. *Miss Bretherton* (London, 1912), p. 327.

15. *Ibid*, pp. 392–3.

16. For Ward's almost suicidal struggle to shorten *Robert Elsmere*, see Peterson, chapter 6 and Sutherland, chapter 10.

17. *Miss Bretherton*, p. 204. (The statement is found in Ward's Introduction to her story, which was published in the 'Westmoreland Edition' of 1912 as a pendant to *Sir George Tressady*.)

18. *A Writer's Recollections*, ii, 15.
19. This letter is held, with the bulk of Ward's surviving domestic and personal correspondence, at Pusey House, Oxford.
20. Mary Ward to G. L. Craik, 5 February 1885, BL Add. MSS. 54928.
21. *Ibid.*
22. Mary Ward to F. Macmillan, 26 February 1885, BL Add. MSS. 54928.
23. G. L. Craik to Mary Ward, 27 February 1885, BL Add. MSS. 55419.
24. Mary Ward to G. L. Craik, BL Add. MSS. 54928.
25. G. L. Craik to Mary Ward, 27 April 1885, BL Add. MSS. 55419.
26. *Ibid.*
27. See Sutherland, *Mrs Humphry Ward*, p. 138.
28. *Henry James: Letters*, ed. Leon Edel (Cambridge: Mass., 1980), iii, 58–60.
29. *Ibid*, p. 17.
30. James's relationship with Lee is examined by Carl J. Weber in 'Henry James and his Tiger-Cat', *PMLA*, LXVIII (Sept. 1953), 672–87; and in Burdett Gardner, 'An Apology for Henry James's Tiger-Cat', *PMLA*, LXVIII (Sept. 1953), 688–95.
31. *Ibid*, p. 66.

8. The Victorian Novelists: Who were they?

1. This project is being undertaken by a team of scholars, under the general editorship of D. F. McKenzie. Simon Eliot's *Some Patterns and Trends in British Publishing, 1800–1919* (London, 1994) supersedes some of my comments here.
2. The purpose for which the material was collected was *The Longman Companion to Victorian Fiction* (London, 1988).
3. These entries, and 876 like them, will be found in the *Longman Companion*.

Index

Plot Summaries are marked by bold Numbers